Changing Child Care

Changing Child Care

Five Decades of Child Care Advocacy and Policy in Canada

Susan Prentice editor

Fernwood Publishing • Halifax

Copyright © 2001 Susan Prentice

Editing: ria julien
Cover art: Doowah Design Inc.
Design and production: Beverley Rach
Printed and bound in Canada by: Hignell Printing Limited

A publication of:
Fernwood Publishing
Box 9409, Station A
Halifax, Nova Scotia
B3K 5S3

Fernwood Publishing Company Limited gratefully acknowledges the financial support of the Department of Canadian Heritage, the Nova Scotia Department of Tourism and Culture and the Canada Council for the Arts for our publishing program.

NOVA SCOTIA
Tourism and Culture

Le Conseil des Arts | The Canada Council
du Canada | for the Arts

National Library of Canada Cataloguing in Publication Data

Main entry under title:

Changing child care: five decades of child care advocacy and policy in Canada

Includes bibliographical references.
ISBN 1-55266-062-1

1. Child care–Canada. 2. Social advocacy—Canada. 3. child care—Government policy—Canada. I. Prentice, Susan, 1961–

HQ778.7.C3C375 2001   362.71'2'0971   C2001-901584-4

Contents

Foreword

The evolution of this book has excited the imaginations of those of us who have spent many years advocating for child care services in Canada. The Child Care Advocacy Association of Canada has adjusted our message and advocacy to the changing political contexts. We have evolved from a regionally based board of representatives into a member council of labour, parents, women's organizations and other social justice partners, with provincial and territorial representation. Where "daycare" was once viewed as a means of allowing the workforce participation of mothers, it is now understood as a range of services that meet many needs. Child care includes full-day, center-based care, family home care, part-day care, extended hours care, preschool programs, programs for children with special needs and many other parenting supports. The importance of the early years is now recognized, as is the contribution of those who work with children. We now can prove that child care contributes to the healthy development of children, supports parental choice in labour-market attachment, promotes women's equality and helps build healthy communities.

The Child Care Advocacy Association of Canada welcomes the opportunity to support research that explores the links between advocacy and policy. It is exciting to think that our collective experience and history in changing child care is great enough to make a book such as this a reality!

Rebecca Kelley Scherer, Chair,
Child Care Advocacy Association of Canada

Acknowledgments

A book such as this is truly a collective product. This anthology was generated through a multiphase research project, Child Care Advocacy and Canadian Policy Processes: History and Practice from World War II to the Present. The Child Care Advocacy Association of Canada (CCAAC) sponsored the project, which was funded by Child Care Visions (HRD Canada). As principal investigator, I had the good fortune of support from an outstanding and intrepid project advisory team, made up of Becky Scherer, Wendy Atkin, Maryann Bird and Cindy Magloughlin. In Winnipeg, I worked with an equally talented crew: Wendy Singleton, Cassandra Brade, Esyllt Jones, Debra Mayer, Sue Law, Jennifer Werhun and Linda Wood. I am grateful for assistance provided by Sandy Froese of the Department of Sociology, and the University of Manitoba.

The project began in April 1999 and culminates in the production of this book in 2001. During that time, the board of directors of the CCAAC has undergone some changes, as has staffing in the Ottawa office—I am indebted to past and current board members, and former co-chair Marta Jurio. Board members played a key hands-on role, interviewing pioneering advocates and sharing their own papers and precious memorabilia. I am especially grateful to the CCAAC executive directors Cindy Magloughlin and Maryann Bird, and to Carole Rivest and Hillary Nangle. Billie Carroll's web work and skills bring the whole project to a cyber-audience through the project's website at www.childcareadvocacy.ca/history.

The remarkable creativity of Winnipeg's Doowah Design brought great visuals to the project. Thanks to Dean Smallwood, Steven Rosenberg and their staff for turning "archival ephemera" into a beautiful poster and book cover. Jocelyne Tougas translated the poster into French and here, too, thanks are in order.

The whole Fernwood team, in Winnipeg and Halifax, are a pleasure to work with. Warmest thanks to Errol Sharpe, Beverley Rach and Debbie Mathers. Special thanks to ria julien and to Wayne Antony for his support at every step of this project, including his continued enthusiasm, beginning at the idea stage and sustained throughout the project. Fernwood is an independent, progressive Canadian book publishing company and they make it possible for books such as this to come to market and find readers.

On the home front, I deeply appreciate the love and support provided by Marty Donkervoort, whose willingness to do more than his share enabled much travel, long nights and considerable distraction on my part. Also on the home front, the outstanding care provided by Claudia Scott and the team at KIDS Inc., headed by Karen Ohlson, allow me to work in confidence that Michaela and Addison are happy.

Over the past two years, assistance came from many quarters and from many colleagues and friends across the country. In particular, the Child Care Resource and Research Unit at the University of Toronto was a great resource to this project. Warmest thanks are due to Martha Friendly and Michelle Turiano.

In addition to this anthology, the larger research project involved interviewing long-time child care advocates across the country, compiling a bibliography, identifying sources for archival research as well as making a visual representation of five decades of child care advocacy. To do this, we relied on the infrastructure of child care advocacy that is woven all across Canada. Its newsletters, journals, bulletin boards and tireless advocates supported our call for people (to interview) and things (to photograph and record). Throughout it all, the good will and energy of the women and men who struggle for better child care made this project possible, and for that, I thank them.

As befits an anthology such as this, all royalties from book sales are assigned to the Child Care Advocacy Association of Canada.

Contributors

Wendy J. Atkin is a consultant and independent writer who has completed graduate studies on the history of women and the child care movement in Canada. She is past Coordinator of the Child Care Advocacy Association of Canada and enjoys a sustained interest in the history of child care activism. She hopes that someday there will be an archival repository for our stories.

Sheila Campbell is retired after a thirty-year career in the daycare field, most recently as Chair, part-time, of the Early Childhood Administration Program at Grant MacEwan Community College in Edmonton, Alberta.

Cheryl Collier holds a degree in journalism from Carleton University and is currently a doctoral candidate in the Department of Political Science at the University of Toronto. Her thesis examines party governments and policies on child care and violence against women in British Columbia and Ontario.

Sharon Hope Irwin is Executive Director of SpeciaLink: The National Centre for Child Care Inclusion, and director of the Special Needs Project of the Canadian Union of Postal Workers. She welcomes responses via the web site: www.specialinkcanada.org.

Jane Jenson is a Professor in the Département de science politique, Université de Montréal, where she holds a Canada Research Chair in Citizenship and Governance. She is also Director of the Family Network of Canadian Policy Research Networks, Inc.

Tom Langford is a political sociologist with ongoing research projects on the historical development of child care in Alberta and the impact of the Cold War on working class politics in the Crowsnest Pass. His term as director of the Graduate Program in Sociology at the University of

Calgary is set to end in 2002. He welcomes comments on his chapter at langford@ucalgary.ca.

Donna S. Lero is an Associate Professor in the Department of Family Relations and Applied Nutrition, University of Guelph, and is co-director of the University's Centre for Families, Work and Well-Being.

Judith A. Martin is the Executive Director of the Work and Family Unit, Department of Labour, Government of Saskatchewan. She was the founding chairperson of the Canadian Day Care Advocacy Association.

Susan Prentice is Associate Professor in the Department of Sociology at the University of Manitoba, a long-time feminist activist, a current member of the Steering Committee of the Child Care Coalition of Manitoba and a former board member of the CCAAC. She can be reached at Susan_Prentice@umanitoba.ca.

Rebecca Kelley Scherer has been an advocate for quality child care for many years, working in local, territorial and national arenas. She has served in a variety of positions on local daycare boards, the Yukon Child Care Association and is currently Chair of the Child Care Advocacy Association of Canada. She recently completed her M.A. at the University of Calgary, with a thesis examining child care policy in Canada.

Vappu Tyyskä is an Assistant Professor of Sociology at Ryerson University, Toronto. She has researched and written about child care policy for a decade, including a book, *The Politics of Caring and the Welfare State: The Impact of the Women's Movement on Child Care Policy in Canada and Finland, 1960–1990*.[1]

Linda A. White is Visiting Assistant Professor of the Department of Political Science and Assistant Director of the Centre for the Study of the United States, both at the University of Toronto. Her research interests lie in the area of Canadian and comparative social and family policy, including child care policy. She welcomes comments on her chapter at lwhite@chass.utoronto.ca.

Note
1. Helsinki: Finnish Academy of Science, 1995.

Introduction

Changing Child Care
Looking Back, Moving Forward

Susan Prentice

A "formidable force," *Ottawa Citizen* editorialists deem the contemporary Canadian child care lobby.[1] They claim the movement's power and undue political influence rests in the convergence of staff, parents, teachers, researchers and an array of other players. The lobby, warns the newspaper, is a "steamroller" that governments must mightily resist. Other observers might query the purported power of advocates, given Canada's piecemeal and patchwork child care system. In fact, it might more reasonably be concluded that the very existence of a child care movement is a direct result of political neglect—certainly advocates' efforts would be unneeded had governments implemented progressive policy and comprehensive services. Still, the *Ottawa Citizen* rightly observes that the child care lobby is a player with which politicians must reckon.

There has been a child care movement in Canada for over half a century—yet surprisingly little has been written about how and by whom child care advocacy has been organized, what the movement has done and tried to do, or what effects it has had on social policy or social change. In this book, we set out to begin to remedy some of these gaps. This project is by, for and about the role of advocacy in the making of a place for child care in the Canadian welfare state. Over the last half century, child care policy and services have changed—quite dramatically—and the child care movement has played a role in that complex, interactive process. Individually, these chapters name some of the particulars of this process; in concert, these case studies accomplish something more.

As a collection, this book makes two significant contributions. First, it explores the history of child care advocacy and policy in Canada from World War II to the present. All too often, these stories have been hidden from history. There are many reasons why child care has been neglected in historical and scholarly studies. One reason is that child care advocacy (in Canada, as elsewhere) has largely been a project of women—and the chapters in this anthology variously propose why this is so. In general, much of women's history has been ignored or has failed to be included in history books. History is usually written from the perspective of the mainstream, and the advocacy groups whose stories are told in this book are still campaigning from the margins to have child care declared an entitlement of the Canadian welfare state. Additionally, this is an anthology about a social movement, and the history of social movements in Canada is still being written. As such, this book directly contributes to the active project of history-making.

The second contribution of this anthology builds directly on the first: the authors work towards developing history as a tool—making the past usable and relevant today.[2] The idea of a "usable past" is sometimes looked down on by those historians who scorn such concerns as "presentist." However, understanding history is essential if the goal is to increase the effectiveness of child care advocates or to specify when and under what conditions advocacy impacts (or fails to impact) on public policy. Exactly *how* a social movement makes a difference is complicated and contested. Strategies and tactics used by advocates have varied enormously over the past five decades: sometimes activists have worked "with" or even "inside" governments, sometimes they have worked "against" governments. At some points, child care advocates have developed broad alliances and messages; other times they have focused tightly on child care services. Sometimes a feminist concern with women has predominated; at other times, the focus has been elsewhere, such as on poverty or children's needs. All social movements struggle with similar questions. Women's groups, for example, must consider the benefits of "going mainstream" as insiders versus the advantages of being unfettered outsiders, free to criticize without fear of biting the hand that feeds them.[3] Tactics, strategies, positions and alliances are perennial questions for all social change groups—and the child care movement is in good company as it debates these questions, and disagrees on the answers.

When and why do some strategies work? When and why do they fail? Since more often than not, advocates are unable to enact the policy they want, assessments of "failures" are especially common and painful. These are the moments when advocates must consider if they could have done things differently or ponder whether their political activity ever has a chance of prevailing. Contributors to this anthology explicitly take up these questions, attempting to not only *describe* child care advocacy (a hard enough job in itself) but also to *evaluate and assess* it. In this way, historical inquiry has value for contemporary political discussion.

There are some clear conclusions that emerge from this collection, despite the many differences between the contributors and the histories they analyze. One overall observation is that advocacy really does matter. It sometimes appears that the small actions of advocates—writing a letter to the editor, planning an educational forum, meeting with politicians, creating an election brochure and so on—make no difference. On the contrary, the long-term view provided by history shows that advocacy does have demonstrable effects. The child care movement, slowly, sometimes almost imperceptibly, helps to shape how parents, politicians, decision makers, bureaucrats, researchers, social justice groups and not least of all, "the public" think about child care. Advocacy contributes to how child care is conceptualized, developed and delivered. However, as these chapters show, the movement does not always make the impact that advocates intend.

In Canada today, there are over five million children aged twelve and under. Close to 95 percent of fathers with children under the age of fifteen are in the labour force, as are more than three-quarters of mothers with children aged six to fourteen and 70 percent of mothers of preschoolers.[4] More than 3,323,000 Canadian children have mothers in the paid labour force.[5] For the country's children, there 516,734 licensed child care spaces (in group centres and licensed homes).[6] Quality, accessibility and affordability vary wildly within and between provinces and territories. The cost of child care and the scarcity of public fee subsidies put the service out of reach for nearly every low-income and most middle-income families. Although much is known about the positive impacts on child development of high-quality early childhood care and education, few children have access to good care. The vast and growing majority of children in Canada need nonparental care—yet our country fails to meet their needs and the needs of their parents. Canadian early childhood education today is character-ized by "inadequacy, fragmentation and incoherence."[7] Child care pro-vision in Canada has actually worsened in recent years.[8] From this broad context, one question emerges: How are we to make sense of this scenario?

History and Politics of Child Care Advocacy

Veronica Strong-Boag and Anita Clair Fellman have argued there is a great deal of promise in rethinking history to understand the participation and significance of groups and areas previously slighted.[9] This is especially true for those who seek to understand child care. Historical work can reassign value, identifying the impact of the welfare state on women, making women visible in welfare state analysis and detailing the role of women as political activists in welfare state development.[10]

In recent years, historians and other researchers have shown how social services vary from country to country. Some countries (such as France and Sweden, for example) have well-developed and generous provisions for children; others (such as Canada and the United States), delegate care arrangements to the market and the family. Within a given country there may also be marked differences: Quebec, for example, has its renowned five-dollar-a-day, publicly funded child care system, while the rest of the country organizes child care largely as a private matter for the free market. Without a sophisticated understanding of how and why such different political choices are made, it can simply appear "natural" that Canadian parents should take care of their own children and equally "normal" that public policy fails to provide child care services just as it provides education, pensions or health care.

The confidence that such political arrangements are "natural" or "normal" has been seriously shaken by recent historical scholarship. New research and new perspectives have enabled historians and activists to look at their national and local arrangements with fresh eyes.[11] Researchers, for example, may now explain how and why Sweden's welfare state differs from that of Canada, why Canada is again different from the United States and how variations within countries develop.[12] In these analyses, scholars examine how political power is created outside the state in social movements—women's groups, environmental groups, advocacy organizations, trade unions and other community associations. Activists, we are learning, intervene in political development—even though, in a strictly formal sense, they are not a part of the policy process. These insights are animating both historical and contemporary studies.

Further, social movement theory posits that conventional understanding of how policy is made and implemented has historically been too narrowly conceived.[13] Social movement theory attends to both *how* and *why* movements form and act. Some social movement analysts focus on resource mobilization, past and present. Resource mobilization is the process through which resources—human and material—are deployed, through collective control, to meet shared goals. This mobilization requires planning and coordination, drawing on social networks of supporters with shared consciousness, alongside human and material resources. Out of such activity, social movement organizations grow, often becoming institutionalized into more formal structures. Their repertoire of action grows.[14] As increasingly structured groups, activist organizations are better able to create and respond to opportunities for action and mobilization. Thus, in lieu of a static focus on structure, social movement analysis introduces a language of agency and strategy.[15] This language of agency and strategy is key to understanding social change.

Although conventional political science assumes that internal institutional arrangements are the decisive factor in welfare state formation, new evidence conclusively demonstrates that factors outside the formal political and bureaucratic system have an important role to play. Social movements are one such group: although their focus is often extra-parliamentary—aiming, for example, to change public consciousness or social attitudes rather than governments)—activists regularly make the state a key target. Well-known historian Charles Tilly, in fact, describes social movements as "a sustained challenge to state authorities in the name of a population that has little formal power with respect to the state."[16] Building on this insight, one wing of social movement researchers has shown how mobilization outside the state influences what happens inside the state, thus revealing how nonstate actors shape public policy and public process. In this literature, class-based identities and trade union organizing often play a starring role.[17] However, social movements are bigger than labour alone, and they include constituencies mobilized on the basis of gender and other affiliations. The women's movement, in fact, is one of the more strikingly effective new social movements, and both its praxis and research branches have been exceptionally active.

The theoretical insights of new social movement analysis have combined with, and been influenced by, feminism. Feminists with both contemporary and historical concerns have sought to connect how women have been, and are, active agents for social change. Their lens has turned to a range of topics that have been traditionally neglected. One topic which has been central to feminists is uncovering the political and public dimensions of "private" life. Tracking this line of inquiry, they have illuminated many aspects of domestic life which were previously ignored. In doing so, they have shown the history of social construction behind gender relations.

The field of feminist scholarship is enormous and growing exponentially. For the purpose of this review, it is particularly interesting to focus on work that examines gender at the intersection of history and social organizing, and to consider what this might have to say about child care. Feminist historians have developed a new and critical understanding of families, work and social welfare, generating a "voluminous literature" that addresses how the welfare state is gendered.[18] Much of this work has focused on women and maternalism.[19] Some feminist historians have shown how the welfare state can foster women's political activism; others have documented how the state undermines women's participation.[20] One of the remarkable findings about the welfare state is how much it has been shaped by women's political activism—especially by elite women, but also by working-class and minority women.

Nevertheless, as Sonya Michel notes in her extraordinary history of child care in America, there is a "curious disjuncture" in historiographic writing that somehow filters out welfare state histories, mother's work and children's lives, with child care seldom appearing or relegated to a minor theme.[21] Her observation applies equally well to Canada, where the grassroots child care movements and the place of child care in welfare state formation have received little scholarly attention. The relationship between the women's movement and the child care movement (in Canada and elsewhere) is complex and contradictory, in part because feminists are still struggling with the vexing meaning and politics of motherhood. Nevertheless, it is clear that child care is a crucial element of a "woman friendly" welfare state—a society where injustice on the basis of gender is eliminated.[22]

This anthology is the first book to focus on the historical relationship between child care mobilization and government policy in Canada. It provides, as a first step, select pieces of a large puzzle. As contributors, we are well aware that for all our work there remains a vast balance of stories to tell. Chapters in this book focus on Alberta, Saskatchewan, Ontario, Quebec and British Columbia, with little mention of Atlantic Canada. Some chapters provide national overviews or reviews of Canadian campaigns, but they too are not a complete telling. For example, there is still much work to be done to understand the meaning and practice of child care and advocacy for racialized communities, as well as for First Nations people, with their unique political relationship to the federal government. Metropolitan areas make up the main focus of this anthology, leaving work to be done on rural, northern and nonurban areas of Canada. Most of the historical focus of this anthology is on centre-based group care, leaving many opportunities for analyses of in-home or family home daycare services. There is a history of school-age care that goes untold in this anthology, just as there are unnarrated tales of caregivers and child care workers. There is more to learn about the role of the second wave women's movement in child care advocacy and also of the work of other social justice organizations (such as trade unions) in child care campaigns. This anthology, moreover, is country specific, and comparative analyses of child care movements awaits. We hope this anthology spurs more historical work on the complex, multifaceted experiences of child care advocacy and policy—and we believe this collection helps quilt together some pieces of that wider history.

Analyzing and Debating Child Care Advocacy

The chapters collected here offer different ways to think about child care policy and advocacy, in what can be thought of as a sampler of current work. The authors do not speak with one voice, and readers will notice differences in interpretation and method. In no small measure, authors disagree with each other. In doing so, they mirror the debates and questions that frame the contemporary child care movement, and in their variances they offer a rare and valuable opportunity for critical reflection. In part, these differences are inevitable in a divided and nonunitary movement. From a bird's-eye view, "the Canadian daycare movement" appears as a singular, cohesive social movement; yet on the ground and close-up, what often takes precedence is a dizzying range of groups, mandates and campaigns within and between cities, provinces and regions of this country.

Contributors to this anthology identify this variegated, nationwide child care mobilization's many contributors to the development of child care policy and services in Canada. They examine the infrastructure and processes of child care mobilization, and they assess the effects of advocacy on public-policy process. Uniting all authors is both a conviction that child care is a necessary element of social justice and a concern that current child care services and policy are inadequate. Unlike those who would claim that child care is primarily a private family matter, the authors argue that child care is better understood as a public responsibility and part of the public good. The contributors arrive, however, at very different conclusions about the work of changing child care, at times even confronting the child care movement itself, challenging advocates to reassess their campaigns, visions and tactics.

For example, the child care movement at the national level has long advanced what some critics see as a utopian vision: a universally accessible, publicly funded, high-quality, non-profit system of care, to which all children, parents and families are entitled. In her chapter, Linda White asks if such demands operate for or against the movement's long-term interests. Her example is the struggle in the mid-1980s over the federal government's proposals to replace one general funding program (the Canada Assistance Plan) with a policy specific to child care. At the time, national advocacy organizations opposing the Mulroney government's 1988 Bill C-144 argued that a bad national policy would have been worse than no national policy at all. In contrast, Linda White critiques the advocates' campaign, pointing out that a "half loaf"—an imperfect, but institutionalized, federal child care policy—offered significant advantages over the status quo.

This assessment raises a related question: Should advocates work for and applaud incremental measures? Or ought they to struggle for wholesale policy reform and redesign? In other fields, this is sometimes termed the "reform or revolution" debate, but it is also relevant to child care advocates and their analysts. Various contributors treat this question in different ways: some explicitly approve of gradual, evolutionary developments, while others hold out for more sweeping and transformative change. Complicating this question is each different level of government's particular responsibilities for child care that campaigns must take into account. In Canada, child care is a provincial responsibility—although many advocates argue that this very fact is part of the problem. On the whole, the historical evidence collected here seems to suggest that local and provincial campaigns have pursued incremental goals; whereas national campaigns have held out for more far-reaching and systemic policy change.

Even when examining the same place and the same time, some authors in this collection arrive at different conclusions. For example, two chapters of this book focus on child care advocacy and policy in Alberta. Tom Langford and Sheila Campbell work from different positions, however, and their respective chapters offer a dialogue on how to think about child care in that province. Where Campbell sees the advantages of working with governments, in coalitions of elite or leading citizens motivated by altruism, Langford proposes that effective advocacy requires a social movement. Campbell's history of the gains made by insiders working behind the scenes with decision makers contrasts with Langford's observations that "special interest group" status weakens the political influence of advocates. Elsewhere in the anthology, Cheryl Collier and Vappu Tyyskä examine Ontario's recent experience, and like the western authors, they too arrive at different conclusions even as they study the same time and place.

Several chapters take up the issue of political parties and elected officials. Jane Jenson's analysis of the fascinating history of child care in

Quebec places considerable emphasis on progressive feminist politicians and "femocrats" (feminist bureaucrats) within the state. Cheryl Collier's analysis of differences and similarities between left-wing and right-wing governments in B.C. and Ontario focuses on the governing party's political platform, concluding that left-wing (NDP) governments are the stronger supporters of child care. Judith Martin, by contrast, is more skeptical about political parties and recommends that activists not be over-confident that the NDP is always an ally.

Is child care made stronger when its message is broader? Or does a less-focused message dilute the movement? This puzzle is taken up by several contributors. Vappu Tyyskä points out the gains and losses from highlighting child care alternately as a women's issue, a children's issue and a family issue. She asks if the benefits derived from successful appeals to conservative concerns about "families in need" outweigh the loss of a feminist social change message. Judith Martin points to a similar quandary: Have advocates been too accepting of a work/family divide and not creative enough in reimagining the workplace?

Even the questions, Who fights for child care? Who are the social actors? do not find unanimous agreement among contributors. Most chapters identify the main locus of political activity in groups and organizations. By contrast, Sharon Hope Irwin and Donna S. Lero's piece points out that advocacy for the inclusion of children with special needs has come mainly from individual parents or pioneering child care directors. Even advocacy groups, they gently chide, have not made inclusion a major plank or significant focus of work. Wendy Atkin raises a parallel observation: the sexism that lies behind the organization of child care is attributable to the active work of women, as well as men. Leading women's organizations, such as the ladies of the board of directors of Toronto's West End Creche, were equally unfriendly to working mothers as were other segments of society. Moreover, Atkin's race-sensitive analysis leads her to conclude that an overconcentration on gender led many to ignore the parallel project of "whiteness" that underpinned notions of child care policy and curriculum in the first half of the twentieth century—and perhaps today, as well. There are important divisions within the child care movement, and historians and analysts must be attentive to these differences. In America, Sonya Michel observes that feminists played a relatively minor role in the struggle for child care, and this collection's contributors offer different assessments of the role of women's groups and others in Canadian child care advocacy.[23]

Some people attribute governments' failure to enact good child care policy to the fault of advocates. Some might read Linda White's critique of 1980s national advocacy efforts this way. Judith Martin underscores a different perspective, pointing out that structural features of Canadian society (chiefly the political and economic climate) have more power than do advocates to shape the landscape of political possibility. Many contributors agree on this point, arguing that although agency and activism make a difference, historical, social, economic and political factors prevail. One of these factors is the role of business and, in turn, government receptivity to for-profit care. Several chapters address the issue of commercial child care and the business lobby's influence in promoting policies favourable to privitized care.

Contributors differ on the relative importance they place on a political division of powers, although all recognize the pervasive effects of federalism. Jane Jenson develops a complex analysis of how and why Quebec has situated child care as a component of comprehensive family policy while other jurisdictions have not. Some authors prioritize the local government (for example, Sheila Campbell on Edmonton and Vappu Tyyskä on two Ontario municipalities). Others identify the provincial government as the key player. Rebecca Kelley Scherer and Linda White make the federal government their focus, Scherer's history chronicling a full half century. These different choices implicitly point to the need to clarify which levels of government have the most power to affect child care—all the while remembering, as the longitudinal stories show, that this "fact" can change with different historical conjunctures. For example, local control over child care had positive effects at some moments and quite regressive consequences at other points.

Across the chapters we can find different conceptions of the state. Authors have different views on whether government is a level playing field in which all voices have an equal chance to be heard or if, to the contrary, government is an unequal playing field where some perspectives predominate and others are systematically marginalized. Some authors see the state as a site of political struggle; others conceive of government as a place of consensus and conciliation in the service of the general good. Thus, contributors recommend different kinds of activities, and they advise different alliances and tactics. Judith Martin, in particular, makes a unique contribution to this collection; like other authors, she identifies the need for political and policy change, yet she simultaneously urges child care advocates to focus on extra-parliamentary sites for social change.

Taken together, the authors provide a mix of analytic tools and insights. Their careful and considered arguments enrich our capacity to understand how and why child care advocacy and policy unfold as they do—their arguments illuminate the possibilities and limitations of future politics.

Changing Child Care

The contributors to *Changing Child Care* debate child care as a political enterprise. The book is an historical retrospective, but as child care advocacy is a still unfinished campaign, this collection inevitably raises questions about the future. What can be gleaned about child care activism in the coming years?

The child care movement confronts significant challenges. In an era of welfare state restructuring, the prospects of comprehensive child care are uncertain. Some of the "debt and deficit" mania is abating in light of a national budget surplus, but there seems to be little political will for public spending on new programs at the federal level, and signals are mixed across the provinces. As I write in this introduction, the progressive legislation passed in 2001 in British Columbia by the NDP looks vulnerable to repeal by the newly elected Liberal government. In Manitoba, over 22,000 people have just responded to a government consultation on a new "vision" for child care, but the provincial NDP appears unwilling to implement fundamental change. Ontario's Conservative government has slashed its child care budget and downloaded costs onto municipalities, fragmenting provincial advocacy into small scale battles with local city councils. On the good news front, Nova Scotia has recently announced new spending of $66 million on early childhood development services, and Quebec seems determined to proceed with its comprehensive policy.

In the era of a Social Union Framework Agreement (SUFA) and a new federal Early Childhood Development Services Agreement, does a campaign for a national child care program make any sense? Should advocates abandon a federal campaign targeting the Canadian government and regroup in provincial or local lobbies? Should they seek broad alliances around a range of family policies, or do they need to continue to make child care a strong focus? Across the country, advocates are struggling with these and other questions. In the meantime, parents who want and need child care can rarely find or afford licensed, high-quality care. The child care workers who care for Canada's children are still paid on a par with zoo-keepers and parking lot attendants.[24] Most Canadians support the idea that governments should actively help parents with their caregiving responsibilities; yet in all of Canada, only in Quebec are child care policy, funding and services are not seriously underdeveloped.[25]

How and why has such a huge gap between public needs, public wants and child care service developed? This collection offers some historical reflections, in ways that may be useful for the future.

Notes

1. *Ottawa Citizen* 2001.
2. Bouwsma 1990; Commager 1967.
3. Briskin 1991.
4. Vanier Institute of the Family 2000: 86–87.
5. Child Care Resource and Research Unit 1998, Tables 1 and 2: 83.
6. Child Care Resource and Research Unit 1998, Table 3: 84.
7. Friendly 2000: 8.
8. Prentice 1999.
9. Strong-Boag and Fellman 1997: 3.
10. Wilson 1977; Gordon 1994.
11. Boggs 1986; O'Connor and Olsen 1997; Olsen 1994; Scott 1990; Touraine 1988.
12. Esping-Anderson 1989; Fraser 1989; Sainsbury 1994.
13. I create a composite entity here out of varying strands, assembling under "new social movement" theory both "old" resource mobilization approaches as well as "new" interpretive identity-based approaches.
14. Tarrow 1998.
15. Carroll 1997: 7.
16. Tilly 1988: 1.
17. Moscovitch and Drover 1982; Moscovitch and Albert 1987; O'Connor and Olsen 1997.
18. Haney 1998: 748; Howe 1996; O'Connor 1996; Orloff 1993, 1996.
19. Brush 1996; Koven and Michel 1993.
20. Gordon 1990.
21. Michel 1999: 7–8.
22. Hernes 1977.
23. Michel 1999: 278.
24. Doherty et al. 2000.
25. Philip 1998, Rebick 1998.

Chapter 1

"Playing Together as Canadians"
Historical Lessons from the West End Creche

Wendy J. Atkin

The history of the child care movement in Canada has only recently become a subject for feminist historians, who have now begun to write accounts focused on the class and gender dynamics of that history.[1] In recent years, as issues of culture and race have taken more prominence in Canadian political analysis, so too have historians become more cognizant of these factors in portraying the past. However, examining cultural and racial topics goes beyond merely including narratives from groups that have been marginalized in the dominant intellectual record; as Anne McClintock points out, we must not view "race and ethnicity as synonymous with black and colonized."[2] A racial analysis yields information on the history of white as well as nonwhite people and we have yet to explore how whiteness (as the dominant race in the Canadian context) has shaped public advocacy for child care.

In recounting the past, historians use context analyses that include the intellectual, geographic and political setting of an era. The story told here recounts the founding of the West End Creche from 1920 to 1940. In it, two main developments will be followed. The first is the transmission of British imperialist values through national women's organizations. The second is the transmission of dominant values of "whiteness" through the day nursery curriculum. Which historical lessons are served by following these stories of national and local day nursery organizing and evolving early childhood education curricula? First, we may be more conscious of how national women's organizations embracing feminism are themselves rooted in ideological systems typified by one-dimensional, rather than kaleidoscopic visions of women's experiences. Second, this inquiry affords an opportunity to unravel the threads of the child care system as we know it and gain a deeper understanding of how facets of curricula and child care arrangements that we may take as given were in fact socially constructed during our collective past.

Today's child care advocate might ask why we need to know this historical information. The intention here is not to blame our foremothers. They sought to fulfill a broader vision for women, carving space for the care of children in public settings and capturing social resources for less-privileged women and their children to enjoy the benefits of early childhood education. Instead, we need to question our founding principles and learn how to include a broader range of people and a larger pool of options for child care. Only then will universality, one of the cardinal principles of the child care movement in the last three decades, have a meaning deeper than universal access to services; universal child care has the potential to embody an understanding of "services" that is as numerous as the many kinds of families, thus including a broad cultural scope of children who stand to benefit.

The modern Canadian child care advocacy movement was founded on a platform calling for the federal government to commit to "a well-organized, universally accessible, publicly funded, not-for-profit, non-compulsory day care system."[3] This is an important story to tell, but there are many other stories of formal and informal child care networks, whose demands for social as well as public support have yet to be told. As we start to write the history of the modern child care advocacy movement, we may be tempted to focus on national and provincial organizations that grew out of the second wave of feminism in the 1960s. However, as historians, we should also be aware of the broad range of child care practices that have been utilized throughout this history.

Origins of Canadian Child Care

The first day nurseries, as they were called, were charities created by social reformers as reactions to the evils of industrialization (such as the shift for many women from the family economy to waged work in factories). This shift often resulted in the onerous burden of arranging for care of young children during mothers' work—hours not necessarily convenient for the neighbours and family members who used to provide informal child care.[4] Canada's first day nurseries were founded by religious groups and women's voluntary organizations.[5] Many also operated employment services that required mothers to work as servants or go to other low-waged jobs at the request of the nurseries' employer clients.[6] These class and gender dynamics of the early day nursery system have been the focus of historical accounts in child and family studies, but we have yet to develop an adequate understanding of how race informs the relevant institutions and the people and political values responsible for shaping those institutions.

British women's historians have demonstrated the close relationship between motherhood issues and social and economic developments, particularly that of imperialism and industrialization. Carol Dyhouse describes how child welfare campaigns in Britain often targeted working-class mothers with criticism and often ineffective education, rather than providing services and supports to replace those that had eroded with the passage of the pre-industrial family economy.[7] Anna Davin brings the campaigns for better infancy and healthier childhood for British citizens into the realm of the Empire by showing how eugenic concerns for preserving the white race were paramount in early-twentieth-century campaigns and programs for infant and child health and education for motherhood.[8] The echoes of these imperialist campaigns reverberated in Canada, as Katherine Arnup describes in her account of the education campaigns designed to prepare mothers in Canada to raise good citizens and healthy Canadians.[9]

There is a correlation between the foremothers of the Canadian first wave feminist movement (national women's groups founded around the turn of the century) and the women who founded voluntary associations that organized the first child care centres in urban Canada during the interwar and post-war periods. Tracing the development of the West End Creche in Toronto, we can identify parallel processes: of the child development experiments being implemented in the Creche, on the one hand, and the dissemination of nationalist political values by its founders, on the other.

The legacy of the period 1920 to 1940, vital to understanding the nature of the child care system that slowly emerged in Toronto after WWII, is certainly contradictory. This was a period in which the best practices of day nursery care emerged. Yet, it was also characterized by a heightened race consciousness that was reflected in the assimilationist goals of social services targeted for recent immigrants to Canada.

West End Creche

The period 1920 to 1940 was bracketed by the end of World War I and the early years of the World War II. It preceded the peculiar chapter in child care history when the Canadian government suddenly—and temporarily—provided direct funding for day nurseries, well before daycare standards of service and training received legislative recognition in the

Ontario Day Nurseries Act (1946). In trying to provide sound developmental care, the directors of the West End Creche faced the constant challenges of an increasingly racially mixed group of children and scant public funds.

Joan Arnoldi and Gertrude Tate were the first Toronto women to take a keen interest in establishing a day nursery in the low-income district southwest of College Street in downtown Toronto. Challenged to undertake this project by a young banker during a dance at a society ball in 1908, Tate approached Arnoldi, and along with a local clergyman, they visited a supportive municipal relief officer. City funds did not flow to the Creche until 1911, and in the interim, Arnoldi and Tate organized seventy-five young women into a club that would support the Creche through voluntary and fundraising efforts. The initiation fee of one hundred dollars and annual membership fees of twenty-five dollars helped to establish the Creche at 521 Adelaide Street West in premises deemed "inadequate but rainproof."[10] In 1912, Arnoldi, her friend Mary Plummer, and Tate embarked on a campaign that raised twenty thousand dollars to construct a new building for the Creche on Euclid Avenue.[11] The paid staff, enlarged to seven, ran the nursery during the war while Arnoldi and Plummer were overseas. While in England, the two became interested in the nursery school movement there. Also during this period, the Creche became increasingly dependent on financial contributions from the Imperial Order of Daughters of the Empire (IODE) Rose fund. After the war, a renewed effort to raise funds saw a series of nine society balls, increased membership and increasing emphasis on child development. By its own account, the Creche "by 1925–26 had changed from being a safe parking place for children of working mothers, to the first nursery school in Toronto staffed with trained workers."[12] This shift may not have been approved unanimously. A new board member from Connaught Laboratories advised in 1929, "as time goes on you will adhere to the application of such scientific methods as are applicable—you will stick to that, no matter what members of the Advisory Committee will tell you."[13]

The economic crisis of the 1930s made it difficult for the Creche to sustain its new direction, however, and the daughters of board members were recruited as volunteers to undertake a range of tasks, including working with the children, repairing toys and painting furniture, as well as selling tickets to the balls.[14] By 1938, the Creche admitted that it could not meet its goals without "fixed sums on a regular, annual basis."[15] The war years, however, were a boon to the Creche, which began to stay open through the summer because of the number of mothers working in war industries.

After 1925, new child development theories began to replace custodial care in the day nursery curricula. The publication of the first scientifically determined stages of early child development by Arnold Gesell "transformed ways of thinking about the period of life called childhood."[16] Closely linked was the notion of mental and physical hygiene, as fostering the development of healthy adult citizens. These ideas were accepted uncritically into the curricula of nurseries such as the West End Creche. With Rockefeller Foundation funding, Gesell's principles were instituted in the newly formed St. George's School for Child Study, which later became the University of Toronto Institute of Child Study. Under the direction of William Blatz, the Institute established both a nursery laboratory and a parent education program for its largely middle-class, professional parents. At the same time, the Institute's students and graduates brought new child development principles into the West End Creche. Institute graduate, Marjorie Burgess, became Creche director in 1928, and her successor Gretta Gordon (also a graduate) was herself succeeded by Margaret Lovatt, an Institute woman with a social work background. Lovatt remained at the Creche as director until the 1960s.[17]

At the Creche, some of the practices of the Institute were followed, but this became increasingly difficult without secure funding. One parent-education class held at the Creche in 1928 brought together seven mothers, all with Anglo-Saxon surnames, most of them able to provide written responses to the tests set for them by the leaders. At these classes, a great deal of emphasis was put on the cleansing effects of fresh air and sunshine. Although the instructors acknowledged that the sun's rays "cannot easily pass through the smokey down town atmosphere," it was considered adequate that Mrs. Brash walked her son to and from the Creche for over one hour each day.[18] Indeed, the amount of leisure time spent outdoors on weekends and in the evenings by the participating mothers would likely have been rarer in families who lacked access to outdoor recreation or who were occupied with domestic pursuits. That the education was aimed at white families was certainly evident in the recommendation,

> that children, even babies ... be exposed to the full sunlight in the open air until they are well coated with tan. This, of course, must be done gradually, a little more each day until the body grows accustomed to it. Sunshine is nature's great cleanser and aids in destroying germs if they are exposed directly to its rays.[19]

Teaching white mothers how to bring up stronger white children was in keeping with the social eugenic values of the early twentieth century.

The principles of the British nursery school movement that had so impressed the founders of the West End Creche were brought to the board of directors in a 1936 address by Margaret Gould of the Child Welfare Council of Toronto. She recalled the lessons learned in Great Britain, where the poor performance of soldiers in wars had revealed "how degenerate was the physique of Britain's manhood":[20]

> "A child grows up only once," said Miss Abbott, chief of the United States Children's Bureau. "Life is a one-way street," says the bulletin of the Nursery School Association of Great Britain. "The first five years of the child's life affect his whole future. What the child misses then, in physical, mental and moral growth, can never be made up to him."[21]

The speaker challenged the West End Creche to overcome the "limitations" of a day nursery and instead play a lead role in the movement to bring nursery education to all preschool-aged children just as the McMillan nursery school had done in Britain. Why such a grand challenge would be issued to a single day nursery struggling to survive the fiscal strains of the depression poses the interesting question of how the Creche came to be associated with nationalist political values in the first place.

Little Immigrants/Little Citizens

The West End Creche, like many social services of its day, would not have survived without the voluntary commitment of the mostly women directors and volunteers—women like Joan Arnoldi and Gertrude Tate. This voluntary effort was fueled by a complex set of values peculiar to upper-middle-class white women of the time, whose intellectual origins date back to their Victorian predecessors and whose feminism and social commitment was entangled with imperialist ideology.[22] This is clear in the role played by the IODE.

The Imperial Order of Daughters of the Empire (IODE), founded in 1900 under the motto "One Flag, One Throne, One Empire," carried British imperial values into Canadian women's political circles. At the twentieth annual meeting, Joan Arnoldi was elected national president of the IODE. She also was diligent in ensuring that the Order maintain its commitment to the Child Welfare Council of Canada, and subsequent to her presidency she was active in the Girl Guides, the vetting of films especially for children and exposing the plight of the so-called Barnardo children. In her presidential address, Arnoldi drew inspiration from her own experiences overseas in World War I, declaring, "we went into the war a body of organized women. We emerged from the war a body of organized citizens."[23] She also put forth her vision for the year ahead, stressing "one of our most important works is the Canadianization of our new citizens."[24]

The 1921 annual meeting highlighted the number of immigrants living in Canada and noted that their presence was strong in cities as well as in the West:

> Slowly the order has been awakening to the fact that it is not only the West that has so many strangers who need to be made into good citizens of Canada and the Empire, but in the cities of the East there are literally thousands of foreigners living their own lives independently of the Canadian people all around them, often not speaking a word of English. The possible dangers to our nation of such a situation, and the equal possibilities for good, have led many Chapters to undertake the stupendous task of educating this foreign-born population in all parts of the country.[25]

The IODE's immigration, education, and child welfare committees advanced a campaign during the 1920s to ensure that Canada remained British, by advocating for immigration policies designed to privilege British emigrants. Chapters distributed citizenship cards, pamphlets, books and other materials promoting the Empire and assisted with social services that focused on family maintenance, prenatal care and agencies that practised modern social work. In 1920, the IODE had endorsed representation at meetings of national child welfare organizations in order to cooperate on common concerns. Over time, the Girl Guides proved a responsive organization, and Joan Arnoldi oversaw the founding of several Girl Guide chapters of the IODE. For Arnoldi, the link between organizations was a natural progression, and she pointed out that "the girls are brought up to the age when they join the IODE or other women's organizations."[26] The links with the Girl Guides were the realization of the IODE's goal to foster good women citizens, and their efforts paralleled the larger cultural project to "Canadianize" foreign-born children and youth, especially as a means to Canadianize their immigrant parents.

The IODE tried to ensure that the influence of British imperial values counterbalanced the cohesion of immigrant communities. They repeatedly lobbied the Canadian government to discourage immigrants from settling in blocks, be they in rural environs or urban neighbourhoods. Many IODE activities, however, also included measures designed to reach immigrants who had already established communities in Canada. The IODE established mothers' clubs for immigrant women, based on the rationale that children, "especially young babies," were a good avenue for cultural transmission into families.[27] The establishment of non-British children's chapters was made possible after a constitutional amendment passed in 1922 allowed "that the children of foreign-born parents who are not naturalized British subjects ... become members of the Children of the Empire Chapters, as this would be a great factor in the Canadianization work of the Daughters of the Empire amongst our foreign-born citizens."[28] However, the Alberta executive member complained that it would not be easy to reach the parents of these children since they "seemed not to wish to learn English, at least the women, and there was a tendency for them to keep to themselves, and try to persuade their children to retain the usages and customs from their own land."[29]

Charlotte Whitton, in her first year as convenor of the IODE Child Welfare Committee, delivered a report of unprecedented length (nineteen pages) to the IODE national meeting at the King Edward Hotel in Toronto. Openly putting aside a request to report solely on the activities of local child welfare committees, Whitton instead focused on exposing the plight of British juvenile immigrants (the so-called Barnardo children). After lambasting the federal government for "nation-building on the backs of children," while placing "little wage slaves on Canadian farms," Whitton concluded her lengthy address by citing the League of Nations Children's Charter in its entirety and delivering the following emotional plea:

> What shall be the unspoken watchword of the Order's child welfare endeavor for 1924–25? May it not be our pledge as the Daughters in Blood, and the Daughters in Soul, of this old Empire.... May not we, this sworn band of the Daughters of the British Empire—an Empire whose very being was born in the triumphant dream of a woman, Elizabeth, the childless mother of Empire—may we not pledge ourselves to this mighty [Children's] Charter, and in so far as it may be given us, to influence our day and generation, dedicate ourselves to the high duty of living it, into the life of this Dominion?[30]

Whitton's address put the notion of children as new or young citizens in a different light; although she managed to capture the political will of the Order to lobby on behalf of these British-born children, the Children's Charter did not distinguish between foreign-born and Canadian children, but assured that every child would be entitled to safety, security and well-being. The question of whether these values were realized in the social services created and run by the class of women represented in the IODE in the interwar period remains unanswered. In the day nursery curricula, however, the emphasis clearly lay in assimilation.

"Playing Together as Canadians"

A special pamphlet published by the West End Creche in 1959 to commemorate its fiftieth anniversary included photos of children in a nursery setting. It stands out not for its depiction of diverse children sharing toys at a play table, but for the accompanying caption:

> In 1954, 101 children from 20 national groups attended the Nursery. Born in 16 different countries, they played together as Canadians.[31]

The Creche was proud of its record in grouping together children from many national origins; a poster depicting a table-top globe of the world entitled "Circling the Globe" was carefully filled in with the numbers of children from various countries. As mentioned earlier, actively engaging with immigrants on very particular terms has long been a project of the Creche:

> Down through its 50 years of history the Creche has continuously filled a vital need among newcomers to Canada. The area surrounding the Creche has provided a first home in Canada to thousands of newly-arrived settlers of almost every nationality. As new families began to make their way they moved out to other areas and their place was taken once again by other newcomers in quick succession. And to each successive group in turn the Creche offered friendship and the opportunity they sought for self-help which enabled them to establish themselves in their new life here.[32]

For much of the Creche's first fifty years, the numbers of immigrant children hovered around 50 percent, reaching an all-time high in 1938 of

85 percent. It is less surprising that this racial mix existed—given that the Creche operated on behalf of low-income children and their parents, alongside the University of Toronto Institute for Child Study that catered mainly to white families— than it is that the Creche boasted of the fact. This is especially surprising since there are few references in Creche records to the difficulties that may have been experienced by children facing language and cultural barriers to the assimilationist goals of the time.

In the quest to develop scientific approaches to caring for children, the founders of the Creche, with the best of intentions, adopted a set of theories on child development that did not account for culture and race beyond the Anglocentric norms from whence they derived. The transmission of child development principles into the Creche curriculum was echoed during the 1950s, when maternalist values crept into the child development canon, tending the Creche policies toward minimizing infant care and encouraging mothers' involvement with the daycare provided. In contemporary writings, Lind and Prentice have demonstrated how patriarchal values permeated the day nursery system in Canada.[33] We have little sense, however, of how whiteness has influenced the curricula of the day nurseries. In the post-war period, there was a widespread lack of awareness that child development notions were racially based and culturally specific. The result was less the promotion of Charlotte Whitton's vision of universal entitlements than a system that shaped the child as a white child, regardless of national origin.

Our collective history is instructive, and as child care advocacy evolves in Canada it is important to examine the race and culture biases of the child care curriculum. We cannot assume that the present-day understanding of "universality" (meaning universal access to high-quality not-for-profit child care services) is embraced by all. A more self-conscious examination of the soil in which our child care institutions have grown can only assist today's child care advocates. Refuting the one-dimensional notion of universality that informs the legacy of the women who founded Canada's first public child care institutions, a kaleidoscopic vision better serves advocates and children—nonwhite and white—alike.

Notes
1.   Historical writing on child care in Canada is sparse. An article by the late Schulz 1978 remains the authoritative survey. See also Pierson 1986 on the wartime day nurseries and Prentice 1989 on the struggle to keep the day nurseries open in Toronto once the war had ended; and Lind and Prentice 1992, Friendly 1994, and Varga 1997, who provides a useful account

focusing on the professionalization of the field. For the 1970s, see Atkin 1998. Marilyn Barber's study of immigrant domestic servants in Canada reminds us that the story of child care includes the many immigrants who have cared for children in other people's homes (Barber 1991).

2. McClintock 1995: 7.
3. Friendly 1994: 150.
4. See especially Scott and Tilly 1978 on the nineteenth century transition from the family economy to the factory system and Ross 1993: 223 on the importance of feminist historians' "rediscovery of housework and childcare as forms of productive work."
5. In Montreal the first nursery in Canada was founded by Roman Catholic nuns in 1854, followed by the Montreal Day Nursery in 1887, and in Ontario the Victoria Day Nursery was created three years later, with East End Day Nursery founded in 1892 and West End Creche in 1909. Both West End Creche and the Ottawa Day Nursery (1911) exist to this day, under different names. The early day nurseries have been characterized as providing minimal or custodial care of children. Typically, a matron, one or two nurses and a cook would staff a centre housing forty-five children and infants. Margaret Hewitt, writing about British day nurseries from the vantage point of the 1950s, has written: "to leave a tiny baby to the care of others was a hazardous business till well into the twentieth century" (Hewitt 1958: 128).
6. Lind and Prentice 1992: 89.
7. Dyhouse 1978: 248–67.
8. Anna Davin 1978: 9–65.
9. See Arnup, Levesque, and Pierson with Brennan 1990 and Arnup 1994.
10. Province of Ontario Archives, B. Corbett, 1965, "The West End Creche." West End Creche papers.
11. Province of Ontario Archives, B. Corbett, 1965, "The West End Creche." West End Creche papers.
12. Province of Ontario Archives, B. Corbett, 1965, "The West End Creche." West End Creche papers.
13. Province of Ontario Archives, B. Corbett, 1965, "The West End Creche." West End Creche papers.
14. Province of Ontario Archives, B. Corbett, 1965, "The West End Creche." West End Creche papers.
15. Province of Ontario Archives, B. Corbett, 1965, "The West End Creche." West End Creche papers.
16. Varga 1997: 41.
17. Varga 1997: 81–82.
18. Provincial Archives of Ontario, West End Creche papers, untitled, March 15, 1928.
19. Provincial Archives of Ontario, West End Creche papers, untitled, March 15, 1928.
20. Provincial Archives of Ontario, West End Creche papers, "Nursery Schools

in Great Britain," November 18, 1936.

21. Provincial Archives of Ontario, West End Creche papers, "Nursery Schools in Great Britain," November 18, 1936.

22. This will not explore fully the ideology of middle-class "whiteness" but relies on a general notion of the meaning of imperialism as that "'ideological cluster' that was made up of 'a renewed militarism, a devotion to royalty, an identification and worship of national heroes, together with a contemporary cult of personality, and racial ideas associated with Social Darwinism'" (Mackenzie cited in Vron 1992: 119).

23. Provincial Archives of Alberta, IODE papers, Annual meeting minutes 1921–1923, Volume 12 (Part 1)/3.

24. Provincial Archives of Alberta, IODE papers, Annual meeting minutes 1921–1923, Volume 12 (Part 1)/3.

25. Provincial Archives of Alberta, IODE papers, Annual Meeting minutes, May 31, 1921.

26. Provincial Archives of Alberta, IODE papers, National Executive minutes, December 1, 1920.

27. Provincial Archives of Alberta, IODE papers, Annual Meeting minutes, June 2, 1921.

28. Provincial Archives of Alberta, IODE papers, National Executive minutes, January 4, 1922.

29. Provincial Archives of Alberta, IODE papers, Annual Meeting minutes, June 2, 1921.

30. Provincial Archives of Alberta, IODE papers, Minutes of 24th annual meeting, June, 1924, Volume 12 (Part 1)/4.

31. Provincial Archives of Ontario, West End Creche papers, "West End Creche," 1959.

32. Provincial Archives of Ontario, West End Creche papers, "Circling the Globe," 1959.

33. Lind and Prentice 1992: 28.

Chapter 2

Family Policy, Child Care and Social Solidarity
The Case of Quebec

Jane Jenson

Quebec's Summit on the Economy and Employment, held in October 1996, brought together employers, unions and a broad selection of popular sector groups to reflect upon plans for the medium-term future of the province.[1] At the summit's end, Premier Bouchard announced a major revision of family policy. Eventually, the process launched at the summit would create a system of Early Childhood Centres to provide centre-based care and oversee family daycare providers while delivering services that cost parents no more than five dollars per day. Maligned by students for his refusal to freeze tuition fees, pressured by anti-poverty activists and socially marginal groups to embrace the goal of *appauvrissement zéro* (zero poverty) rather than striving to achieve a "zero deficit," Lucien Bouchard might simply be accused of searching for a theme that would unite rather than divide.[2] But the decision to announce a major reform of family policy, with universal and affordable child care at its centre, was much more than an effort to get out of a sticky political situation. It represented the victory of a coalition of activists and officials seeking to address the needs of families and children within Quebec's societal strategy (projet de société).

Indeed the summit was only one moment, albeit a crucial one, in a long discussion about family policy in Quebec. Child care and family policy have been subjects of explicit debate for over two decades. By the mid-1990s positions were aligned, in part, with reference to the government's Third Family Action Plan (1995–1997). Elaborated after broad public consultations in the 1995 International Year of the Family, the action plan was multi-faceted: its focus on prevention addressed preventing spousal abuse and inducing greater participation of fathers in child rearing; its focus on balancing work and family addressed the needs for greater child care and adolescent education about the importance of both parents sharing family responsibilities; its focus on financial support for parents and family environments addressed improving housing, valuing solidarity across families and emphasizing the family dimension in all services.[3] This list, while not exhaustive, represents responses to the demands of a wide range of actors and interests involved with family policy: feminists, the family movement, anti-poverty activists, social workers and experts on development and early childhood education, as well as government bureaucrats. While some of these actors are located in the private sector and involved in policy development through consultations, others are located inside the state's "structure of representation" in particular parts of the public-service sector and para-public bodies.

Family policy is a key element in a broader process of social reform, as is social assistance and labour-market policy. This multidimensional reform sought (1) to improve parents' capacity to balance work and family life; (2) to provide both financially accessible and developmentally sound child care services that facilitated school readiness; and (3) to induce parents with low-incomes or on social assistance to find either employment or better jobs.[4] Given this strategic location in the process of modernizing social policy, it is not surprising that the announcement of the new family policy garnered a huge amount of attention. Nor did this abate over the following months. In January 1997, the government published the White Paper, *Les enfants au cœur de nos choix* (Children at the Heart of our Choices) and legislated the following July.

Who were the major actors involved in debating family policy in Quebec? What was at issue in their disputes over the new policy, including the child care initiatives? The story begins with an overview of the history of such controversies—both to set the context and because Quebec is the only province which has had a self-identified family policy for several decades. In Quebec, the more European-style language of "family policy" describes the range of services and benefits available to children and their parents. In the name of social solidarity, Quebec has designed a number of benefits to redistribute income from the childless to those responsible for raising children. However, all these actions have provoked debate about how to achieve this redistribution and express this solidarity. In addition, child care policy and family policy have been, in recent years, increasingly integrated with other policy domains, so that an even wider range of actors is involved in disputing goals, forms and definitions of fairness. Advocates share a view of child care as one part of a larger whole and engage points of access as numerous as they are.

The resulting family policies can set a number of priorities. They may seek, for example, to promote child development, to maximize equality of opportunity and condition among all types of families, or to advance gender equality.[5] Quebec's family policy over the last decades has always had a range of goals, as the Third Action Plan described above well indicates. Nonetheless, promoting parental employment has recently emerged as the top priority. For example, in June 2000, in a speech vaunting the "Quebec way," the Deputy Minister of Child and Family Welfare, Maurice Boisvert,[6] described the 1997 reforms as follows: "We decided that we had to increase our support to families.... As a result we put in place a number of structural measures for the society of the year 2000, the harmonious functioning of which centres on employment." Nor is this statement surprising. The institution responsible for family policy, the ministère de la Famille et de l'Enfance[7] was created in 1997 by amalgamating the Family Secretariat—the Office des services de garde à l'enfance (OSGE) responsible for regulating child care—and the Ministry of Income Security. This new ministry quietly sought advocates' input and approval, creating an advisory board in the spring of 1999.

Child Care After the Quiet Revolution:
From Social Development to Family Policy

As Yves Vaillancourt[8] has stated, Quebec is the province that had the most privatized social services (before 1970) and then created the most public ones (after 1970):

> In the 1970s, the social service system which had so recently depended to a great extent on the commercial or nonprofit private sector, very quickly became one in which the public sector clearly formed the main component, thus relegating the various private agencies and services to a complementary—indeed re-sidual—role.[9]

This pattern remains true today, in the child care field at least, as the province moves against the current, putting most of its money into universal and inexpensive public services.

Quebec's social services were altered fundamentally by the wave of reforms initiated by the Quiet Revolution of 1960. Previously, services had been provided either by the Catholic Church (to Catholic Quebecers), or via a network of charitable and non-profit agencies (to non-Catholic communities). This changed dramatically as a new team of reformers, based in both the Quebec Liberal Party and the Parti québécois, took the reins of power in the next decades. Modernizing politicians, bureaucrats and other experts have had a major influence over the shape of policy since 1960, but they have also had to contend with a mobilized civil society that has sometimes had different assessments of the best direction for change. The 1960s reform thrust also intersected with initiatives from Ottawa that were setting all the provinces down some new paths.

During this period in Quebec, the combination of internal and external forces for change was dramatic. The *Social Assistance Act* of 1969 was Quebec's response to the Canada Assistance Plan (CAP), while the *Health and Social Services Act* (1971) established Quebec's universal healthcare system. Both pieces of legislation followed in the tracks of the Castonguay-Nepveu Commission, a major investigatory body that framed the terms of debate about health and social services for several decades. The commission consulted most of the province's key specialists on social policy, both conservative and reformist, and heard from almost every sector of Quebec society.[10]

Despite a new non-categorical social assistance regime that adopted an individualized approach to social security,[11] there was a concomitant concern about families. One result was a provincial family allowance regime, elaborated in 1969, that did not share with Ottawa the distrust of large families that had shaped federal family allowances since 1946.[12] These family allowances, altered at each moment of reform over the last decades, remain a key pillar of Quebec's family policy.

The Castonguay-Nepveu Commission was very critical of private services, whether non-profit or commercial; it clearly put the accent on public services.[13] Nonetheless, opposition to non-profit provision was somewhat tempered because of the non-statist approach of Quebec's highly mobilized civil society. In the 1960s and continuing today, this movement was traversed by a dense network of community groups, agencies, projects and popular initiatives whose *political project* was and remains to provide services "differently." From the early 1960s, citizens' committees were actively intervening in the social policy domain. They were equally critical of the individualistic "case work" approach of social workers and the charity-based models of religious organizations. They sought instead to provide collective solutions and services that would build local leadership and develop community capacity. While they turned to local governments, as well as to Quebec and Ottawa, for funding and support, their take on social services, as mentioned earlier, was never statist. By the late 1960s these popular-sector groups' (*groupes populaires)* political project was quite explicit. Rather than lobbying for public services, they mobilized self-help groups and community action, creating infrastructure such as legal aid, literacy training and family budgeting programs, child care centres and people's clinics.[14] Unions were also active participants, backing local self-help groups that promoted financial independence among low-income communities by setting up food, child care or other co-ops.

This mobilization, both in cities and rural areas, might have gone the way of contemporaneous collective action throughout North America—that is, towards obscurity—had it not been institutionalized in important locales, two of which are of central importance to this chapter. A central action of the popular-sector movement was establishing daycare centres *(garderies)*. These centres were incorporated as non-profit organizations and run by councils of parents and staff that embraced both democratic and child development goals.

The establishment of such services had also been a major goal of the second wave of the women's movement, since the movement's appearance in the mid-1960s. The Fédération des femmes du Québec (FFQ) at its founding in 1965 included state-provided child care on its list of six demands and continued to agitate for child care, for example, in its brief to the Royal Commission on the Status of Women (RCSW).[15] The Confédération des syndicats nationaux (CSN) also presented a brief to the RCSW centred on child care. Taking things in their own hands, women's and other popular-sector groups used funds from the federal Local Initiative Programme (LIP) to set up non-profit, democratically run, parent-managed centres in disadvantaged areas and other neighbourhoods.[16] These first politicized child care centres have been reclaimed as the model for today's central institution for child care and development, the Early Childhood Centres,[17] created by the 1997 reform.

A second important institution created at this time was the Centre local de services communautaires (CLSC). Modeled on the people's clinics, the CLSC serves as a point of entry to the healthcare system—providing home care (including postpartum care for multiple births), peri-natal care, parenting support, and so forth—and is intended to be a pivotal actor in community development projects.[18] The CLSC is in many ways an institutionalized expression of the community-based, progressive approach to health and social services—an approach suspicious of "medical" solutions, professionals, centralization and commercialization. Employing social animators as well as social workers and healthcare professionals, the CLSC has official responsibility to liaise with the voluntary sector and the community.[19] The CLSC remains a key partner in virtually all programs for children and families, with local CLSCs becoming a crucial link in the family policy chain, working closely with Early Childhood Centres in their catchment area.

In contrast to the popular-sector movement, the government of Quebec was not quick onto the child care field.[20] Its first formal involvement was in 1974, when the temptation of CAP dollars led to subsidies for low-income parents using regulated child care. New legislation in 1979 continued subsidies to low-income parents, established direct subsidies to centres, and created an allowance for the care of children with disabilities. At the same time, the regulatory and licensing body, the Office des services de garde à l'enfance, was created.

Over these same years, despite the philosophy and rhetoric privileging non-profit and community groups, the commercial private sector was not at a standstill, in part because of governmental foot dragging. When the supply of public and non-profit services could not keep up with demand, commercial providers rushed to expand.[21] The mix was always an uneasy one, however, with ministers frequently expressing an aversion to commercial expansion and even seeking to halt it.[22]

Setting Family Policy: Juggling a Variety of Purposes and Multiple Instruments

There has never been consensus on family policy in Quebec. Opinions vary over the most desirable types of services, to be sure. Some vaunt non-profit while others argue for a level playing field for commercial services. Some claim public financing is sufficient, while others believe services must also be publicly delivered. Beyond these controversies, there is always the issue of the birth rate, and whether public policy should be natalist in its goals.

We have already described the positions of the late 1960s and emphasized their continuity with those underpinning the 1997 reform. However, before those community-, child- and democracy-centred positions could become sufficiently strong to launch a new regime, Quebec passed through a controversial period when other ideals triumphed and alternative goals were promoted. In these debates the actors remained the same, but the balance of forces was different. Thus, by the 1970s the women's movement was an important force supported by "femocrats" (feminist bureaucrats and other civil servants) within several ministries as well as the Conseil du statut de la femme. But demographers and the family movement also were influential actors, as were outside experts and bureaucrats from a range of social and economic ministries.

Three years into its first term in office, the Parti québécois (PQ) government launched what would become a long and vibrant debate about family policy: one that continued through the terms of the succeeding Liberal government, culminating in 1987–88 in a new family policy and two new institutions—the Conseil de la famille (a para-public body responsible for advising the minister) and the Secrétariat à la famille.[23] While it began as a focused discussion of economic growth, including the population size needed to sustain development,[24] the discussion, prompted by the PQ government's economic strategy statement, *Bâtir le Québec* (1979), soon became a wholesale public debate about families, equality and social equity.[25]

Before going any further, it is important to understand the policy context of the mid-1980s, particularly surrounding the 1984 Green Paper, *Pour les familles québécoises*, that framed the debate and positions later adopted by major provincial actors. In 1984 the PQ government was already actively considering tax reform and strategies for protecting the French language and Quebec culture in the face of a declining birth rate. The tax reform process was tending in the direction of favouring two-parent and working families, while a parliamentary commission, headed by Richard French and reporting in 1985, had a mandate to analyze the demographic situation in the context of cultural policy. The commission proposed a dualistic approach of increasing immigration and fostering a higher birth rate.[26]

Seeing both these policy developments emerging, women's groups were anxious. Despite guaranteeing gender equality in Quebec's 1975 Charter of Rights and Liberties and despite a progressive program to advance equality between the sexes put into place in 1978, in an attempt to deal with cultural challenges the province appeared to be moving back towards traditionalism, via the tax treatment of families.[27] In response, in 1985–86, feminists coming from both the FFQ and the more traditionalist Association féminine d'éducation et d'action sociale (AFEAS) actively intervened in provincewide consultations organized by the touring three-person Consultative Committee on the Green Paper. Women were optimistic that their voices would be heard, because one member of the committee, Nicole Boily, was a feminist who had worked with the FFQ, and another member, Christiane Bérubé, had just ended her term as president of AFEAS.

In addition to tax reformers, natalists and feminists, the debate engaged professionals who had a stake in establishing clear, new norms and gaining additional resources for social work, psychology, health and other social fields.[28] Last but never least, the family movement too was actively involved. This movement of individuals and groups promoting healthy families and family life, has been an important actor for decades. Renée B. Dandurand describes its two wings:[29] "There is a conservative and Catholic one, very close to the Church. But there is also a liberal wing, which looks to the state to support families, in their diverse needs and their diverse situations." It was with this second, progressive branch of the family movement that the third member of the consultative committee, author Maurice Champagne-Gilbert, was associated.

The consultative committee's reports[30] came down strongly in favour of the principle of shared responsibility between parents and the community. They recognized the variety of situations in which families live, and they downplayed natalism. More generally, the committee argued that there was no crisis of the family. The real challenge, they proposed, was instituting new forms of solidarity between the sexes. In its recommendations, the committee sought to avoid supporting natalist policy, proposing higher levels of spending and more coherent support for families, as well as improved parental leaves, conditions of part-time employment and family allowances. It was strangely silent on the matter of child care, only recommending that (1) the current regime be better organized and that everyone, including employers, do their part and (2) the existing subsidy for low-income families using services be retained.

With the Liberals in government by the time the second report was issued, some adjustments to expectations were inevitable. However, the change from one party to another did not mark a major policy reorientation. The 1987 statement on family policy issued by the ministère de la Santé et des Services sociaux stood on four principles, most of which reflected the general thinking of the consultative committee. The fourth principle was, of course, the exception to the above generalization. The four principles were: (1) providing public support for the costs of child-rearing; (2) fighting poverty; (3) encouraging parents to seek employment; and (4) supporting a higher birth rate.[31]

The second and third principles provided the rationale for needs-based subsidies for child care; tax credits; recurring funding to child care centres; generous maternity and parental leave packages; as well as allowances for young children and income support for working parents. Thus, 1988 also saw the creation of the Parental Wage Assistance program, known as APPORT in French. This program sought to draw both parents into the labour force by providing a wage supplement to families with even a tiny amount (now $100 per month) of earned income and offering extra support for child care expenses.[32]

Principles one and four generated four types of family allowances. One was universal. Others addressed the particular needs of young children and the disabled. Perhaps best known was the birth allowance, whose amount increased to very generous levels for the third child and subsequent children.[33] Birth allowances favouring "the third child" never gained unanimous support ,and controversy surrounding them touched all the central issues of Quebec politics. Sustained from the 1980s, these issues ranged from economic development to the role of the state, from immigration to linguistic protection; conservative demographers debated feminist demographers; proponents of social spending confronted neo-liberals; natalists verbally sparred with familialists and feminists. The controversy shook all the major players: the National Assembly; government agencies, such as the Secrétariat à la famille; para-public bodies, (including the Conseil du statut de la femme and the Conseil de la famille); the press; and intellectuals.

The post-1987 system was coherent, in the sense that it stood on the four principles listed above, but it was complicated, with a wide variety of different programs. Moreover, while coherent in themselves, as an expression of the goals of family policy, the design did not always mesh well with other governmental goals. There were still problems of linking it to employability measures; there was mounting concern about the "poverty trap" and intergenerational reliance on social assistance.

After its election in 1995, the PQ government, as did its Liberal predecessor, undertook to reform social assistance programs, eventually tabling the very controversial Bill 186 (only passed in June 1998). In one decade, Quebec transformed its social assistance regime into one based on both income support and its own notion of "employability."[34] Because of the limited results rendered from training and other programs and due to rising rates of unemployment and welfare, another large debate on the subject of social assistance was opened. From the beginning, due to policy makers' concerns for single mothers and poor families, child benefits were part of this discussion as was the idea of expanding child care.

In preparation for reforming social assistance, the government asked a group of experts to make proposals for redesigning the system. Eventually, when the experts failed to agree, two disparate reports were published: one by the majority (headed by psychologist Camil Bouchard and hence coined the *Bouchard Report*) and one by the minority (headed by economist Pierre Fournier).[35] Nonetheless, despite their disagreements on a range of other matters, both groups agreed that "children should be removed from social assistance" and both recommended the creation of an integrated family allowance.[36]

Also, the estates-general of Education, after months of touring the province for consultations, in their 1996 report recommended increased and more accessible child care for young children and extended preschool education services. Such services were deemed imperative to combat high drop-out rates and curb school failure in general. The Conseil supérieur de l'éducation made similar recommendations, as did the majority *Bouchard Report*. The experts reminded Quebecers that these proposals were by no means new, citing the *Parent Report* (the Quiet Revolution blueprint for secularizing and modernizing education) that decades earlier recommended kindergarten for four- and five-year-old children.

During this time, the women's movement had also mobilized and the 1995 march for *Pain et Roses* (Bread and Roses) identified child care as a key goal, as did the later interventions of the FFRQ during the Quebec summits of 1996.

The claims and proposals of these expert studies, consultations and groups addressing poverty and promoting gender equality all fed into the major reform of family policy announced at the Summit on the Economy and Employment in 1996. Also, they particularly influenced the White Paper released the following January. That wide-ranging document became the basis for the redesign of family policy and the creation of several new benefits and institutions: unified family allowance, reorganized child care sector, new parental leave and insurance schemes, housing subsidies for low-income families and insurance for prescription drugs.[37] Hence, several decades of engaging debate culminated in one comprehensive document.

Towards a Family Policy with "Children at the Heart of Our Choices"

As we have seen, changes to child care programs in Quebec have always been located in a broader set of family policies. The 1997 reform, perhaps best known for its five dollars-per-day spaces, is no exception here. This shift in funding arrangements, as well as the emphasis on universality and a developmentally appropriate curriculum, is part of a much broader effort to reform social assistance, develop broad-based support for the PQ's political vision, promote gender equality and demonstrate Ottawa's recalcitrance with respect to the federal principle. With such an all-encompassing agenda, it is not surprising that a number of actors considered the reform to be of consequence to their interests.

The first of these actors were the fiscal conservatives, who wanted to achieve a zero deficit and deemed universal family allowances and generous birth allowances a "waste" of state funds. Provided as they were to families whether they "needed" them or not, these allowances prompted those who shared Finance Minister Bernard Landry's overwhelming fear of deficit spending (at least on social programs) to look for a change.

Next on the list of actors was the women's movement. The 1995 March for Bread and Roses mobilization had visited increasing prominence on the movement, and FFQ president, Françoise David, was an important player at the Summit on the Economy and Employment. Movement women now also had ties to women within the state; feminists and social democrats, such a Pauline Marois and Louise Harel, had risen to high cabinet responsibility, and femocrats were scattered throughout the bureaucracy, but perhaps of equal influence was the PQ's desire to assure that no gender gap would interfere with its support in the next referendum.

Other crucial actors in this policy network, often providing the glue that allowed all the parts to hold together, were child development experts. Camil Bouchard, for example, had published a formative document in 1991, *Un Québec fou de ses enfants (Quebec, Mad about its Children)*[38] that it made the case, well before Fraser Mustard had arrived on the scene, that early childhood education was crucial to proper development. Moreover, it argued that poverty and disadvantage were the factors most likely to place children at risk of negative developmental outcomes. In the preparations of the 1997 White Paper, Bouchard helped link domains such as social assistance (recall, he had signed the majority report of the 1996 expert consultation on social assistance reform), early childhood education and social solidarity.

The White Paper was not preceded by any formal public consultation. It was written by the secretariat of the Committee of Priorities of the Executive Council and signed by one of its members, Pauline Marois, Minister of Education.[39] The government had judged it important to keep the drafting process under firm control for a number of reasons. First, the major lines of the reform had already been announced at the summit; the government knew what it wanted to do. Second, the direction of reform was not universally popular. The natalist wing of the family movement was not happy with the threat to the birth allowances that the paper posed. Commercial child care operators were also opposed to the reform. Indeed, Minister Marois' concern about the rising importance of commercial child care providers in the system and her decision immediately after the 1995 election to place a moratorium on new licences, both informed the paper. It was, therefore, obvious to the commercial sector that its future was on the line. Third, the government was facing resistance to its parallel reform of social assistance and did not want to open up another line of attack. Finally, the government, as well as the bureaucrats and experts who supported the reform, understood that it made sense only as a package. None of the parts in and of itself was a compelling reform, but together they created a momentum for positive change. Therefore, the whole had to hold together and be held together.

The White Paper made an argument for coherence, presenting a strong case for "integration" across social, educational and employment domains. As a result, family policy is now described as having four main objectives: (1) to ensure fairness by offering universal support to families; (2) to give more assistance to low income families; (3) to facilitate the balancing of parental and work responsibilities; and (4) to foster children's development and equal opportunity.[40]

In the White Paper there was a somewhat great emphasis on promoting employment and equal opportunity. Despite such differences, however, the policy has a number of clear principles; some continue past practices while others break with the past.[41] Family policy pursues its objectives through the following programs: an integrated family allowance, targeted to low-income parents, covering the estimated costs of raising a child from birth to age 18; universality in the tax regime, including a tax exemption for dependent children's basic needs and a non-refundable tax credit for dependent children; parental insurance providing paid parental leaves to virtually all employed new parents; educational and developmental child care services organized by Early Childhood Centres; accessible child care services, via fees of five dollars per day and reduced-cost child care for low-income working parents and 23.5 hours per week free child care for social assistance recipients, in order to ensure that children at-risk use the developmental service; full-day kindergarten for five-year-old children; half-day kindergarten coupled with child care for four-year-olds living in Montreal's disadvantaged neighbourhoods.

The focus on equal opportunity, equity and solidarity across classes is expressed in the integrated family allowance, available to all low-income families with dependent children under eighteen years. It replaces three family allowances[42] and those parts of the social assistance regime that had been paid with respect to children. The amount varies according to the birth order of the child and the number of parents living with the child as well as according to family income. The Family Allowance supplements the Canada Child Tax Benefit (CCTB) that Revenue Canada pays to Quebec families. In other words, if necessary, it tops the CCTB up to Quebec's preferred supplement level. Until 2000 at least, Quebec was among the eight provinces taxing back the CCTB going to families on social assistance. When the federal government increased the amount paid out in the CCTB and its supplement in the 2000 budget, Quebec decided not to tax back all the increase. According to some, the province extended this generosity in an attempt to maintain its financial involvement—that is, visibility—with many families.

The overall assessment of this unification of programs suggests that they keep low-income parents more or less where they were in terms of benefits, as long as these parents stay on social assistance.[43] However, because the benefits are neutral as to employment, there is a gain made by those who are working in a low-paying job. Therefore, reflecting the link to employability goals, the policy offers an incentive to seek employment.

The major losers in this shift to a single, targeted family allowance are middle-income families with more than two children. They no longer could count, for example, on a birth allowance injecting up to $8000 into the family treasury. While middle-income parents lost the previously universal family allowance, they acquired less costly child care. This was a gain for those who used the services, but families who cared for their own children or used informal care received no benefit. Therefore, there has been some dispute about the fairness of the new system, and about whether it recognizes the diversity of family needs.[44]

In contrast to the targeted Family Allowance, an emphasis on universality is evident in several programs maintained by the 1997 reform: the tax exemption for dependent children, the non-refundable credit for the first child of single-parent families and the non-refundable tax credit to all families.[45] This third credit is the only universal tax credit in the country for families with children[46] and it is worth $598 for the first child ($897 for a single-parent family) and $552 for subsequent children. These tax advantages are a key expression of solidarity in the form of universality; the same principle underpins the child care programs.

The 1997 family policy announcement continued Quebec's established tradition of providing the most generous programs of paid maternity leave and unpaid parental leave in Canada.[47] The White Paper also announced that the government would institute a new program of Parental Insurance. This idea of redesigning parental leave, to extend coverage and cleave it from eligibility for Unemployment Insurance, had been promoted by the PQ for almost a decade. It was part of the 1981 election campaign, promoted primarily by Lise Payette, and in 1996 Louise Harel took up the idea once again. The Conseil du statut de la femme had also been pushing for such a change since 1988, when it published a detailed analysis of the gaps in coverage.

Ottawa's 1971 decision to link eligibility for both maternity and parental leave to Unemployment Insurance and the ongoing restructuring of the labour force were of grave consequence to many Quebec women. According to the estimate of the Conseil du statut de la femme (CSF), fully 50 percent of women who gave birth in Quebec in 1988 were not eligible for paid leave, despite the fact that 72 percent of Quebec women between ages twenty and thirty-five were employed. This gap resulted from many workers' failure to meet the eligibility requirements of the federal regime. Still, this problem has not been solved by the shift to Employment Insurance, which has further reduced eligibility in some cases, while increasing it in others (such as for part-time employees).[48]

It was in response to this family policy that the White Paper proposed to completely break the link to employment. A new regime, based on earned income rather than duration of work, would make leaves available to any parent who earned at least $2,000 in the year prior to birth. Management of the program would be transferred to the Régie des rentes, with the funding rate set at 75 percent of the previous year's income.[49] It also proposed a paternity leave of five weeks, with the rate calculated on the father's income. There would also be an adoption leave of twelve weeks.[50]

In addition to a paternity leave of five weeks, the draft bill sets out two options for parents: forty weeks at 75 percent replacement of the previous year's earnings or fifty weeks at 70 percent for the first eighteen weeks and 55 percent replacement for the remaining thirty-two weeks.[51]

Parental Insurance has not been implemented but it is on its way. Intergovernmental negotiations broke down in March 1997 when Quebec asked Ottawa to transfer a portion of the Employment Insurance funds to the province, while noting that Quebec parents using five-dollar-per-day child care would no longer claim the Child Care Expense Deduction (CCED); thus saving federal dollars. In the face of this failure (and a number of others in the following years), Quebec began to mobilize support. The PQ twice promised a new regime—in the 1998 election campaign and at the March, 1999 National Assembly opening. In May 1999, consultations with employers, unions, and family organizations began on a go-it-alone strategy, and in fall 1999, ministry-led consultations with employers brought agreement in principle.[52] The February 2000 Youth Summit endorsed a "made in Quebec" plan; included in the consensus were not only youth groups but also employers, unions, women's groups and so on. In the face of continued rejection by Ottawa and a growing mobilization in Quebec, Minister of State, Pauline Marois, tabled Bill 140 on June 6, 2000. In presenting the bill, the minister cited as her impetus the "historic demand of women's groups" and other socio-economic groups, as well as the consensus expressed at the summits of 1996 and 2000.

Getting to Five-Dollar-per-Day Child Care and the Early Childhood Centres

Of course the White Paper did not only address parental leave; a major dimension of the family policy reform of 1997 was the redesign of child care delivery. Until 1997, Quebec shared with most other provinces a mixed-bag approach to child care services, providing regulated daycare centres *(garderies)* and family daycare *(garde au milieu familial)*, as well as unregulated nursery schools, drop-in centres *(haltes garderies)* and school-based child care all under the jurisdiction of the Ministry of Education.[53] In 1995, the licensing body (the Office des services de garde à l'enfance— OSGE) imposed a moratorium on new licences because department officials and the minister responsible were concerned about the commercial sector's increasing role in the overall system. The 1997 reform ended that moratorium but, more importantly, it created a new institution, the Early Childhood Centre *(Centre de la petite enfance)*.[54]

Once up and running as intended throughout the province, these centres will mark a major shift from established thinking about young children, about work and family and about the transition to school. The centres are governed as a non-profit corporation, with parents a majority on the governing council. Offering different kinds of child care, they incorporate under a single roof both the traditional centre-based *garderies* (for at least seven children) and the supervisory responsibility of family daycare.[55] The family daycare option tends to be selected for infants (almost half of all children under twelve months old are in a family daycare) and older children who are in kindergarten part of the day. Centre-based care predominates among two- to four-year-old children,[56] and centres may also take school-age children who do not have access to an after-school facility. Efforts have been made to make Early Childhood Centres widely available. There are twenty centres operating in Aboriginal communities, and an agreement is being developed to transfer administrative responsibility for governing these services to the Kativik Regional

Government. Services are also available in the far north, including in Inuktitut.[57]

Other family daycare providers have access to the resources and educational programs of the neighbourhood Early Childhood Centre. The centres, in collaboration with other agencies, offer a variety of programs to the broader community. Most often these collaborations include that other important Quebec institution, the CLSC (Centre local des services communautaires).

Probably the best known result of the child care reform is the provision of truly affordable child care, set at a standard rate—paid by all parents regardless of their income—of five dollars per day, or twenty-five dollars per week for full-time daycare, up to ten hours a day. The province fills the gap between fees and operating costs with direct grants to the centres. The money for financing the program was found, among other places, in the cancellation of the tax deduction for child care expenses. As sufficient low-cost spaces become available, parents can no longer deduct child care expenses from their provincial income taxes. Nor can they claim the federal CCED, as providers do not issue receipts.

Beginning in 1997, four-year-olds were offered low-cost spaces, with care for three-year-olds and after-school care covered in September 1998. The program aimed to reach newborns by the year 2001, but the schedule was sped up, so that, as of September 2000 the five dollar-per-day rate was universally available to parents of any child in a centre, family daycare or after-school care.[58]

Parents on social assistance, with preschool children over age two or children with a medical certificate prescribing attendance, have access to free child care for twenty-three and a half hours a week in a centre or in family daycare. Clearly, the goal here is to prevent parents' exclusion from the labour force from hindering their child's development. The Ministry of Social Solidarity will pay for child care hours in excess of twenty-three and a half for parents on social assistance participating in employability programs. Finally, parents eligible for the income supplement program (the Parental Wage Assistance Program) receive a three dollar-per-day subsidy that reduces their fees to only ten dollars a week per child.

Such encouragement, by means of free or very low-cost care, illustrates child care policy's direct and unabashed basis on the principle of enabling all parents, even those with low earning capacity to enter the labour force. All parents on social assistance with children aged two and older are now classified as "employable." But there are also induce-ments—and significant assistance—for these parents to use not only regulated child care but care with a strong educational content.

Early childhood education and development is clearly a focus of this reform, promoting school readiness for all children and seeking to overcome the learning disadvantages often associated with low income and poverty. Early childhood education is defined as the key program for successfully integrating children into society, for school readiness, and for preventing problems later in life. Thus, Early Childhood Centres have a strong educational mandate, based on a new, provincewide program. Tailored to different age groups, the program is based on techniques of learning through play.[59]

Developmental priorities also underpin the extension of kindergarten in September 1997 to a full day for five-year-olds. While compulsory schooling is begun at age six and kindergarten attendance is optional, over 98 percent of five-year-old children do attend full-day programs. In addition, four-year-olds living on the island of Montreal in areas designated as "disadvantaged" have access to half-day junior kindergarten and educational child care. This differential treatment of certain four-year-olds is the only part of the program which is not universal.

This new educational emphasis demanded some serious attention be paid to improving the credentials of child care workers and raising their wages. The former is long overdue; Quebec's regulations for staff ratios and training are among the least demanding in the country. Indeed, in 1999, 23 percent of Early Childhood Centres did not meet the licensing requirements for trained workers.[60] In response, new training programs are being developed. For example, managers of child care facilities may enroll in a program developed by the Université de Québec à Montréal (UQAM), while family daycare providers can now be trained in a provincewide distance learning program through Quebec's Télé-Université.

Wages have been paid some attention—they were raised after workers threatened to strike in the spring of 1999. Seeking to avoid the disruption such a strike would provoke, the government settled with the union, affiliated to the CSN, after a series of short stoppages and well-publicized threats. Wages have been improved by an average of 38 percent, and the ministry has allowed Early Childhood Centres to increase the income of family daycare providers.[61] Despite the hoopla, the starting salary of a child care worker with a junior college (CEGEP) diploma will be only a modest $25,000 (currently it is $20,293). Nevertheless, the ministry reports a 56 percent enrolment increase in such programs.[62]

Critics and Responses

The new family policy, along with the child care component, has many supporters, not least of which are its designers and promoters inside the state. However, there is also a good deal of popular support. During the 1998 election campaign, Jean Charest criticized the five-dollar-per-day program as "not meeting the needs of all parents." In less than thirty-six hours the item had disappeared from the campaign agenda, as negative reactions and objections swamped the Liberal leader.

This said, there are still critics. First are those parents who cannot get a space for their child. While any parent may use child care, centres still ration access, via waiting lists and so on, as there are not enough spaces to meet demand. In 1998–99, for example, the number of spaces increased by 17 percent overall. There were major differences across regions, however, with rural and peripheral regions benefiting particularly. For example, spaces in Montreal increased by 6 percent, while those in the region Nord du Québec rose from 356 in 1996–97 to 712 in 1998–99. Spaces in Nord du Québec rose again by 68 percent in 1999–2000, and that same year spaces in the Côte Nord increased by 35 percent.[63]

Often parents with "atypical needs" still do not have their needs met, and they must resort to all the usual forms of unregulated care, including drop-in centres or unlicensed kindergartens. However, several pilot projects announced in 2000 sought to provide services twenty-four hours a day for shift workers. This promise had been included in the 1997 White Paper but was previously left aside.

The constant pressure to create new spaces remains. Waiting lists continue to grow, despite the increase of spaces. Indeed, the auditor general reported a shortfall of 135,213 places in March 1999; of the 229,323 children needing a space, only 94,110 had one.[64] In response, the government claimed, in June 2000, to have added 34,000 spaces over the previous two years, or 300 a week for the years 1999–2000.[65] The government's future target is 12,000 new early childhood educator jobs by 2005.

This juggling of numbers and targets represents, in part, the difficulty of predicting demand. The initial calculations that informed the White Paper were based on a survey done under the old regime, in 1993–94.[66] Many more parents than anticipated appeared at the doors of Early Childhood Centres seeking to transfer their children into educationally focused programs from the informal care or other arrangements they were currently using.

Among critical parents are those who have lost ground under this new program. And they have not hesitated to make their voices heard. One such group is those who saw their tax deductions disappear; parents employing nannies and in-home babysitters or using unregulated but receipted care could no longer deduct those expenses from their Quebec taxes (of course they retained the federal deduction). Parents also complain that, in this competitive market for spaces, centres are charging additional fees (registration fees are an example) or hiding higher costs in "program fees." Therefore, parents charge, the promise of fixed costs may in some cases be illusory.

A second important critic has been the auditor general, who issued a damning report in 1999. The report criticized the ministry for general mismanagement, as well as for its lack of evaluation criteria of the central goals, that is, child development and school readiness. Beyond these somewhat accountantlike criticisms were others going to the heart of the matter. The auditor general found an increased use of family daycare—from 26 percent of spaces in 1996 to 34 percent in 1999.[67] Yet, the oversight, with respect to educational content, sometimes appeared more "virtual" than real. The report also pointed out that Quebec still lacked the administrative capacity to issue licences to drop-in centres and private kindergartens. Yet this type of service was still providing a fair amount of child care, filling the above-described gap between supply and demand.

The ministry has responded to the criticisms about training and has established a task force to investigate the "contribution" of drop-in centres.[68] Nonetheless, there are still gaps in the capacity to regulate and to manage the system.

A third, vociferous and long-standing critic is composed of the other major losers under the new regime; many commercial operators, with their limited access to grants, have difficulty making ends meet. These actors, whom the minister made no bones about preferring to see play a more diminished role, have been hard hit. The original White Paper had suggested that commercial providers would be phased out, but after a major mobilization and the sobering recognition that without them there would not be enough available spaces, a compromise was eventually struck. Existing commercial operators now receive public funds, but at a lower rate than public facilities, via an agreement in which the government rents spaces. Since 1997, there has been a five-year moratorium on new licences. Owners have also been offered the possibility of transforming their businesses into centres, by selling to a non-profit association of parents that would form the governing body. The mishandling of these transformations forms another of the auditor general's criticisms. The process is cumbersome and slow, and in the meantime the ministry is closing its eyes to illegal operators, as it can not afford to lose spaces.[69]

A fourth set of critics comes from within the family movement. These opponents of the 1997 design do support state spending on children and families. However, they would prefer to see the generosity that Quebec directs toward child care diverted to a universal family allowance, recognizing the contributions to society of all parents. Thus, in a dramatic winter 2000 re-release of a study originally published during the 1998 ice storm, the Institute for Research on Public Policy[70] reported that three-quarters of families received less money under the new regime than under the previous one. The authors were critical of the government's actions in abandoning universal family allowances and substituting allowances targeted at low-income parents. They recommended, as in the traditional French system, generous and universal family allowances for *all* parents, in the name of horizontal redistribution across families, rather than vertical redistribution from better-off to low-income families.

However, this group's recommendation with respect to child care was an about-face. The authors claimed that child care should be universal instead of market driven, allowing parents to chose whether to pay for care or provide it themselves, as well as to select the type they preferred.

These two positions exactly oppose those adopted by the government in 1996–97. The government policy sought to build solidarity via universality and to invest in children's development in the realm of child care, while it expressed a commitment to equity with its targeted family allowances. In part, the divergence comes from differing assessments of two elements of the family policy mix. One is clearly the educational component of child care. The authors of the IRPP study[71] insist that "parents know best" about the quality of care and that governments should not be in the business of establishing standards for credentials or programs.[72] Thus, the editor's note, signed by Carole Vincent of the IRPP, makes a plea not only for greater choice but for re-valuing parental care. She summarily writes, "Indeed it is difficult to argue that the benefits generated by daycare services exceed those generated by parental care."[73]

The government, in contrast, inspired by the literature on child psychology and early childhood development, takes another position. It attributes value added to quality child care services, not only for disadvantaged children but for all children. Thus, the program seeks to overcome the threat to some children posed by their parents' circumstances, such as living in poverty, or from the failure to diagnose and intervene early enough when a child exhibits developmental and other delays. In addition, the government sees the educational content of the program as greatly promoting school readiness for all children.

A second difference between the positions of the IRPP and the government is evident in the attention to matters of equality, especially gender equality. Even if there has been a discernible decline in the rhetoric of gender equality in the post-1997 family policy, as compared to its predecessors, the argument is still present. Therefore, the design of parental insurance, child care and family allowances reflects, *inter alia* attention to gender inequalities in the labour market, for all women, whether low-income single mothers or professionals living in two-parent families. The IRPP report, in contrast, is virtually silent on matters of gender equality—never the strong suit of the family movement.

This last comparison takes us back to the fundamental issues raised for decades by women's movements and experts in child development. From this somewhat lengthy comparison of two positions promoted in the ongoing and lively debate about child care and family policy in Quebec, we can appreciate the fact that these issues are not settled. While the new regime has widespread support, its critics both inside the state and in civil society are not without influence. Childcare in Quebec, as elsewhere, remains a work in progress.

Notes

1. This chapter is part of a larger project supported by a SSHRC research entitled Citizenship Regimes and New Social Unions: Learning from Caring.
2. The press at the time made such arguments. See, for example, Cloutier 1996 and Charette 1996.
3. "Family Policy History." Available at www.famille-enfance.gouv.qc.ca.
4. See the press at the time. For a recent review of the Summit declarations, see the Auditor General's 1999 report (Vérificateur Général 1999: para 4.16), available at www.vgq.gouv.qc.ca.
5. Jenson and Stroick 1999a: 2–3 provide one such list.
6. Boisvert 2000: 3.
7. In its own documentation in English, the ministry translates its name as Ministry of Child and Family Welfare. We will use this translation as well.
8. Vaillancourt 1988: 144.
9. Vaillancourt 1988: 151.
10. Lesemann 1981.
11. Boychuk 1998: 84.
12. Bergeron 1997: 261–68.

13. Vaillancourt 1988: 147–49; 151.
14. Bélanger and Lévesque 1992: 715–24.
15. Collectif Clio 1992: 464.
16. Desjardins 1991: Ch 3; Lamoureux 1992: 699.
17. See Boisvert 2000: 5, who says of the new ECC: "I would be remiss if I failed to mention the beginnings of these child care centres. The current network was created out of parent-run day care centres and home day care providers who formed agencies responsible for their management. The collaborative spirit between educators and parents has been maintained, protected—I would even say made a priority."
18. The CLSCs resemble the "people's clinics" in many ways, especially in the emphasis on empowerment of communities through mobilization and action. Nonetheless, several of the groups running "people's clinics" (which were staffed by a mix of medically-trained personnel, social animators and volunteers) opposed Bill 65 which established the CLSCs because they saw them as excessively statist (Bélanger and Lévesque 1992: 721–22).
19. Roy 1987.
20. Baillargeon 1996.
21. Vaillancourt 1988: 161.
22. Jenson and Phillips 2000.
23. A Secrétariat à la politique familiale was set up in 1984, but reorganized and renamed in 1988.
24. The emergence of concerns about the birth rate is hardly surprising, given the fact that in the single decade from 1961 to 1971, the average Quebec family fell from four to two children, while in the mid-1980s the birth rate dropped to 1.4 (Dandurand 1992: 368).
25. Jenson 1998.
26. Academic demographers, always important actors in this policy network in Quebec, had been writing of the demographic crisis for years. The Parliamentary Commission, reporting in September 1985, had a mandate to "study the cultural, social, and economic impact of current demographic tendencies for the future of Quebec as a distinct society" (Dandurand 1987: 354).
27. Dandurand 1987: 353.
28. Dandurand 1987: 355.
29. 1987: 355–56.
30. These were *Le soutien collectif réclamé pour les familles québécoises. Rapport de la consultation sur la politique familiale* (1985) and *Le soutien collectif recommandé pour les parents québécois. Rapport de la consultation sur la politique familiale* (1986). The move from "families" to "parents" signals the shift in perspective that the Committee was trying to provoke.
31. Lefebvre 1998: 221.
32. Beauvais and Jenson 2001: Appendix A, Table 8.
33. The *prime à la naissance* was profoundly natalist in design: $500 for the first

and second births (which in 1989 became $1,000 for the second birth). In 1988, third births brought $3,000, in 1989 $4,500 and, until 1997, $8,000 spread over five years. Prior to the 1997 reform, the basic family allowances and young child allowance also rose with the number of children.

34. Noël 1996.
35. Noël 1996.
36. Lefebvre 1998: 215–16.
37. Rose 1998.
38. MSSS 1991.
39. Her executive assistant and the chief negotiator throughout this process was Nicole Boily, who had been a member of the 1984–86 Consultative Committee and who would subsequently be named President of the Conseil de la famille et de l'enfance.
40. These three goals are constantly reiterated in a range of documents. This English version is from Boisvert 2000: 4. Sometimes, however, the first and second are merged, to generate three main objectives (see, for example, "Family Policy History," available at www.famille-enfance.gouv.qc.ca).
41. Current information about the programs can be obtained from "Family Policy History." Available at www.famille-enfance.gouv.qc.ca.
42. A separate allowance for children with disabilities is still available.
43. Rose 1998.
44. IRPP 2000; Vérificateur Général 1999.
45. There are also a range of other tax benefits for families with children. For the details and comparisons to other provinces, see Beauvais and Jenson 2001: Appendix A, Tables 10, 12).
46. Clarke 1998: 13.
47. In 1978, Quebec created a Maternity Allowance. This benefit provides coverage for the first two weeks of maternity leave not covered by federal Unemployment Insurance (now Employment Insurance). Quebec also has the most generous unpaid parental leave in Canada. In 1990, new parents, both birth and adopting, could access 34 weeks of unpaid parental leave; the unpaid leave was extended to 52 weeks in 1997. For a comparison with the other provinces, see Beauvais and Jenson 2001: Appendix A, Table 4.
48. This estimate of eligibility is also made by the Canadian Labour Congress. It reports that between 1988 and 2000, the percentage of new mothers eligible for UI or EI parental benefits remained at just under 50 percent, despite the extension of EI to part-time workers (Beauvais and Jenson, 2001: 9).
49. This idea of a separate *caisse* for parental leave, as well as extended coverage, had been promoted by the PQ for a number of years. See *La Gazette des femmes* 1996.
50. Lepage and Moisan 1998.
51. See Ministère de la Famille et de l'Enfance 2000.
52. Québec 2000: Vol. III, 133.

53. Childcare Resource and Research Unit 1997: 25.
54. The Ministry's documentation in English calls these "child care centres" but I believe "early childhood centre" is a better translation, both because it makes a distinction between what has become the term in many places for *any* daycare centre and because it makes the link to "early childhood development" which is a major part of their mission.
55. Family day care providers can care for up to six children, or nine if they have an adult assistant. For details about the Early Childhood Centres, see *Les centres de la petite enfance* or the overview in "Family Policy—Educational and Childcare Services," both available at www.famille-enfance.gouv.qc.ca.
56. Québec 1999: 130.
57. Boisvert 2000: 7.
58. Québec 2000: Vol. III, 132.
59. One of the major criticisms launched against Quebec's program is its failure to truly live up to this promise. With most attention paid to creating enough spaces, including at a high rate in family daycare, the spotlight has not be kept consistently on supervising the implementation of the educational program. This is one of the criticisms of the Auditor General, for example (for an overview, see Lacroix 2001).
60. Vérificateur Général 1999: para 4. 65.
61. Québec 2000: Vol. III, 132.
62. See Ministère de la Famille et de l'Enfance 2000.
63. Lacroix 2001: 90.
64. Vérificateur Général 1999: para 4.45.
65. The first figure is from Boisvert 2000: 7 and the second from Ministère de la Famille et de l'Enfance 2000.
66. Vérificateur Général 1999: para 4.48.
67. Vérificateur Général 1999: para 4.53.
68. Ministry, communiqué de presse, June 22, 2000.
69. Vérificateur Général 1999: para 4.77 ff.
70. IRPP 2000.
71. IRPP 2000: 28–29.
72. They concede a role for regulation of health and safety, however.
73. IRPP 2000: 3.

Chapter 3

From Social Movement to Marginalized Interest Groups
Advocating for Quality Child Care
in Alberta, 1965–86

Tom Langford

In this chapter, I will analyze child care advocacy in Alberta between 1965, when the provincial government first made a financial contribution to a day nursery, and 1986, when the province ended a period of rapid expansion of licensed child care spaces by restricting operating allowance payments to existing centres.[1] I argue that, whereas advocacy in the late 1960s and early 1970s emanated from a social movement for quality child care, advocacy in the late 1970s and early 1980s was carried out by marginalized interest groups. In analyzing this historical change in advocacy, I address two general questions: first, how did the structure of political opportunities at different points in this period affect the relationships between advocates and state officials and the influence of advocates on child care policies and programs in Alberta? During this twenty-two year period, the key dimensions of the political opportunity structure for quality child care advocacy were the roles of elite state allies in policy development, the political influence of commercial child care operators and the responsive, accessible climate of the institutionalized political system. The effects changes in each of these dimensions visited on Alberta advocates are discussed.[2] Second, what were the major strategic initiatives of child care advocates during these years, how successful were they, and might alternative strategies have proven more successful?

The span between 1965 and 1986 can be divided into two distinctive periods. 1965–77 represents the "glory days" of quality child care in Alberta. Alberta's *Preventive Social Services Act* (PSS), in conjunction with the cost-sharing arrangements of the Canada Assistance Plan, encouraged many local governments, often on the insistence of and in collaboration with community groups, to begin establishing non-profit child care services. A total of sixty PSS daycare centres were in existence as of May 1977.[3]

In contrast, the years 1978–86 represent the "glory days" for day care capitalists in Alberta, under the sponsorship of the provincial government.[4] In the beginning of this period, child care services, with the exception of school-age programs, were removed from the PSS program. This eliminated municipalities' previous abilities to initiate new services while paying only 20 cents on the dollar and to insist on quality standards as a prerequisite for public funding. Commercial and non-profit centres were equally eligible for two new provincial funding programs. The first program, inaugurated in 1978, paid portable, income-tested subsidies to any licensed service in which a subsidy-approved child enroled. The second program, initiated in 1980 and frozen in 1986, paid daycare centres and satellite family day homes a monthly allowance for each child enroled in the service. These programs promoted a rapid increase of licensed child care spaces, particularly in Edmonton and Calgary, as capitalists recognized the profit potentialities of this heavily subsidized industry where there was an abundant supply of low-wage labour. Throughout this period the province refused to legislate training standards for those who worked with young children; thus, the market for child care workers was wide open, creating an elastic supply of labour.

Because these two periods are so different in terms of provincial government policies on child care, I contrast advocacy in 1965–1977 with advocacy in 1978–1986.

Conceptual Orientation

My central argument—that daycare advocacy changed from a social movement to a marginalized special interest—raises two conceptual questions: How is a social movement different from an interest group? What defines a condition of marginalization vis-à-vis state officials?

Social movement organizations (SMOs) and interest groups both engage in conventional types of advocacy (such as lobbying) and undertake organizational activities (such as membership drives). What distinguishes SMOs from interest groups, however, is the support they enjoy from a significant number of ordinary citizens who are willing to engage in contentious as well as conventional political action and the longevity of these citizens' commitment to the movement's cause.[5]

The second conceptual question has to do with marginalization. A typical approach to this issue divides the universe of pressure groups which a government department might deal with into those with "insider" status versus those with "outsider" status. My focus, however, is on distinguishing three types of insider status, since Alberta advocates never constructed their goals in such a way as to qualify as outsiders. A "core" insider group is consulted on a broad range of issues in a particular policy area and has appreciable influence on state policies; a "specialist" insider group is consulted and influences policy on a narrow set of issues; and a "peripheral" insider group "has the insider form" (i.e., access to state officials and being actively consulted) but "little, if any, influence."[6] All three of these types of insider status are part of the history of child care advocacy in Alberta, 1965–1986.

1965–1977: Quality Child Care Flourishes
Provincial Support Won for Quality Programs in Edmonton
In January 1964, there were thirty-eight licensed day nurseries in the province of Alberta; most of these were commercial businesses, with a few run on charitable grounds.[7] The provincial government made no financial contribution towards these services. After the 1964 controversy over the Edmonton Creche Society's plans to close its centre after almost thirty-five years in operation (described in Sheila Campbell's chapter in this anthology), in June 1965 the province agreed to contribute funds to a day nursery that would replace the Edmonton Creche. The very conservative provincial Social Credit cabinet would only approve the expenditure after being assured that government funds would not be subsidizing those who could afford to pay.[8]

After the creche controversy was resolved, the City of Edmonton continued to study the need for government involvement in the provision of child care services. In response to the provincial government's passage of the *Preventive Social Services (PSS) Act* in 1966, the city announced its plans to build a number of daycare centres and to hire a director of daycare services. Howard Clifford, a social worker previously employed in the mental health area, began this job in February 1967. Within a short time, Clifford had raised the city's daycare standards to meet the Child Welfare League of America standards.[9]

Throughout 1967 the city of Edmonton proceeded with its plans to construct a city-run, demonstration daycare centre. However, a new Public Welfare minister was installed after the provincial election in May of that year. A.J. Hooke was a veteran of the Social Credit government who had been a member of the provincial Executive Council (along with

Premier Manning and four others) that had decided on May 2, 1944 to refrain from participating in the wartime day nursery program.[10] In October of 1967, the city received word that the province would not approve the demonstration centre as a PSS project. Subsequently, Minister Hooke told the *Edmonton Journal* that full-scale, government supported daycare programs "are for the birds," and the paper ran the story with an eyecatching headline. Demonstrating his ignorance of the philosophy of PSS child care, he remarked, "There are a lot better places the government can put its money than into babysitting services."[11]

Letters opposed to Minister Hooke's position flooded into the premier's office; the writers included eight women's organizations, three church groups, three non-profit social service agencies, two community groups and thirty-four citizens, including six prominent citizens. In contrast, there were only four submissions in support of Mr. Hooke's stand, two of which came from the Edmonton Day Nursery Association and its most outspoken member. One month later, Premier Manning overruled his minister. Howard Clifford commented that there would have been no hope for the demonstration centre without public protest.[12]

Public protest capitalized on two favourable political opportunities. First, the main opponents of Edmonton's plan to sponsor a number of quality child care centres were commercial operators. However, they were a weak pressure group as there were only twelve licensed commercial centres in the city. Second, the provincial cabinet was quite isolated among state elites. Its own civil service bureaucrats supported using the PSS program to fund quality child care services, and urban municipal officials throughout the province were of like mind. Advocates thus had allies in secondary elite positions in the province. Indeed, in the case of municipal civil servants such as Howard Clifford and Al Hagan (hired as Calgary's daycare counsellor in 1969), an important part of their job was public education and advocacy for quality child care. For instance, in 1968, speeches made by Clifford to a variety of groups numbered eighty-four.[13]

By 1968, a child care movement had emerged in Edmonton. This movement counted social workers and other professionals among its leadership and was supported by numerous social service and voluntary organizations (particularly women's groups) and even by the city's major daily newspaper. At the same time, there was a ferment of interest in child care at the community level, and many women (and some men) were willing to put in long hours of activism to support quality child care initiatives. It is also clear that, collectively, this movement was challenging dominant cultural views of women's roles in society and of community responsibilities to young children.

Well-Organized Opposition from Commercial Operators in Calgary

By early 1971, five non-profit daycare centres were functioning in the city of Calgary as PSS projects. At the same time there were forty-three licensed commercial daycare centres in the city; neither the commercial centres themselves nor their clients were eligible for any government funding. The PSS centres were viewed as unwelcome, subsidized competition by commercial operators who, through the Day Care Association of Calgary, began lobbying against them in public forums in early 1970 and hired prominent Calgary lawyer, Irwin Blackstone, Q.C., to argue their case.[14]

In January 1971, an oil industry executive who was an appointed member of the city's social service committee stated in a committee meeting that the city-funded daycare programs were "gold-plated" and "too blasted expensive." The committee immediately established a subcommittee to study "the costs and standards of day care services" and published an announcement inviting written briefs on the subject of daycare.[15]

Unqualified opposition to the city's involvement in provision of child care was restricted to four submissions from commercial operators and twenty-seven from parents and grandparents whose children were in commercial centres (some of them with multiple signatures). Support for Calgary's daycare policies came from a wider coalition of groups than did the opposition. It included twenty-two clients of PSS centres and four PSS boards, as well as four other categories of advocates. The first was voluntary organizations, such as the University Women's Club, the Junior League and the Calgary United Fund. A second category was scientific authorities, offering expert opinion in areas such as medicine, psychology, economics and social work. Third was citizens (eleven submissions), many of whom explicitly framed their arguments in a way that emphasized their publicmindedness rather than self-interest. Finally, the Social Service Department defended its existing approach to daycare.

There is a great deal of overlap between the categories of supporters of quality daycare in Calgary in 1971 and in Edmonton in 1967. The one exception is the increased prominence of scientific authorities in the Calgary debates. These authorities included the head of pediatrics in the Faculty of Medicine at the University of Calgary as well as the director of pediatrics at the Foothills Hospital.[16]

The majority on the seven-person subcommittee supported the city's existing standards. In a 1996 interview, former daycare counsellor, Al Hagan, stated that he was never worried about the outcome of the 1971 inquiry. This perhaps is understandable given the strong movement of

Calgary residents in favour of government-supported, quality child care. Evidenced in the submissions to the inquiry and also in the strong expressions of community support for a child care centre and family day-home program in Bowness-Montgomery (opened in May 1970), this movement was a formidable force. In a characteristically pioneering action, they established the first child care centre at a community college in Canada, opening at Mount Royal College in February 1970—some six months before any government funding had been obtained. Furthermore, in 1970 the use of civil disobedience was threatened by daycare supporters. In September of that year, after the University of Calgary failed to initiate child care on campus, the Women's Liberation Group threatened to occupy a dining room on campus for the purpose of cooperative child care. This event indicates that second wave feminists had started to join the movement for quality child care, bringing with them a more confrontational approach to authorities than had traditional advocates.[17]

At the same time, the inquiry revealed that even in 1971 the commercial daycare business in Calgary was profitable enough that its owners could in fact justify hiring a high-profile lawyer.

The Heyday of Quality Child Care in Alberta

The 1971 inquiry into Calgary's daycare program concluded just after the province experienced its first change in government in thirty-six years. The Progressive Conservatives under Peter Lougheed had made improvements to daycare one of the planks of their provincial election platform.[18] This meant that the institutionalized political system was open to innovation and change in the field of child care. A mere six weeks after the election, a provincial conference, funded by the Clifford E. Lee Foundation,[19] was held in Edmonton. This was the founding conference of the major advocacy group in Alberta, the Alberta Association for Young Children (AAYC), and among the keynote speakers were the new Social Services and Education ministers.[20] Because of the auspicious timing of its founding, the AAYC had a core insider status with the new provincial government nearly from its inception.

The primary public activity of the AAYC was its yearly conference. In the early 1970s the conferences were intended to feed directly into provincial government policy. For instance, government ministers requested that the AAYC submit policy recommendations coming out of its 1972 conference, The Child and His Family in the Context of Today.[21] The core insider status of the AAYC is further suggested by a number of its activities in 1973: a meeting with members of the legislature to explain its recommendations; the presentation of a brief to a legislative committee on regulations; the appointment of an AAYC representative to the Provincial Early Childhood Co-Ordinating Council; the active involvement of provincial social service bureaucrats on AAYC committees; and the very public actions taken by the AAYC board opposing a government initiative. The board vigorously protested the way in which the Early Childhood Services proposal had been developed by bureaucrats before the formation of a Policy Advisory Committee, urging public protest meetings and sending letters to all the Members of the Legislative Assembly and a special bulletin to all AAYC members. This protest fits the mode of action of a "high profile" insider group which feels confident enough about its place in the policy-making process to mobilize the public to pressure government.[22]

By 1974, the province had struck a day care review committee, chaired by a civil servant who was also an AAYC member. The AAYC was invited to have a representative on a committee "to plan a province-wide workshop to be held at Government House, Edmonton, sometime in September." Significantly, however, the Calgary Private Day Care Operators Association received a similar invitation. AAYC activists also spent considerable time doing detailed work on a proposed child daycare Act for the province and on a committee concerned with early childhood training programs. Undoubtedly the provincial government viewed the AAYC as a core insider group because of its expert knowledge in many policy areas, as well as its provincewide representation base. In contrast, the rising status of Calgary's commercial operators was grounded on the increasing prominence of large and very profitable centres, as well as the conservative government's preference for "free enterprise" arguments.[23]

The other major thrust of advocacy for quality child care during the early- to mid-1970s came from the different groups associated with the PSS daycare programs, particularly municipal social service bureaucrats, the boards of directors of those centres, centre employees and parents. Alongside the expansion of the PSS program, however, there was a noticeable decline in the public concern about and agitation for quality child care and other social services. This point was made by Al Hagan just before he left Calgary to take up a position in Medicine Hat: "It used to be that I'd come to work and there'd be about six people in my office to bug me about some issue or other." By 1978 this was no longer the case.[24]

By 1976 at least one prominent AAYC activist (Sheila Campbell, a contributor to this book) had concluded that the group had lost its status as a core insider. She noted that the AAYC did not have access to the minister and senior departmental bureaucrats and it was not routinely consulted concerning social policy on young children; furthermore, she suggested department civil servants "are not making our position as clear to the Minister as we would wish."[25] Nevertheless, in January 1977 when the province struck a task force to make recommendations on child care standards and subsidies, three of the seven members, including Chairman Myer Horowitz, had been leading members of the AAYC. Their input on the task force was countered by at least one owner of a commercial daycare (with a capacity of 119 children) and by other "private citizens." The advocates on the task force thought to compromise with the others in order to come up with a set of recommendations that could be endorsed by all members. Their stated hope was that the proposed minimum standards would be improved over time.[26]

After the task force reported, the Social Services Department prepared a new daycare policy that was considered by the cabinet's Social Planning Committee in September of 1977. The committee accepted the idea, long promoted by commercial operators and endorsed by both the task force and the department, of portable daycare subsidies tenable at any licensed centre. The committee also accepted the department's recommendations to phase out all deficit operating funding for PSS centres over five years and approve no new PSS centres. Finally, it recommended "that the Province set realistic minimum standards for day care operators"; this language indicates that quality of care was far from being of paramount importance.[27]

The new policy, announced in March 1978, proved to be very popular with commercial operators and the thousands of Albertans for whom child care subsidies now became accessible. For quality-care advocates, however, the policy was a disaster; not only did it fail to significantly raise the minimum licensing standards for child care centres, but also it signified that provincial support for Alberta's innovative experiment with high-quality child care would soon end.

The prospects for quality child care in Alberta had looked very promising when the Lougheed government was elected in 1971. However, the openness in the provincial political system occasioned by the change in government lasted at most through Lougheed's first term in office (1971–75). These were the years when the AAYC was a core insider group in policy discussions on young children, when many new PSS daycares were established throughout the province and when significant across-the-board improvements in licensing standards seemed attainable. Yet by 1975 the political opportunities for quality child care advocacy had markedly declined. One reason for this has to do with Lougheed's electoral success. In the election of that year the Progressive Conservatives won 63 percent of the popular votes and sixty-nine of seventy-five seats; it no longer needed to appeal to left-of-centre urban voters in order to overcome the Social Credit opposition, as many Social Credit voters now endorsed the PC government. As well, the commercial operators' lobby became more successful over time, in large part because of its ideological compatibility with the government, but also because its idea for portable subsidies assisted many more Albertans with child care costs, while it only moderately increased overall spending by the provincial government.

1978–1986: Advocates Marginalized as Daycare Capitalists Prosper
The Origins of Operating Allowances
Despite committing substantial new funds to child care, the province's 1978 policy changes actually increased public controversy. There were two main reasons for this development. First, the new program was initially proposed as a funding partnership between local governments and the province, with local governments taking on the administrative tasks of subsidy administration, licensing inspection and others. Many municipalities found it difficult to support the program, however, because of its failure to raise the standards of care. Consequently they delayed in getting it going. Opposition was strongest in Edmonton, where city council did not decide to participate in the provincial program until August 15, 1979, even then refusing responsibility for licensing.[28] This municipal recalcitrance, along with the regional inequalities created by a decentralized social program, caused the province to modify its approach in April 1980; local governments would no longer be involved in any way in operating the province's child care programs (although it eventually was decided to leave out-of-school programs in municipal hands).[29]

The second source of controversy was the continuing low standards of care. Particularly problematic was the staffing requirement of just one worker for every twenty children. Three events in 1979–80 demonstrated the political liability of the province's low standards policy. The first occurred when, in the spring of 1980, a parent's group began organizing against the low quality of the care at a chain commercial centre in Calgary. Some of the parents were former clients, while other parents still had their children enroled in the centre. Upon learning of the parents' group, the centre's manager expelled a child whose father was part of the group, incorrectly declared the parents' group illegal and threatened lawsuits against parents who had made critical remarks about the quality of care in the centre, accusing them of trying to "discredit private day care."[30]

The second controversy concerned research which demonstrated that Alberta's child care standards were among the lowest in the country. This information was available to the government in 1979 and was leaked to the press in June 1980.[31]

Third, the low standards meant that considerable pressure was placed on licensing officers to ensure children's well-being. In a case in early 1980, the province's director of licensing attempted to use the court system to revoke a poor-quality centre's license. He was overruled by the Social Services minister and fired from his position.[32]

These controversies sparked the provincial government to introduce a new funding program to improve staff-to-child ratios. In September 1980 the province began paying licensed child care centres a monthly allowance for each child enroled in the centre. This allowance was meant to enable centres to meet improved ratios without appreciably increasing the cost of child care for parents. Initially the allowance was fixed at $55 per child, regardless of age. However, within two years the monthly allowance paid for infants up to eighteen months of age was increased to $257 and the allowance paid for toddlers between nineteen and thirty-five months of age was increased to $131 per month. Soon the staff-to-child ratios were improved to levels which were among the best in Canada. Further, the payment of operating allowances enabled licensed daycare centres to charge fees for the care of children up to three years old that were competitive with many unlicensed caregivers, and it encouraged considerable commercial investment in child care centres. By 1986, the province was spending over $30 million per year on operating allowances: that is, more than it was spending on fee subsidies for children of low-income parents.[33]

Advocates as Marginalized Interest Groups
If the Alberta Association for Young Children was a core insider group in the first half of the 1970s, its status in the last half of the decade is harder to decipher. Evidence presented above suggests that the AAYC was a peripheral insider group in its dealings with the Social Service Department from as early as 1976. Other evidence suggests that the group sometimes filled a specialist insider role. This was the case in its liaison with the Department of Education over training requirements for child care workers. It was also as a specialist insider that the group was asked to name a representative to a 1978 advisory committee on the qualifications of daycare workers. The AAYC hardly endeared itself to the government when its representative refused to endorse the report.[34]

The latter event confirmed the AAYC's status as a peripheral, marginalized insider in its dealing with the government and social services bureaucrats. When the Day Care Advisory Committee was formed by the province in 1980, neither was the AAYC invited to nominate a representative nor were any leading AAYC members invited to join. This was an about-face from the close consultative relationship that the organization had previously enjoyed with the provincial government between 1971 and 1974. By 1986, with little influence on the government, the AAYC was reduced to contemplating whether it should initiate a centre accreditation program which parents could use as a supplement to basic governmental licensing.[35]

With the end of PSS funding for child care centres, municipalities were forced to decide whether to continue to support some or all of the old PSS centres using money raised by taxation. The debates in each community over this issue were complex and lie beyond the scope of this chapter. But, to be sure, municipal social service bureaucrats could no longer play the same advocacy role for preschool child care as they did in the 1970s; the provincial government was running its own show and was not reliant on municipal expertise or goodwill. Like the AAYC, city bureaucrats had become peripheral insiders, eager to contribute but unlikely to be heeded.

A further development in quality child care advocacy in Alberta was a multiplication of interest groups. For instance, in 1982 the Early Childhood Professional Association (ECPA) of Alberta was formally established (although child care professionals had discussed forming the organization as early as 1978).[36] Other advocacy groups also emerged, such as the Calgary Regional Association for Quality Child Care. Hence, advocates' efforts were no longer channeled through a single organization, but tended to be diffused.

The Rise of Daycare Capitalists
The new policy directions in daycare, introduced between 1978 and 1982, had different effects throughout the province. In smaller communities, often the loss of PSS funding threatened the only licensed child care centre, as the market was not large enough to attract commercial investment. In Alberta's cities, in contrast, the policies led to many commercial child care centres being opened in a very short period of time. The investors' motive was to capitalize on the profit opportunities occasioned by the availability of government subsidy and operating allowance funds, in particular. Consequently, operators established chains of centres in Calgary and, to a lesser extent, in Edmonton. Some of the

chains were relatively small (less than four centres) while others included more than ten centres. In Calgary, by the mid-1980s, the prominent chains were Canadian Kindercare (distinct from the KinderCare chain in the U.S.A.), Panda and Educentre. Concurrently, the capitalists who controlled these chains assumed the specialist insider role for daycare planning. The new-found influence of daycare capitalists was demonstrated by their capacity to gain government support for development of the commercial sector's own staff educational programs, independent of the college system. Social Services Minister Bob Bogle provided $25,000 in seed money for this project in 1981. By 1984 the first classes had graduated from private training programs in Edmonton and Calgary.[37] On occasion the AAYC enjoyed access to senior officials, such as when three executive members met the new Social Services minister, Neil Webber, in 1983.[38] Nevertheless, PSS advocates no longer had much influence because the government's agenda was well defined and quality child care advocates generally were not speaking the same language as the government.

Prior to the 1978–86 period, two types of daycares predominated in Edmonton and Calgary: PSS-funded centres run on a non-profit basis (most by non-profit boards); and commercial centres run by an owner-operator. Because of the resources available to the PSS centres and the high standards set by the municipalities, the quality of care was uniformly high; indeed, Edmonton and Calgary were recognized as daycare leaders across Canada. In contrast, based upon considerable anecdotal evidence, the quality of care in owner-operator centres normally ranged from abysmal to barely adequate, although occasionally it was good. Was the rise of daycare chains in the early 1980s a good thing for Alberta's children? Fortunately, we have some systematic evidence to help answer this question.

Bruce Friesen studied the quality of care provided by different types of centres in Calgary in the early 1990s. He measured the quality of care in forty-five centres using the Infant/Toddler Environment Rating Scale. Of the thirteen non-profit centres in the sample, 62 percent provided good care while only 15 percent provided poor care. The percentile was almost reversed for the seventeen independent commercial centres, where only 23 percent provided good care, while 65 percent provided poor care. An entirely different pattern emerged for the fifteen commercial chain centres: the majority (54 percent) provided adequate care, while a mere 6 percent supplied good care and the remaining 40 percent, poor care.[39] These findings indicate that at best, daycare chains aspired to provide an adequate level of care; in almost all cases, profit was put ahead of building a high-quality program. In contrast, good care was more likely to be found in independent commercial centres (because of the commitment and expertise of some commercial owner-operators) and much more likely in non-profit centres (where quality of care is often of paramount concern). The rise of daycare capitalists between 1978–1986 thus institutionalized a new model of caring for young children in Alberta: treating child care as a profit-making investment necessitated a downgrading of the ideal standard of care from good to adequate. After the heady years between 1965 and 1977 when high-quality, non-profit centres flourished throughout Alberta, developments between 1978 and 1986 represented a devastating blow to the dreams of advocates for quality child care.

Conclusion

Although a new model of child care was introduced in Alberta between 1978 and 1986, the old model survived in the form of dozens of daycare centres and family day home programs that started as PSS projects. Many Alberta municipalities continued to support these child care programs in order to maintain "lighthouse" models of quality care. This is much like the situation in Quebec, described in Jane Jenson's chapter, where politicized child care centres established in the 1970s survived to be reclaimed in 1997 as the model for Quebec's new system of early childhood centres. Unfortunately, many Alberta municipalities ended or reduced their support for lighthouse projects in the 1990s, and at no time in the past fifteen years has the provincial government signaled any interest in returning to the PSS model of high-quality child care. That said, many of the non-profit PSS centres still survive, and through the incredible dedication of staff and parents, they provide a measure of quality care and community that is beyond the vision of all but a handful of commercial centres. After years of government neglect, the non-profit centres still represent a model for an alternative provincial policy. This demonstrates the importance of nurturing institutional alternatives even when the political tides are flowing in the opposite direction.

For child care advocates in Alberta, the political opportunity structure underwent some dramatic shifts between 1965 and 1986. Important openings for new initiatives were provided by the *Preventive Social Services Act* of 1966 and by the electoral victory of the Progressive Conservatives in 1971. In 1971–1975, leading advocates held the status of core insiders as the government reviewed its children's policies. By the mid-1980s, however, the structure of political opportunity for advocacy was fundamentally changed, and advocates were entrenched in a peripheral insider status. This situation resonates with that found in Ontario in the later part of the 1990s when, as recorded in Vappu Tyyskä's chapter, a closed opportunity structure meant that different advocacy strategies were equally ineffective in influencing policy outcomes. This finding suggests that advocates need recognize the limiting potential of particular historical junctures and that decisions about whether to engage in oppositional or pragmatic child care politics are best made in light of the available political opportunities. My analysis runs counter to Linda White's argument, which asserts that oppositional politics are an anachronism. Indeed, I would go so far as to propose that pragmatic politics are most appropriate in a situation of bountiful political opportunities, not when pragmatic advocates are equally marginalized by government as their more idealistic colleagues.

The central argument of this chapter is that whereas advocacy in the late 1960s and early 1970s emanated from a social movement for quality child care, advocacy in the late 1970s and early 1980s was carried out by marginalized interest groups. Perhaps the defining feature of the earlier social movement was its broad base of supporters, including many altruistic women without professional or even personal links to the issue. Sheila Campbell captures the spirit of these altruistic women in her chapter on the history of daycare in Edmonton, and Judith Martin also points to their importance in her analysis of the genesis of advocacy in Saskatchewan. The rise of this movement and its importance in Alberta's early history of government involvement in child care were the product of a unique set of circumstances (such as the relatively low employment rate of professional women, the lack of provincial government expertise in child care and the inadequacy of most of the existing care options). And it is naive to suppose that any amount of creative strategy or hard work could have preserved the same movement into the 1980s. Nevertheless, there is an important lesson for advocacy: strive to broaden the base of support by involving groups and individuals who have nothing to gain materially from the adoption of child care policies. This is as important for community-based, non-profit centres as for provincewide advocacy organizations.

My final point concerns advocates' strategy in response to the regressive policy initiatives taken by the Alberta government between 1977 and the early 1980s. The initial provincial proposal involved ongoing partnerships between municipalities and the province, with municipalities taking on administrative responsibilities for subsidies and licensing. It is fair to say that unrelenting opposition to this plan by the city of Edmonton was a major factor in the 1980 decision to eliminate the municipal role in preschool child care. The mistake made by these advocates was not in voicing opposition to the regressive elements of the plan but rather in administratively blocking the plan's timely implementation in Edmonton. The end result of their intransigence was the exclusion of highly knowledgeable municipal bureaucrats from ongoing internal discussions of provincial daycare policy and administration. Alberta thus lost an institutional counterbalance that could have helped to moderate the influence of daycare capitalists in the 1980s.

Notes

1. This study was supported by a Social Sciences and Humanities Research Council grant (410-94-0477). I thank Kristin Lozanski, Lynne Malmquist, Rachael McKendry and Janine Smith for their research assistance.
2. For a conceptual overview of political opportunities, see McAdam 1996: 23–40.
3. For historical background on PSS, see Bella 1978.
4. Daycare capitalists include owner–operators of commercial services (excluding those small services where family members do much of the work) and investors in commercial services. The financial goal of daycare capitalists is to realize a profit on their commercial investment through the employment of workers to care for young children.
5. Tarrow 1998: 4.
6. Maloney, Jordan and McLaughlin 1994: 31, 27.
7. Provincial Archives of Alberta. 83-386, "Alberta Nursery Schools, Play Schools and Day Nurseries Licenses, yearly data, 1959–1973."
8. City of Edmonton Archives, Day Care Letter files, Public Welfare Minister L.C. Halmrast to Edmonton Mayor Dantzer, June 7, 1965.
9. *Edmonton Journal,* June 29, 1966; *Edmonton Journal,* July 5, 1966; *Edmonton Journal,* August 26, 1967.
10. Provincial Archives of Alberta, 70.429, Box 2, item 16, Executive Council Minute book November 15, 1943 to October 23, 1945.
11. *Edmonton Journal,* October 23, 1967 and *Edmonton Journal,* November 25, 1967.
12. Provincial Archives of Alberta. 77.173, f702, Day Care Centres. *Edmonton Journal* 1967a. Clifford tells a story that indicates good fortune was also at work. In a meeting with City of Edmonton officials, Manning was at first opposed to funding the demonstration centre. One of these officials happened to mention that daycare programs were better for young children than sitting in a babysitter's home watching TV. This argument changed Manning's mind on the issue since the CBC had recently aired a show that was highly critical of Manning's government (interview with Howard Clifford on February 20, 1996).

13. Edmonton Social Services Department 1968.

14. Statistics on daycares in Calgary are from City of Calgary Archives, Barbara Scott, 1971, "The Need for Good Quality Day Care in Calgary: A Brief Submitted to the City of Calgary Day Care Study Committee," Social Services box 9566, ff Parents' Group Committee.

15. *Calgary Herald,* January 19, 1971; *Calgary Herald,* February 15, 1971.

16. City of Calgary Archives, Social Services Box 9566, ff Parents' Group Committee, Batch 1 submissions, items 19 and 25; Batch 2 submissions, items 14 and 15; Batch 3 submission, item 3; Batch 4 submission, item 1.

17. *Calgary Herald,* September 9, 1970; *Calgary Herald,* September 15, 1970; *Calgary Herald,* October 1, 1970.

18. This is demonstrated by the resolution which the Progressive Conservatives had sponsored while in opposition which called for more government assistance to daycare centres. It passed in November 1968 with the support of the governing Social Credit Party. Sometime before the 1971 election, Calgary's daycare counsellor, Al Hagan, recalls Lougheed telling him that daycare was an important issue for his party (interview with Al Hagan, April 16, 1996).

19. Clifford E. Lee had been a leader of the Alberta CCF during World War II. After the war he made a large amount of money as a land developer and house builder. The Foundation has been an important supporter of initiatives for quality child care virtually since its inception.

20. Campbell 1997: 1, 7–8.

21. Provincial Archives of Alberta, AAYC Fonds, 1972. "A Brief to the Government of the Province of Alberta. Recommendations Pertaining to Young Children and Child Development Programs in the Province of Alberta, December 1972." See also Campbell 1997.

22. Campbell 1997; Maloney et al. 1994: 28; Provincial Archives of Alberta, AAYC Fonds 1973 "The Need for Consolidation and Improvement of Legislation Pertaining to Programs for Young Children."

23. "The Alberta Association for Young Children Information Bulletin"; *Altachild* 1987:8. In July 1974 there were sixty commercial centres in Calgary, an increase of seventeen in three years. By July 1976 commercial centres numbered seventy-one. Among these centres were two with licensed capacities in excess of 100. Their total capacity was greater than the capacity of the sixteen centres that were licensed for fewer than twenty children in 1974 *(Calgary Herald* 1976).

24. *Calgary Herald,* "'Day Care Has Turned Full Circle,' Says City Consultant," August 23, 1978.

25. Provincial Archives of Alberta, AAYC fonds, 1976, memo from S. Campbell to Dr. M. Horowitz, "Re: Meeting Friday with M. Finlay, et al.," March 1.

26. Provincial Archives of Alberta, AAYC fonds, 1978, "Report of the Day Care Task Force, April, 1977," *Submission of the AAYC in Response to the 1978 Day Care Regulations and Subsidy to Low Income Families,* May.

27. Alberta Provincial Cabinet Minutes, September 13, December 13, 1977, with supporting documentation (obtained through a freedom of information request to Executive Council, Government of Alberta).

28. Letter from Mayor C.J. Purves to the Minister of Social Services and Community Health, Bob Bogle, Edmonton Community and Family Services records, undated.

29. *Calgary Herald,* May 2, 1980a: A16.

30. *Calgary Herald,* May 20, 1980; *Calgary Herald,* May 26, 1980:B2.

31. *Calgary Herald,* June 5, 1980: A1.

32. *Edmonton Journal,* April 2, 1980.

33. Public Archives of Alberta, Press release from Minister Bob Bogle, Day Care Initiative. September, 1980, 93.188/Box 2, Minister's Correspondence. Alberta Provincial Cabinet Minutes, 1980, 1981. Discussions of Day Care, December 16, 1980 and April 14, 1981, (obtained through a freedom of information request to Executive Council, Government of Alberta) *(Calgary Herald,* April 12, 1986).

34. Provincial Archives of Alberta, AAYC Newsletter, December 1978; Provincial Archives of Alberta, AAYC Newsletter, April 1979.

35. Provincial Archives of Alberta, AAYC Newsletter, Spring 1986. Report by president Malcolm Read.

36. Provincial Archives of Alberta, AAYC fonds, 1982, letter from Michael Phair, ECPA president to Andi Dinsmore, AAYC president, April 30. For an early reference to the ECPA, see *Calgary Herald,* June 3, 1978.

37. Provincial Archives of Alberta, Day Care Advisory Committee, minutes, June 12, 1981 and February 9, 1984, 90.438, ff "Correspondence, Private Day Care Society of Alberta." *Edmonton Journal,* February 13, 1984.

38. Provincial Archives of Alberta, AAYC Newsletter, 1986, March.

39. Friesen 1995.

Chapter 4

Acting Locally
Community Activism in Edmonton, 1940–1970

Sheila D. Campbell

Background[1]

Throughout Canada, child care activism had its beginnings at the local level. Patricia Schulz describes the beginnings of daycare in Toronto and Montreal as a movement with women—usually acting in concert with a group—as its driving force.[2] The story in Edmonton is similar. Organizational and individual activism caused municipal politicians to enact and enforce policy to fund non-profit daycare services and to ensure services' effectiveness through appropriate standards and enforcement. Drawing its inspiration from local pioneers of child care, this chapter poses the question: What factors make for successful activism at the local level?

The 1999 National Children's Agenda, issued by the Federal-Provincial-Territorial Council of Ministers on Social Development, recommended the community as the best place to identify problems and find solutions.[3] Yet, J. Masson, for example, cautions that such action is always subject to constraints imposed on municipalities by provincial and federal policy.[4] Still, the history of daycare services in the city of Edmonton in the early part of the twentieth century and then especially in the years from World War II to 1970 affords strong evidence for the proposition that activism can indeed be effective at the local level.

The main focus of this chapter is on daycare policy from World War II to 1970. Prior to this period, there were children in need of care while their mothers worked. However, there were not very many of them, and their mothers were mostly from very poor families. These women were not high-powered, sophisticated political lobbyists, so others acted on their behalf to provide the early subsidized, non-profit daycare which had important implications for later advocacy activities in Edmonton; this charitable, early work institutionalized child care policy, and by example, legitimized later programs (see White, Chapter 5 in this volume).

The Beginnings of Daycare Service in Edmonton

There were two early instances of particularly successful advocacy for Edmonton daycare services. The earliest occurred in 1908 when members of the local Council of Women, spurred by a genuine concern for children of poor working mothers, established a committee to develop and operate a daycare centre. These prominent local women or "worthies" (as Wendy Atkin calls them in her chapter) secured the cooperation of a large number of local organizations and important citizens, along with the support of the local press. They appealed directly to the mayor and councillors, persuading them to accept token fees, because of the parents' poverty, and to provide financial support of seventy-five dollars per month.[5] Soon, the first Edmonton Creche opened its doors with the stated goal of making a place "where the children of working women are properly cared for."[6]

Before it could again advance, Edmonton daycare services suffered a setback. Following an attempt to integrate daycare with full-time residential care for children without families, daycare services temporarily disappeared from the scene. The reasons for the integration failure were twofold: lack of public knowledge of the Children's Home Society provisions for kinless children and working parents' unwillingness to associate their children with "destitute and neglected children."[7]

Many years later, in 1929, the second successful instance occurred when a dramatic event created public awareness that the need for daycare was not being met. Five small children, left home alone while their mother worked, were barely rescued from their burning house by a passerby.[8] A group of prominent local women investigated the need under the able leadership of Lady Rodney, convenor of Child Welfare in the Local Council of Women. She personally visited rooming houses and homes in the inner city and described what she found: unsanitary conditions, children locked in rooms while their mothers worked, irresponsible caregivers, overcrowded care situations and, in one case, six or seven babies in a home, some lying on the floor holding their bottles.

Urged by this women's group, the mayor called a public meeting which led to the establishment of the Edmonton Creche Society under a board of prominent citizens that included both the lieutenant governor and the premier as honorary members.[9] This board received excellent support from the local media and was able to pressure local organizations and businesses to generously contribute money, furnishings and foodstuffs.

The board even succeeded in persuading city council to provide a building and some funding.[10] Furnished with donations, the new Edmonton Creche opened in 1930 with the goal "to look after the children of working mothers during the day time."[11] The Creche provided Edmonton's only subsidized child care until 1965.

This early advocacy was successful for several reasons. It occurred in a small setting; Edmonton's population was 18,500 in 1908 and 74,298 in 1929. Advocates were socially and economically important, putting them into direct contact with the decision makers. Their demands were limited and altruistic in nature. These people had no vested interest in daycare services as users, staff or professionals. Finally, the decisions were entirely within the purview of the city itself, as the senior governments had no policy on these services.

The childcare issue arose again in Edmonton during World War II over attempts to expand daycare. The Edmonton Creche was hard pressed to meet the needs for care, and, in 1943, a number of local groups including the Edmonton Council of Community Agencies urged city council and the province to take advantage of the new Dominion-Provincial Wartime Agreement, a cost-sharing agreement to provide new care centres for the children of wartime working women (this agreement is described in more detail by Scherer in Chapter 10).[12] Despite their ad hoc lobby, the groups were unsuccessful, and a provincial government committee recommended against accepting federal funding as they saw no need for care.[13]

The city continued its traditional relationship with the Edmonton Creche, although the Creche Society was in an ongoing battle to garner adequate facilities and funding from the city. In 1947, community support broadened to include funding from the Edmonton Community Chest, the agency coordinating collection of charitable funds. In 1949, the city authorized an extension of the Creche premises to better accommodate the sixty children in attendance.

These early efforts to provide daycare services left an important legacy by establishing precedents in the years after World War I, when the demand for daycare increased beyond a philanthropic service for the children of the poor working mothers into a broader demand for services for children of working parents in general. These precedents legitimized community support for daycare services and subsidized care. Daycare was recognized as an independent service need.

The Beginning of Change

Two major trends affected daycare services in the years following the World War II. As in the rest of Canada, the number of working mothers in Edmonton increased dramatically during this time.[14] Regionally, this increase followed the 1947 discovery of oil. As men flooded into the high-paying jobs of the oil industry, the demand for women workers increased in Edmonton, especially in the service industries. As well, the increasing cost of living required that both parents of low- and middle-income families draw an income.

Also, with women's growing desire for equality, more professional, middle- and upper-income women remained in the work force after marriage. Consequently, the composition of the families in need of daycare came to greater reflect the population in general and to include people with more knowledge of the political process and greater resources to create change.

In a second trend, local groups who had focused on wartime matters during the war, turned their attention to child welfare. Following stories of exploitation and maltreatment, there was growing concern about the general welfare of children placed by the government into foster homes.[15]

Although "legislation on day care of children in Canada is a provincial matter and is entirely a post-war phenomenon," welfare matters in Alberta were originally considered the responsibility of local government.[16] Legislation in respect to child welfare was very limited and in respect to daycare or non-ward care was non-existent. *The Child Welfare Act* of 1925 [17] began the process of provincial centralization, a process furthered by the creation of the Bureau of Public Welfare, in 1936.[18] Unfortunately, the division of responsibilities between local and provincial government remained ill defined and somewhat contentious.[19]

In 1947, in response to growing concerns about child welfare, the Provincial Imperial Order of Daughters of the Empire (IODE) brought Charlotte Whitton, a former director of the Canadian Council on Child Welfare, to Alberta to direct an investigation into foster care and adoption in the province. They were unable to obtain the cooperation of the provincial government, which insisted that it alone should be responsible for such an investigation.[20] Whitton's report had an important effect in Edmonton. Highly critical of all aspects of child welfare in Alberta, her 1947 report was rejected by the government but found support from a provincial commission of inquiry established to look into her claims.[21] The *Child Welfare Act* of 1944 had applied only to children who were wards of the provincial government. The Whitton study revealed serious problems for children who did not come under the Act, but were being cared for outside their own homes by persons other than their parents. It castigated the government for weak standards and poor monitoring of child welfare. In respect to the city, the report recommended a "detailed examination of the civic welfare needs, services and standards" by a committee of city council. [22]

When there was little follow-up government action, public pressure mounted to force either the provincial government or the city government to extend and improve child welfare legislation. The Family Service Bureau and the city Welfare Department urged an investigation into services for Edmonton children. As an indicator of the grave need, they cited the case of one woman who single-handedly looked after her own child, tended to two children for twenty-four-hour care and provided daycare for fifteen to twenty children under age six.[23]

The Edmonton Council of Community Services (ECCS), recognized by the city council and most local organizations as responsible for social welfare matters, set up an investigating committee. The Edmonton Community Chest requested that the investigation be extended into local child care facilities including the Edmonton Creche and the few for-profit centres.

The ECCS brief to city commissioners in 1956 reported daycare services' inadequacy in both number and quality. It recommended that the Welfare Department license private homes to give daycare as a means to initiate service to children who were not wards of the government but were being cared for outside their homes. The city Legal Department contended that Edmonton did not have the authority to pass such a bylaw, and the superintendent of Welfare cautioned the city that there would be no provincial funding to help with the services to non-ward children.[24] This caution combined with widespread opposition to limiting service to private home auspices resulted in the city taking no action.

The ECCS continued its efforts by bringing representatives of other groups (including the Family Welfare Study Group of the Edmonton University Women's Club (UWC) and the Edmonton Study Group on Family Welfare (SGFW), an informal group of local women) to its committee. Reciprocal memberships enabled these groups to coordinate their actions. The young women members of both groups, trained and directed by Margaret Norquay, a sociologist and a member of the Welfare Council Committee, visited all the homes and agencies advertising child care services and found many facilities exhibiting deplorable conditions. There were several instances of one person caring for a large number of children and infants. One facility located in a storefront was freezing cold. Some homes refused admission, requiring that children be brought to the door and handed over. The Creche, too, was reportedly badly overcrowded.

The UWC, concerned by the poor conditions found in these visits, presented a brief to the Child Welfare Commission of the Government of Alberta in 1959.[25] Endorsed by the Junior League and publicized by the media, the brief recommended several improvements to the legislation, including an annual inspection and licence for day nurseries and the prohibition of all related advertising, unless the nursery was licensed and approved. The UWC then reproduced its brief for SGFW to distribute to its extensive mailing list of MLAs, provincial bureaucrats, council members, heads of organizations and other important decision makers. These measures achieved a small success when the government advised the club that all day nurseries would be licensed and also promised to investigate advertisements for daycare.[26]

Before this step was actually accomplished by the provincial government, the University Women's Club Family Welfare Study Group joined other groups who met with the city by-laws committee to discuss the possibility of a business licence for day nurseries. The city did nothing, claiming that provincial authorities had promised to take action.

Coincident with the concern about standards was a growing awareness of the need for additional daycare services. In a report to the University Women's Club membership in 1961, the Family Welfare Study Group revealed the extensive need for daycare discovered in its survey of working mothers with preschool children.[27] At the same time, the Edmonton Welfare Council (formerly the Edmonton Council of Social Agencies) had set up a daycare planning committee, which also studied need and recommended creating a network of community-based daycare centres and upgrading standards in city daycare services.[28]

Finally, the provincial government was prodded into action. In early 1960, the *Child Welfare Act* was amended to more clearly define institutions as including day nurseries. A nurse, Frances Ferguson, was appointed responsible for setting up, maintaining standards and inspecting institutions and foster homes in Alberta. In 1961, the provincial government published a set of very general and minimal standards. For example, standards for staff required only that they be "sympathetic to the welfare of the children, suitable in point of age, health and personality to occupy the position."[29] The next change occurred in 1963 when the standards were augmented, including the specific daycare requirement of twenty square feet per child.[30] Still, the groups advocating change continued to view these standards as totally inadequate.

Edmonton citizens were not about to let the matter drop. Efforts were coordinated informally through occasional public meetings and a network of individuals involved in various groups. The Study Group on Family Welfare continued to circulate a periodic information newsletter. One study group member succeeded in obtaining the endorsement of the Edmonton Presbytery of the United Church Women for a resolution on daycare recommending that civic authorities be petitioned for higher standards and subsidy and educational authorities for training programs.[31]

Throughout this period, advocates utilized a new crop of publications to develop their background knowledge and to provide information about appropriate daycare policy and standards. New theory and research helped to reduce public concerns about daycare programs.

The writing of John Bowlby, originally interpreted as supporting the conventional wisdom that mothers should stay at home with their children, was re-evaluated and determined to apply only to institutional-ized children lacking a permanent primary caregiver.[32] Psychologists began to understand the importance of play and peer interaction oppor-tunities. New research showed that appropriate environments with sufficient space and equipment, well-trained staff and child-centered programming did not harm young children. Multiple-mothering theory attributed developmental strengths to children exposed to several good caregiver situations.

Growing concerns about child welfare were reflected in the creation of new international and national organizations like the United Nations Educational, Social and Cultural Organization (UNESCO), which pro-vided material on the welfare of the world's women and children. The Canadian Council on Social Development had some concerns for chil-dren, and the Canadian Council on Children and Youth had a small Alberta Committee. Still, there were no provincial organizations con-cerned with children.

The Report of the Royal Commission on the Status of Women in 1961 provided invaluable information about Canada's 2.5 million work-ing women, over half of them married, many with young children, many earning very low pay.[33] The Women's Bureau of the Federal Department of Labour, in 1964, published a report on its studies of daycare and working mothers,[34] which was credited with demonstrating to the federal government that the number of working mothers was sufficient to warrant immediate attention.[35] The World Health Organization book

Care of Children in Day Centres[36] provided an important international perspective on the provision of quality daycare. This information alerted the general public and even some in the for-profit daycare community to the need for better provision of daycare in terms of public funding, number of spaces and standards for care.

All around, on an international, national and civic level, specialists, policy makers, advocates and ordinary citizens alike began to see the need for and benefits of quality child care services.

The Creche Crisis

Efforts to create change bore fruit in the mid-sixties through a fortuitous combination of events. The precipitating event occurred on April 1, 1964, when without prior indications, the board of the Edmonton Creche and Day Nursery announced its intention to close the Creche immediately. The board made the threefold argument that it did not agree with subsidizing child care for mothers "where the parents are both working through choice rather than necessity"; that there were other agencies to provide for paid care; and that it would be cheaper for the city to subsidize care for needy mothers in these agencies.[37]

There is no doubt that the board was also influenced by the continuing problems with the city during preceding years: the temporary closing due to condemnation of the building by the city fire marshall and the city's criticism of Creche services when attempts were made to find a new building. At one point, the Creche Society had indicated its ambivalence when its lawyers sent a letter to the city expressing concern about the criticism of the Society and insisting that it might very well be a municipal or provincial responsibility to provide care.[38]

The closing announcement precipitated a great deal of concern. Not only was the Creche the sole subsidized care available in Edmonton, but also only six small for-profit daycares existed. Action followed immediately. The Save the Creche Committee was formed and a public meeting was called by the Council of Community Services.

The publicity resulting from the threatened closing of the nursery created a general public awareness of daycare issues. Occurring at the same time as changes in federal funding practices, the closure brought pressure to bear on the province and the city to meet the need for more and better services.

1966—A Watershed Year

The events in Edmonton were heavily influenced by the actions of the federal and provincial governments. In January, responding to the pressures created by the huge increase in women working outside the home and the resulting public concerns, the federal government introduced the Canada Assistance Plan,[39] to assist in funding non-profit daycare programs for needy families.

In a move designed to take advantage of the federal plan, the Alberta government followed in the same month with the *Preventive Social Services Act*.[40] Under this Act, the province subsumed the daycare program as part of child welfare. The province agreed to pay local municipalities up to 80 percent of the cost of establishing, administering and operating preventive programs, including daycare. The municipality was required to provide the remaining 20 percent of funding and to hire a qualified social worker as program director.

Edmonton's citizens took the partial decentralization of power, related to preventive non-profit daycare, as an opportunity to force the city to implement their demands for improved service. During a period of five months, there was a flurry of activity. First, a large public meeting informed the city council and the provincial government of citizens' general concerns, despite the ongoing controversy about the desirability of daycare. Next, the Edmonton Welfare Council[41] and the Family Service Association[42] made representation to the city council urging them to implement a daycare administration within the city government, extend daycare services to suburban areas and develop quality services and staff, including properly trained caregivers. These recommendations received support from the University Women's Club and others.[43] All of this activity was widely reported in the local media, which also ran a series of articles on daycare.

As a consequence of all these activities, the former Creche was reborn as the Community Day Nursery (CDN). The United Community Fund (formerly the Community Chest) agreed to fund the Creche for an interim period and appointed an interim board with representatives from the UCF, the city and the Edmonton Welfare Council. The city agreed to provide new facilities in a former city-owned garage and the former Creche Society agreed, after negative publicity, to contribute its old equipment— purchased entirely from public donations. The CDN Society, with a broadly based community board, was incorporated in 1966 with the mandate to offer a public, non-profit, subsidized daycare service in Edmonton. The board then hired Mary Hull, a trained nursery nurse from

England, as the new executive director to introduce a play-based, developmental program into what had been a merely custodial care setting. Thus, a new standard of daycare programming was established in Edmonton.

In July, following prior recommendations and utilizing the new legislation and funding, the city established a daycare branch, with Howard Clifford as Director of Day Care Services. In partnership with other social work professionals in the city's Social Services Department, he provided a supportive link to city administrators and councillors. It was not long before Clifford implemented a set of guidelines.[44] Based on the newly published Child Welfare League of America Standards for Daycare,[45] these guidelines were a comprehensive list of requirements for adequate daycare programs and they exceeded the provincial standards by a considerable margin. Although these standards applied only to the non-profit centres subsidized by the city, they marked a first for Alberta and provided an example for other cities and the province in general. Not one to sit on his hands, Clifford also actively promoted non-profit care through public speaking, working with local groups and fostering the development of new centres in unserviced areas by quietly approaching local citizens to form an organizing committee and carry out the necessary advocacy to establish a needed centre in the city.

With the number of care facilities on the rise, trained staff were in very short supply. Largely as a result of a University Women's Club brief (supported by other groups) to the University of Alberta,[46] a four-course, non-credit preschool training program was established in the Faculty of Extension in 1967. Workers in both for-profit and non-profit centres took advantage of this opportunity to acquire training. In 1971, the Edmonton branch of the Canadian Committee on Early Childhood was successful in persuading the new Grant MacEwan Community College to establish an accredited two-year diploma program for daycare staff. It would be the second such training program in Alberta.[47]

After the 1960s

Under the guidance of Howard Clifford and the administrators who followed him, daycare services expanded throughout the 1970s to a total of thirteen city-subsidized centres also providing infant and school-age child care. During this period, with the addition of parents to daycare boards, daycare services were finally democratized. Special groups composed largely of parents, administrators and staff became active in dealing with the city to retain funding and augment services. The involvement of the general public declined and the prominent citizens and interested groups of the early days were no longer much represented in advocacy activities.

Unfortunately, the city was not allowed to continue its involvement in providing daycare services. Concerned about the low standards of care in the nonsubsidized centres, advocates changed their focus from the local level to the provincial arena, joining with others to form a provincial organization, the Alberta Association for Young Children, devoted to agitating for improved daycare services and better provincial standards. In response, commercial daycare owners organized themselves and lobbied the government to keep standards low, so as to reduce their costs and to allow subsidized parents to use their centres.

In 1981, the provincial government, committed to private enterprise, gave in to these demands and changed the structure once again.[48] Subsidy was provided directly to parents to use wherever they wished, and supervision and monitoring was recentralized in an effort to implement provincewide standards. Standards for staffing were slightly upgraded and a basic operating grant independent of registration was provided to centres to support this change.

This attempt to eliminate local involvement was resisted by Edmonton City Council. Backed by widespread public support, it refused to agree to provincial demands, arguing that the provincial daycare standards were too low and would undermine the existing Edmonton services.[49] Eventually, the city was forced to compromise but was allowed to continue its subsidy arrangements with thirteen daycare centres with which it had "historical association," but was precluded from expanding services. At present, the city continues subsidy to eleven of those centres. School-age programs which were placed in a separate category by the province are still managed by the city.

During this period, Edmonton emerged as a leading community in respect to public involvement in the daycare debate, the level of tax-based funding and support for daycare and the emphasis on quality care in subsidized facilities. The high level of support for public daycare services was part of a larger climate of approval for the use of public resources in the best interests of all citizens. This climate resulted from a number of factors—Edmonton had a large university community,[50] a large unionized, working-class-community[51] and a diverse multi-ethnic population with many folk from strong social democratic traditions. The local press generally reported favourably on and endorsed social action to provide daycare. It also provided useful public information on the growing body of research about child development and caregiving.

The Relevance of History

The history of daycare in Edmonton demonstrates that the actions of ordinary citizens can be an effective form of daycare advocacy. Many factors are involved in achieving success: altruistic motivation; thorough background knowledge of the issues; concerted, cooperative effort; persistence; local media involvement; plus good timing and luck. As illustrated in the case of Edmonton, precedent plays a significant role and should be more emphasized in contemporary advocacy activities.

The potential for success in the current era, even with these factors present, appears to be very limited. Having already removed preschool care from the control of local government, the province has once again changed the structures. Since 1998, Edmonton advocates must deal with the newly appointed Edmonton Regional Children's Services Authority (ERCSA), responsible for daycare services and child welfare in the Greater Edmonton Area, encompassing several municipal governments.[52] Operating under a board appointed by the province, the ERCSA is still attempting to establish itself administratively. There is uncertainty about how much autonomy the province will allow and how much funding will be provided. The province still determines the daycare budget and sets the standards—which are still not equal to those previously established by the city. The ERCSA approves funding and licences and monitors child care agencies.

The city of Edmonton no longer sets its own standards for daycare services. The eleven centres with the "traditional" relationship receive additional funding from the city under a generalized program only if they provide specialized preventive services.[53] Their impact as example-setting centres has been severely diluted by the sheer extent of for-profit care and by considerably reduced media coverage. The changes in provincial funding resulted in a rapid expansion of for-profit centres in Edmonton. With lower standards, they have been able to undercut the fees of the subsidized centres, many of which are presented with serious funding problems, especially when they attempt to provide better staff salaries.[54]

The provincial government, entrenched and devoted to its policy of private enterprise, seems to have lost any sense of responsibility for the traditional function of protecting the public through standard setting and monitoring of services. It utilizes shifting structures and apparent decentralization to deflect and confuse critics and advocates. Advocacy for children's services has become fragmented among the many interest groups devoted to various aspects of safety, health, childhood diseases, early intervention, preschool care and school-age care. The non-profit daycare community has become ingrown, lacking the support of outside groups and any social elites who can speak directly to decision makers. The for-profit daycare community, which now provides the bulk of care, is well organized and its practices to limit expenditures and endorse private enterprise are compatible with government policy.

In the light of these changes, it is difficult to recommend where and how to conduct effective advocacy action. A variety of strategies have been successful, but the same strategies may not be useful in a different time and setting. Advocates may need to devise new techniques.

However, this review of child care history in one locality does suggest that one critical factor in successful advocacy is timing. Sometimes success can be created through persistent efforts of advocates bringing pressure to bear on local politicians, as in the establishment of the earliest daycare service. More often success is the result of a precipitating event, such as the aforementioned fire or the threat to close the Community Day Nursery—an event that enlists media attention and widespread local interest to support advocacy activity. Sometimes successful advocacy results from coordinating efforts to coincide with a revision in government policy, such as the period of the Canada Assistance Plan and *Preventive Social Services Act*. It may also occur when a government becomes vulnerable due to an election or a need to regain public support or a combination of all of the above.

Obviously, advocacy must proceed on many levels. In between critical times, we may need to be content with carrying on maintenance activities which provide the underpinning upon which critical action is based: pushing public education, lobbying policy makers, seeking media coverage and networking to build a broad and coordinated support base from which to launch into action at a propitious time. Advocates should always keep watch for the critical time that best offers the possibility of success.

Notes

1. Ellen Derksen and Anne Lightfoot assisted in research for and review of this chapter.
2. Schulz 1978.
3. Federal–Provincial–Territorial Council of Ministers on Social Policy Renewal 1999.
4. Masson 1985.

5. City of Edmonton Archives, letter from City Secretary-Treasurer, April 17, 1909, RG8, Class 21, File 13.
6. *Edmonton Bulletin,* "The Edmonton Creche," December 5, 1908 City of Edmonton Archives.
7. *Edmonton Bulletin,* "To Extend Creche Work," April 14, 1910 City of Edmonton Archives.
8. City of Edmonton Archives, letter from Lady Rodney, May, 1929, RG11, Class 32, File 2.
9. City of Edmonton Archives, letter to City Commissioners, March 20, 1930 RG11, Class32, File 2.
10. City of Edmonton Archives, Edmonton Creche Society, First Annual Report, 1930–31, MS58, Box 1, File 1.
11. City of Edmonton Archives, letter to City Commissioners, March 3, 1930 RG11, Class32, File 2.
12. City of Edmonton Archives, letter and brief to Mayor Fry, September 24, 1943, RG11, Class 32, File 7.
13. Provincial Archives of Alberta, letter from Premier Manning, September 24, 1944, 69.22/52.
14. City of Edmonton Archives, Edmonton Welfare Council, Day Care Planning Committee, "An Assessment of the Need for Day Care Services for Children of Employed Mothers in Edmonton." Brief to City Council, December, 1965. RG11, Class 32, File 7.
15. Provincial Archives of Alberta, University Women's Club, Minutes, 1943, 69.22/12:496.
16. Canadian Council on Social Development 1971.
17. Government of Alberta, *Child Welfare Act,* 1925.
18. Government of Alberta, *Bureau of Public Welfare Act,* 1936.
19. Provincial Archives of Alberta, IODE, Alberta Provincial Chapter, 1947, *Welfare in Alberta: The Report of a Study,* 95.187/7.
20. Provincial Archives of Alberta, letter from the Minister of Public Welfare, October 31, 1946, 95.187/4.
21. Provincial Archives of Alberta, IODE, Alberta Provincial Chapter, 1947, *Welfare in Alberta: The Report of a Study,* 95.187/7.
22. Provincial Archives of Alberta, IODE, Alberta Provincial Chapter, 1947, *Welfare in Alberta: The Report of a Study,* 95.187/7.
23. City of Edmonton Archives, Edmonton Council of Community Services, *Brief to the City,* September, 1956, RG11, Class32, File 12.
24. City of Edmonton Archives, memo to the Mayor, January 21, 1957, R.G.11, Class 32, File 12.
25. Provincial Archives of Alberta, University Women's Club, "Continuing Interest in Day Care," Appendix to "Standards for Training in Day Care Services," Brief to the Government of Alberta, May, 1966, 78.476/G.
26. Provincial Archives of Alberta, University Women's Club, Minutes, November 16, 1959, 69.22/52.

27. Provincial Archives of Alberta, University Women's Club, "Day Care Centres for Children: Family Welfare Study Group Report," February 20, 1961, 69.22/52.
28. City of Edmonton Archives, Edmonton Welfare Council, 1964, "Annual Report," MS 323, Class 1, Subclass 4, File 1-27.
29. Provincial Archives of Alberta, Alberta Department of Public Welfare, 1961, "Minimum Standards for Operating and Licensing of Institutions and Nurseries."
30. Provincial Archives of Alberta, Alberta Department of Public Welfare, "Minimum Standards Governing Operation and Licensing of Institutions and Nurseries," June 28, 1963.
31. *Edmonton Journal* 1966b.
32. World Health Organization 1962.
33. Government of Canada 1961.
34. Department of Labour 1964.
35. McCord 1988.
36. World Health Organization 1964.
37. *Edmonton Journal* 1964.
38. City of Edmonton Archives, Edmonton Creche Society letters, 1951, RG11, Class 32, File 11.
39. Government of Canada, *Canada Assistance Plan*, 1966.
40. Government of Alberta, 1966. *Preventive Social Services Act*, 1966.
41. City of Edmonton Archives, Edmonton Welfare Council, Day Care Planning Committee, "Brief to the City of Edmonton on the Establishment of Day Care Services," March, 1966.
42. City of Edmonton Archives, Family Service Association, "Day Care Study, A Brief," March, 1966.
43. *Edmonton Journal* 1966b.
44. City of Edmonton, n.d, "Guidelines for Day Care Services," (Edmonton: City of Edmonton).
45. Child Welfare League of America 1965.
46. Provincial Archives of Alberta, University Women's Club, "Brief to the University of Alberta," May 1966.
47. Edmonton Branch, Canadian Committee on Early Childhood—OMEP Canada, 1970, "Brief to the Board of Grant MacEwan Community College," Child Care Program Proposal, Edmonton.
48. Government of Alberta, *Family and Community Support Services Act*, 1981.
49. *Edmonton Journal* 1978.
50. Masson 1985.
51. Dolphin 2001.
52. Interview with Doris Badir, Capital Region Services Authority Board, February 15, 2001.
53. Interview with Kathy Barnhart, Edmonton Community Services Department, February 14, 2001.
54. Mahaffy 2001.

Chapter 5

From Ideal to Pragmatic Politics
National Child Care Advocacy Groups in the 1980s and 1990s

Linda A. White

This chapter's core question addresses how the results of decades of child care advocacy measure up against advocates' ideals: what level of success have advocates achieved in their push for government–funded, accessible, high–quality care in relation to their ideal vision of child care in Canada? The chapter critically analyzes child care advocates' efforts to lobby the Canadian federal government in two recent decades: the 1980s and 1990s.[1] The first part focuses in particular on advocates' opposition to the National Strategy on Child Care, introduced in 1987 by the Conservative government under Prime Minister Brian Mulroney and further entrenched as Bill C–144, the proposed *Canada Child Care Act*. It poses the question, did advocates make the right strategic choices in the 1980s to fight for a "whole loaf" and reject the "half loaf" proposal offered by the federal government? The second part of the paper analyzes observed shifts in advocacy strategy in the 1990s and evaluates the comparable success of this shift.

This chapter argues that daycare advocates' oppositional strategy adopted in reaction to the Mulroney government's proposals was counterproductive to achieving their ultimate goal of federal funding for a national daycare program. This argument rests on scholarly observations of the impact of policy institutionalization in shaping and constraining later program development, as well as the importance of normative institutionalization.[2] Child care advocates' continued demands in the late 1980s for a high–quality, universal, federal child care policy led them to reject then-Prime Minister Mulroney's promise of more money alongside greater commercial involvement in child care. While the child care lobby felt it necessary at the time to oppose this perceived "half loaf," their opposition to the federal plan, in hindsight, was costly; that is, it resulted in "no bread."

Not only did the federal government not come through with more monies, but also the demise of Bill C 144 and the lack of new legislation in the Progressive Conservative government's second term prevented the establishment of a greater institutional role for the federal government in child care, beyond what existed under the Canada Assistance Plan (CAP). The existence of a specific federal child care program would have offered an institutional bulwark against later program erosion (though funding erosion is another matter) that occurred in the 1990s under the federal Liberal government, with the shift to the Canada Health and Social Transfer (CHST) and to block funding for health and social programs. The failure to accept such federal child care offers also pre-empted the institutionalization of legitimating norms that comes with policy implementation. Advocates' acceptance of the limited child care funding that the Mulroney government offered would have institutionalized the idea of child care as a legitimate area of government activity and provided both the normative and institutional foundation for future policy expansion and development.

Advocacy groups' strategy in the 1990s, in contrast, has been to endorse a broader approach to policies for children that emphasizes early child development and support for parents. This approach promotes high-quality child care as one means by which to provide support for children and parents. The child care advocacy community has also been willing to applaud incremental measures leading toward their ultimate goals, rather than criticizing governments for their less than wholehearted embrace of child care. Child care advocates, for example, have lauded the current government's proposal to expand the length of time parents can claim parental benefits as a step toward creating programs that reconcile work and family life. Advocates have also broadened their rhetoric from one supporting child care to one supporting child care as part of an early childhood education or development program. In the 1980s, these programs would have been seen as poor substitutes for child care.

This new 1990s strategy should lead to greater long-term success at achieving some forms of targeted child care, in that it better responds to dominant norms in society regarding care outside the home and the role of women in the labour market. It should also prove more successful with governments than the earlier strategy, as broader "early years"-based child care programs provide a solution to the problem of child poverty that governments seek to resolve. Additionally, such a broad-based approach to child care delivery responds well to recent accountability demands: demands that the success of government programs be measured according to outcomes (which early child development programs purport to affect.) Third, it responds to ideological concerns about the role of government in the provision and funding of child care programs, in that child care is not being demanded solely to benefit women or to provide "socialized" care, but rather to balance work and family life, as well as to promote early child development, and thus, prevent problems later in life. Finally, the strategy fits well with provincial (and now federal) concerns about flexibility in program design and delivery in an increasingly decentralized federation. Thus, factors such as timing—as governments search for solutions to child poverty and child development—and fitness—deriving solutions from already-legitimate norms and institutions—will go a long way to program acceptability.

This more conciliatory, pragmatic approach, however, has pitfalls as well. It will not build universal, full-time, formalized child care that facilitates women's (parents') labour market participation and such facilitation has been the thrust of lobbying efforts since the creation of the child care advocacy movement. In fact, it could result in a very watered down and less comprehensive version of child care—the very fear of child care advocates in the 1980s. Thus, trade-offs are inherent in both the old and new strategies.

History of the Contemporary Child Care Advocacy Movement

The child care lobby is very vibrant in Canada. Advocates have mobilized at both the provincial and federal levels since the late 1970s and early 1980s to push for a national policy on child care. At the municipal level, local groups mobilized even earlier to encourage policy development and expansion at the provincial level. Federalism arrangements, in fact, require advocates to target their efforts at all three levels of government—federal, provincial and municipal—since the latter two are often responsible for program delivery. Although child care is substantively an area of provincial responsibility, child care advocates also focus their attention on the national level, pushing for funding and national standards in program delivery and program support. Targeting so many levels of government, however, drains advocates' energy and resources.[3]

The child care lobby has been very strong in Canada, in part because the state has traditionally provided a great deal of funding support for interest group activity.[4] However, child care advocacy organizations have faced greater constraints recently because of cutbacks in funding support at both the federal and provincial levels.[5] Their influence has also been tempered due to the increasing momentum of conservative groups lobbying against centre-based care and by a continuing generally conservative ideological climate in Canada that remains ambivalent both about care of children outside the home and the role of women in the paid labour force. Fiscal and federalist concerns have more recently kept child care "off the table," to a large extent.[6] Advocacy organizations' strategies adopted over the past decades, however, have also constrained their effectiveness.

The child care advocacy lobby generally supports the establishment of a publicly funded, comprehensive, high-quality system of child care accessible to all families. This position has been modified from that of the 1970s, when many in the movement argued for state-run as well as state-funded daycare. At that time, it was believed that a socialized form of child care would transform relations between women and men and thereby counter patriarchal power structures in society.[7] In the late 1970s and early 1980s, advocacy groups adjusted their demands to gain more mainstream support. For example, Action Daycare formed in Ontario in 1979 as an organization of parents, daycare workers, community activists and trade union representatives.[8] It lobbied for free, universal, quality daycare. In 1981, when Action Daycare became the Ontario Coalition for Better Child Care (OCBCC), its mandate shifted from promoting free and universal daycare to promoting a well-organized, universally accessible, publicly funded, not-for-profit and non-compulsory daycare system.[9]

The lobby movement became more sophisticated over time, moving from simply asking for more and better child care to proposing just how to do it. At the national level, a key event in this regard was the September 1982 second national conference. Held in Winnipeg, it was sponsored by Health and Welfare Canada and organized by the Canadian Council on Social Development. Over 700 delegates from across the country attended the conference, including child care workers as well as representatives of trade unions, women's groups and social service agencies. This conference added further momentum to the idea of universal, as opposed to targeted, child care access.

The Canadian Daycare Advocacy Association, now the Child Care Advocacy Association of Canada (CCAAC), formed in 1983, out of this conference. Its declared mandate has moderated from advocating for free daycare to its current goal of "accessible, affordable, high quality and non-profit child care services."[10] In 1986 also formed was the Canadian Child Daycare Federation; now the Canadian Child Care Federation (CCCF), it began as more of an apolitical and professional association focused on issues of training, professional development, and so on. It has taken on more of an advocacy role and now coordinates some advocacy initiatives with the CCAAC.[11] Finally, other advocacy groups have lobbied on behalf of child care, such as the National Action Committee on the Status of Women (NAC) and trade unions such as the Ontario Federation of Labour (OFL).[12]

Until recently, all the groups involved in advocating child care supported a number of core principles upon which a child care system should be based. First, child care should be national in scope. Second, it should be publicly funded. Third, access should be universal and equitable, that is, regardless of family income, region, ethnic, linguistic or racial background, ability or disability. Fourth, it should be comprehensive, providing a range of services. Finally, it should be of high quality, often meaning non-profit, with appropriate regulation and adequate salaries for staff.[13] Strong support for these core principles led the advocacy associations to oppose the child care reforms proposed by the Conservative government in the late 1980s.

The 1987 Proposed Reforms

The federal Progressive Conservative government under Prime Minister Brian Mulroney first announced its plans to reform federal child care funding in December 1987. The biggest component of the National Child Care Strategy was a promise to commit $3 billion over seven years, or $429 million per year, to develop child care where needed and to change the federal-provincial cost-sharing arrangements by removing child care from the Canada Assistance Plan (CAP). The Conservative strategy effectively proposed a ceiling on child care, as federal funding until then was open ended under CAP. The government also proposed to loosen requirements that existed under CAP, which had been until then offered operating cost funding exclusively to non-for-profit centres. Instead, Bill C-144[14] would allow funding of operational costs to commercial daycare centres as well.

There were other components of the strategy. First, was a promise of more generous tax deductions for child care expenses for parents with young children and refundable child tax credits for parents who cared for their children at home. That program would cost an estimated $2.3 billion over seven years, or $329 million per year. Second, the government announced a new Child Care Initiatives Fund of $100 million over seven years, or approximately $14 million per year, for research and child care development. It later announced a third component, of $60 million over six years for support to child care on aboriginal reserves.[15]

Many child care advocates and groups immediately mobilized against the government's National Child Care Strategy.[16] They found fault in a number of areas. First, they objected to the ceiling that would be imposed on cost sharing. Second, they disliked the idea of funding for commercial spaces. Third, they complained that the Act would impose no national standards. Fourth, they argued that monies directed to tax benefits would divert funds from those to establish spaces in daycare centres. Since the advocates' ideal was universally accessible, publicly funded, comprehensive, not-for-profit and high-quality daycare, they saw the changes as a huge step backward in their fight for a national daycare system.

The federal ceiling on cost sharing, while portending a future ceiling on federal spending in 1990, was unusual at the time and thus was fiercely resisted. The cap on federal funding, advocates argued, would hurt provinces with well-developed programs. It would impair provinces that had plans to expand programs, as Ontario and Quebec did at the time. Critics pointed out that under then-existing fiscal arrangements, child care spaces would likely continue to expand at an annual rate of between 10 and 16 percent, meaning an increase in federal government spending of $1.8 billion over seven years.[17] If growth continued as it had between 1985 and 1988, expenditures would be even higher, at $3.9 billion. But, if changes were made along the lines that the Mulroney government proposed, that expansion could not occur. Furthermore, a portion of the funds that would otherwise go to create new spaces would instead be directed to already-existing commercial daycare services not then eligible for subsidization. Thus, the fixed funding ceiling and the plan to support commercial care were two main issues advocates tackled. Their view at that time was that it was better to have no child care system at all than a deeply flawed, commercial one with no national standards.

In addition, they opposed the emphasis placed on tax benefits, which advocates felt would undermine their main goal of developing child care services. Tax measures would not address the issue of lack of spaces for children. Furthermore, "tax measures create no opportunity for [a] public authority to shape the quality, availability, or affordability of child care services." Neither would they "offer a vehicle through which government might address the issue of child care providers' wages and working conditions."[18] Tax programs tend to benefit higher income earners, and they require parents to pay for child care services up front.

Other, more conservative groups such as REAL Women opposed the

legislation in principle, rejecting nonparental care of children and participation of women in the labour market.[19] REAL Women instead argued
that governments should be providing more support to those who chose
to stay at home with their children.[20]

The federal government went ahead with only part of its strategy: the
cost-sharing component and the block-grant formula. The government
introduced Bill C-144, the *Canada Child Care Act*, in the House of
Commons in July 1988. By then, the provinces had persuaded the federal
government that the promised $3 billion was inadequate, so the federal
government increased its financial commitment to $4 billion, with the
hope of creating 200,000 new spaces. The federal government gave the
provinces the option of either retaining the existing funding under CAP or
moving to block funding. Once provinces moved to block funding,
however, they could not go back.

The Senate Standing Committee on Social Affairs, Science and
Technology was in the process of reviewing the legislation when Parliament was dissolved for the November 1988 election. Although Prime
Minister Mulroney declared during the election that he would reintro-
duce the *Child Care Act* if re-elected, the debate over free trade overshad-
owed the child care issue. In its second term in office, the Mulroney
government announced it would not go ahead with its cost-sharing plans.
It also announced the end of universal family allowances, substituting
instead the Child Tax Benefit, targeted to low-income families with
children. It also increased the Child Care Expense Deduction from a
maximum of $2,000 to $4,000 for families with one child under seven
years old and increased the refundable child tax credit. It also established
paid parental leave benefits of ten weeks. Not one of these measures did
anything to develop child care services.

Meanwhile, the Conservative government implemented its planned
cost cutting by other means. In 1990, it placed a ceiling of 5 percent
growth in contributions under the CAP to "have" provinces—that is,
Ontario, Alberta, and British Columbia. The cap meant those three
provinces no longer received 50 percent federal funding for monies spent
above the 5 percent ceiling. If those provinces chose to expand child care
and other social services, they would have to shoulder the entire cost above
the 5 percent cap. In 1995, the federal Liberal government went even
further and eliminated the CAP entirely, replacing it with a block-funded
program for health and social services under the Canada Health and Social
Transfer (CHST).

At the end of the Mulroney government's terms in office, child care remained a solidly welfare-based and income-based program. After a debate of more than fifteen years in which advocates promoted child care as part of a broader public policy for children, parents and women's equality, they failed to persuade the federal government to expand funding and other support for child care on advocates' own terms.

Assessment of Movement Efforts around Bill C-144

One major failing of the advocacy movement until the 1990s was in its an all-or-nothing attitude to child care—accepting nothing less than the ideal. This strong stance stemmed in part from a lack of trust, given their perception that past government actions undermined the movement's goals. In many ways the advocacy groups saw themselves as struggling against the state, not working with it.[21] Thus, child care activists felt it necessary to oppose all government initiatives that did not meet their ideal of free or at least universally accessible child care. In addition, child care advocacy groups in the 1980s were more optimistic that governments would eventually respond to their demands; thus, halfway measures, they felt, should not be accepted if they hoped to continually press for governments to meet their full demands.

In hindsight, this position appears costly, especially with regard to Bill C-144. First, the legislation proposed by the Mulroney government included a proposal to remove child care spending from CAP and make it a separate program for cost-sharing arrangements. As a separate program, child care might have been exempt from the later ceiling on CAP introduced in 1990. One federal official interviewed in 1996 stated:

> I think some advocates would argue that [the Department of] Finance would have included that piece of legislation in the cap. I would argue that probably would not have happened because the *Vocational Rehabilitation for Disabled Persons Act*, which is very similar to CAP, was open-ended but not subject to a cap. Now that is not to say that when the federal government introduced the CHST, it would not have rolled it [child care funding] in too. I suspect it might have, although again the VRDP has been exempt from that for political reasons.

Second, a highly visible, separate program could have led to a reconceptualization of child care from a welfare program to an institution-alized service for all parents with children, something child care advocates have promoted for some time. The same federal official interviewed in

1996 also argued that:

> With the passage of C-144, you would have had something much more visible to the public and something that the advocates could have focused on in terms of amendments for improvement. What you would have done for the first time under that act is you would have isolated and focused the attention on child care as a discrete service as opposed to one of a number. It was in legislation that is highly visible, and even though it had its flaws, I think that there might have been an opportunity over time to improve some of those flaws.

Given the cuts to child care that occurred federally with the elimination of the CAP and the move to block funding, a fixed commitment to child care funding would be far superior to what exists today where provincial governments have no obligation to spend any federal monies on child care. In 1988, for example, many groups strongly criticized the promised long-term funding for daycare operating grants and subsidies to parents of about $600 million per year, which would have kicked in after the initial seven-year funding period.[22] Currently, though, the federal government provides no explicit funds for operating grants or subsidies to parents, programs that go a long way to develop formalized child care.

At the time, child care advocacy organizations feared that once the changes were made and the money was committed, they would be difficult to reverse.[23] For example, Bill C-144 would have allowed federal funding of commercial care for the first time. In Australia, the tremendous expansion of child care in the late 1980s and early 1990s came at the price of allowing commercial care.[24] The child care lobby's stance in Canada, by contrast, was absolute opposition to commercial expansion. Child care advocates feared that large U.S. commercial care companies would move into Canada, diluting quality. Advocacy groups felt (and still feel) it was their role to maintain quality in child care services. They have had to push governments continuously on issues of quality, rather than rely on governments themselves to promote it. Thus, commercial care had to be opposed.

While institutionalization of bad policies can constrain future policy development, this is not always the case. For example, until the late 1980s, the government of Ontario provided subsidies to both for-profit and not-for-profit child care centres. The percentage of commercial child care centres dropped dramatically in Ontario from the late 1980s onward, through the explicit policies of the Liberal and NDP governments to decrease the amount of commercial care.[25] Thus, programs that are in place can be reformed.

In commenting on the oppositional stance by child care advocates, Katheryne Schulz of the OCBCC stated in 1996, "Well, I don't think we were wrong. We didn't want the CAP to be capped, and we were also concerned about conditions." She went on to argue:

> In a way it's actually better that they are trying to do this [eliminate funds] now on a broader scale because ... if you attack something bit by bit by pulling this out of CAP and that, which would be a smarter strategy in a way, then you wouldn't get the same unified opposition to what you were doing. If you're taking CAP apart and replacing it with the CHST, at least everyone can see that they are all in jeopardy as a result.

Unfortunately, cuts to federal funding under the CHST were so devastating to other social and health programs, the general public has largely ignored cuts to child care.

As their defence, advocacy groups argue that neither they nor anyone else could have foreseen the level of cutbacks Canada experienced in the 1990s that has prevented the expansion of any major social programs. When asked, in light of what happened to child care funding in terms of the CAP, would CUPE's perspective on Bill C-144 have been different, child care representative Jamie Kass responded:

> I don't know at this point. [Back then] it was a decision to oppose going from unlimited funding to limited funding, and not enough limited funding. There was such a fear that we would end up in fact with so much less. You couldn't have told us back then [about the demise of CAP]. They hadn't even frozen CAP yet.... You know, it would drive you crazy because you couldn't rewrite it. Now we have limited funding, in fact we have no funding because we'll be at the bottom of [the list]. What people are so concerned about is that the impact of the CHST will be devastating on child care because health, education, welfare will all be picked up first. The real impact of the cuts will be in terms of child care.[26]

In hindsight, however, it should not have been difficult to forecast government cutbacks. The Mulroney government was already engaged in government streamlining at the time and had completed the Task Force on Program Review that prescribed a number of government cost-cutting measures.[27] The problem was that the advocates saw these moves as partisanship when, in hindsight, they foretold major economic and ideological shifts.

The lack of institutionalization of child care policies at the federal level means that governments at both levels have little normative or policy basis upon which to legitimately build child care programs today. Institution-alization can narrow the range of possible options, but it also provides the basis for future growth along the institutional paths set previously. Policy institutionalization is important for legitimation purposes as well. As Krasner argues, "once new institutions are in place they can assume a life of their own, extracting societal resources, socializing individuals, and even altering the basic nature of civil society itself."[28] Institutionalization encourages the public to accept the basic legitimacy of the program.

The Evolution to Pragmatic Politics

The 1990s have witnessed a major evolution in child care advocates' position and an increasing recognition that, in order for policies to be institutionalized, they must have support at the political, economic, administrative and public levels. Public support is especially important in the realm of social policy, where policy solutions and policy problems are more contested and as it is often difficult to build governmental support when faced with societal resistance. Research demonstrates that this support can be built if policies are seen to serve some purpose, such as offer a solution to a perceived policy problem.[29] Furthermore, it helps if policies can be linked to values and norms already embedded in society and accepted as legitimate.[30]

For the longest time, child care advocates did not recognize the importance of linking child care to other established policies and pro-grams. Because the lobby's main concern was, and still is, quality child care, advocates resisted linking child care to other policies, such as parental leave and benefits and early childhood education.[31] Given limited resources, advocates devoted their time and money to lobbying for the ideal form of care. In the 1990s, however, advocates became increasingly aware and accepting of the importance of these linkages. Child care must be "pitched" as a policy that (1) helps society, (2) fits well with other policy goals and (3) does not undermine—or clash with—dominant norms about gender roles.

A further weakness in the child care lobby's strategy until the mid-

1990s was that it tended to frame its support for child care in terms of equality for women and, in particular, equality for working women. However, a large percentage of the population is hostile to such gender arguments as, "if a woman has the right to participate equally in the job market then she must have child care. If a woman bears children, then she must have child care. If a woman bears children, then she must have support to raise them."[32] Many Canadians believe that it is better for children if mothers do not work outside the home, and/or that child care is not the state's role.[33] Concentration on women's equality arguments alone has been a hindrance to the development of societal support for child care, especially with the mobilization of right-wing groups to counter women's rights advocates' arguments.

The shift in child care advocates' stance thus came partly as a response to the enormous resistance to child care mounted by organized social conservative groups. By the mid-1990s, a number of groups defending "the family" had proliferated: REAL Women of Canada, along with the Calgary-based Kids First Parent Association of Canada, Westcoast Women for Family Life, Families First and Foremost, the National Family Network, and Women for Life, Faith and Family.[34] These "familist" groups have two arguments: first, that mothers should take care of children and, by implication, leave the labour market; and second, that centre-based care is harmful for children. Both of these arguments found support among Canadians and resulted in resistance to the expansion of public funding for child care.[35] As a result, child care advocates have encountered less resistance to the idea that child care services are but one aspect to an overall family policy that supports parents' work *and* home life.[36]

Child care advocates' increasingly pragmatic stance has in part responded to shifts in governmental positions as well. The federal government's position has shifted dramatically from 1995, when then-Human Resources Development Minister Lloyd Axworthy attempted to keep national (and federal) daycare on the table, to what is now being articulated: "early childhood development" and "support for parents." Programs under these labels include income-support policies (such as the national Child Tax Benefit); improved maternity and parental-leave programs and benefits; other measures that support parents' efforts to balance work and family life (such as flexible employment hours and schedules); measures to support effective parenting and child health, such as community resource centres and recreation programs, well-baby and well-mother programs; and developmentally based rather than custodial child care and early childhood education aimed to help *both* employed and stay-at-home parents.[37] In other words, governments no longer support an explicitly national "daycare" program but endorse child care as one aspect of a broader child- and family-centred approach.

Child care advocates in general tend to embrace these programs as well, but insist that the cornerstone to any child and family policy is high-quality child care services.[38] Some child care advocacy organizations did not have as far to move to this position as others. The Canadian Child Care Federation (CCCF), Dianne Bascombe argues, has always focused more on service delivery and has avoided taking an ideological position on child care—for example, allowing workers from commercial as well as not-for-profit centres to join the organization. Furthermore, because its main concern was support for child care workers and quality of service provision, it tended to focus less on gender issues raised by women's rights organizations such as NAC or cost issues raised by parents using the services. Yet, even the CCCF had a difficult time embracing the idea of including independent childminders or family daycare under its rubric.[39] Cindy Magloughlin of the Child Care Advocacy Association of Canada (CCAAC) argues that its ultimate goal has always been achieving a coherent family policy and public recognition that people who are raising children are doing something valuable. Child care is an absolutely critical part of that policy, but so too are other pieces such as maternity and parental benefits, pre-natal and post-natal services, and family-friendly workplaces. The error child care advocates made was in simplifying the message to only include child care.

Magloughin argues that child care workers at the local level recognized for some time the need for a broader message but that the evolution of awareness at the national level took some time. Indeed, she argues, the existence of the Canada Assistance Plan funding in some ways narrowed the position of advocacy groups since the federal government insisted that funding had to go to non-profit licensed care. The elimination of the CAP allowed advocacy associations to broaden their focus. The CCAAC has not given up on universal, publicly funded child care but has increasingly recognized that other small measures can occur along the way.

Advocates have resigned themselves to the idea that universal, publicly funded child care is not going to happen overnight. They have also recognized that the battle must be fought at an ideological level: that child care must be "sold" by connecting it in some way to other policies or programs. Research on early childhood development, therefore, has come at a most opportune time for the movement. Support for child care as part of early childhood development at both the societal and governmental levels has been buoyed by a number of studies and policy documents released in the past few years. These studies argue that child care is a "good thing" for children developmentally and thus a sound economic policy.[40]

These early-years studies have generated a remarkable amount of attention that can be attributed to three factors. First, research on early childhood development boldly suggests that the first three to five years of a child's life are critical to his or her physiological, emotional, and psychological well-being. Second, think-tanks, such as the Canadian Institute for Advanced Research and the Canadian Policy Research Networks, have picked up these researchers' message and carried it to governments.[41] Other advocacy groups, such as the National Council of Welfare and the Invest in Kids Foundation,[42] have embraced the findings of this research as well. All of these groups advocate a holistic approach to programs for children, in line with the research's suggestion about stages of early child development and the influences affecting that development.

Third, that kind of outcomes-based approach has fit well with the new emphasis on accountability techniques.[43] It works to set goals for what governments are trying to achieve and to measure successful implementation via outcomes such as shifts in poverty and literacy rates, reduced crime and so on. Early childhood development-based programs thus fit nicely with shifts in administrative thinking. Administrators argue that these kinds of programs will generate observable outcomes: if you build them, the results will come.

These programs also represent a logical extension in governmental concern with child poverty, which it began to address vigorously at the federal level in the 1990s with the introduction of the targeted Child Tax Benefit and the provincial level, as well, with the National Child Benefit. Early child development (ECD) holds out the promise of especially helping at-risk population groups. ECD can also be connected to crime prevention programs, as signaled by justice officials' involvement in the working group connected to the National Children's Agenda.

Finally, child care advocates have acknowledged the need to generalize their message in order to meet the needs, not just of all players, but also of all provinces. Federalism concerns require that both the federal government and child care advocates pitch programs for children which are very broad, very flexible and do not commit any one province or territory to a specific program design; rather, provinces and territories must have the freedom to work out their own "detailed program design and mix best suited to [their] own needs and circumstances," as per the requirements of the recently negotiated Social Union Framework Agreement.[44]

Conclusion: Assessment of the Movement's Efforts in the 1990s

Given the ideological underpinnings of social policy issues in Canada, the measures that policy makers adopt need not only have political, economic and bureaucratic viability, they need also to have societal viability. Thus, ideas must have a certain degree of normative acceptance or societal "fitness" to be successfully implemented. That fitness needs to respond to prevalent economic and fiscal conditions in Canada, the strength of oppositional groups, federalism concerns, and dominant ideas about the family and women's roles in society and the labour market.

As outlined above, advocates have demonstrated a growing awareness of the difficulty of "selling" child care to governments and the electorate in Canada. Governments, in effect, need a reason to intervene—usually with some policy problem they are trying to solve. Child care advocates have been unpersuasive in the past, partly because the reasons they have offered to government have not been palatable (such as support for women's equality) and also because the measures they have proposed have been narrowly cast to focus on daycare services exclusively. Their shift in rhetorical stance in the 1990s thus goes a long way, first to provide a legitimating rationale for the policies proposed (that is, "save the kids"); and second, because the measures proposed are more broad, flexible and can respond to fiscal, administrative and jurisdictional/federalism concerns, all of which are necessary in a changed political, economic and administrative climate. The risk involved is that the measures eventually adopted, for example, under a negotiated National Children's Agenda, may be a vastly watered down version of what advocates want. Thus, child care advocates might achieve success—that is, the establishment of some kind of child care and early childhood development programs in each province and territory—only by sacrificing their core goal, which is to achieve a comprehensive national daycare system.

The political terrain has changed so much, with fiscal, administrative, federalism and continued ideological concerns pushing policies in the directions documented above, that a more pragmatic politics is really the only possible route to success. Thus, it makes little sense for child care advocates to return to the solely oppositional politics of the past. However, they must continue to present strong arguments for the need for comprehensive, accessible, high-quality child care programs as a core part of early child development and learning. While supporting provincial and territorial broad-based programs for early child development and parental support initiatives, child care advocates should continue to press for a nationwide system of daycare services. However, advocates must now endorse such services as a central part of early child development and learning, as they have in the past, while recognizing the need to "sell" those programs in ways that are ideologically, politically, economically and administratively palatable.

Finally, it should be noted that, as child care advocates' message has become more persuasive, their ability to communicate those arguments has been impeded by cutbacks in government funding and shut-outs from federalism negotiations. The current failure to establish a coherent family policy in Canada at this point, therefore, lies in large part with continued lack of political will on the part of policy makers and not with the advocates' message. This lack of political will is indeed disheartening for, as Dianne Bascombe points out, "if we can't get federal and provincial governments to agree on programs for kids, we don't have any hope for social programs, period."

Notes

1. The chapter draws on interviews completed in 1996 with child care advocates and government officials regarding the 1980s period, as well as recent interviews with advocates regarding current directions in child care policy. It also draws from dissertation research that compares child care policy development in France, Canada and the United States. See White 1998.

2. Goldstein and Keohane 1993; Krasner 1984; Pierson 1993.

3. Katheryne Schulz of the Ontario Coalition for Better Child Care (OCBCC) argues that dealing with shared responsibility for funding and provision is difficult. Often the result is that service delivery varies from region to region and funding is never permanent. Municipal involvement is double-edged as well, Schulz argues. Some municipalities have a good track record on child care and push the province for provision. Others do not. (Interview with Katheryne Schulz, Public Education Coordinator, Ontario Coalition for Better Child Care, Toronto, Ontario, June 4, 1996.)

4. Burt 1997: 482 argues that funding is vital for interest groups in that it gives the groups a measure of legitimacy, it guarantees them a voice in policy discussions and it provides them with the financial resources to survive.

5. For example, in the early 1990s, the OCBCC received funding from the federal Secretary of State Women's Program, Human Resources Development Canada, Labour Canada, the Ontario Ministry of Community and

Social Services, and the Ontario Women's Directorate, along with membership fees and donations (OCBCC 1994). Mary-Anne Bédard reports that over the past half decade, the OCBCC has lost all base funding from Status of Women Canada, which now only provides project funding. Other organizations have told the OCBCC that they no longer fund advocacy organizations, even for projects. Because of the loss of base funding, the OCBCC has to focus more on research rather than advocacy to justify project funding, spend more time fundraising, and get by with a greatly reduced staff (interview with Mary-Anne Bédard, Executive Director, Ontario Coalition for Better Child Care, Toronto, Ontario, June 6, 2000).

6. See White 2001.
7. Prentice 1988b.
8. Colley 1981.
9. Colley 1983: 310.
10. For the CCAAC's current mission statement, see its website: http://home.istar.ca/~ccaac. Its earlier mission statement can be found in CCAAC 1995. The then-CDCAA moved away from the demand for free child care in 1985, a move NAC did not immediately endorse (NAC 1986: 13).
11. Interview with Cindy Magloughlin, Executive Director, Child Care Advocacy Association of Canada, Ottawa, Ontario, May 19, 2000.
12. Bédard notes that, with the loss of a great deal of government and foundation funding, trade unions such as the Canadian Auto Workers have been enormously helpful to the child care cause, either by providing funding to child care advocacy organizations such as the OCBCC, or by launching their own campaigns. (Interview with Mary-Anne Bédard, Executive Director, Ontario Coalition for Better Child Care, Toronto, Ontario, June 6, 2000.)
13. CACSW (Canadian Advisory Council on the Status of Women), 1986, *Caring for Our Children*, Brief Presented to the Special Committee on Child Care, Ottawa: CACSW; CCAAC 1995; Léger and Rebick 1993: 17–18; OCBCC 1981.
14. *Canada Child Care Act*.
15. Phillips 1989: 166–67.
16. Groups that mobilized against Bill C-144 included the Canadian Day Care Advocacy Association, trade unions, including the Canadian Labour Congress, the Public Service Alliance of Canada, the Canadian Union of Public Employees, the National Union of Provincial Government Employees/Canadian Teachers' Federation, The Federation of Nurses, women's groups such as NAC, the Canadian Advisory Council on the Status of Women, anti-poverty groups such as the National Anti-Poverty Organization and the National Council of Welfare, and other interest groups such as the Canadian Jewish Congress and Canadian Federation of Students (Phillips 1989: 172).
17. NAC 1988: 1. The National Council of Welfare cites the amount of $2.6 billion over seven years (NCW 1988: 15).
18. Teghtsoonian 1996b: 12.

19. Phillips 1989: 172.
20. Teghtsoonian 1996b.
21. See Prentice 1988b.
22. See, for example, NAC 1988
23. Phillips 1989: 201.
24. Brennan 1998.
25. White 1997.
26. Interview with Jamie Kass, former Union Education Officer and Elected Representative on child care for Ontario, Canadian Union of Public Employees and head of child care programs, Canadian Union of Postal Workers, Ottawa, Ontario, May 13, 1996.
27. Canada, Task Force on Program Review 1986: 30. Ironically, though, the Nielsen Report did *not* suggest radical changes to the CAP. It stated, "since CAP alleviates the needs of people caught under adverse economic circumstances, solutions to those problems [the fact that "nearly half of all Canadians currently on welfare are employable but unable to find work"] must be found elsewhere."
28. Krasner 1984: 240.
29. See, for example, McNamara 1998.
30. Keck and Sikkink 1998.
31. Gallagher Ross 1986: 31–33, for example, takes the Task Force on Child Care to task for not going far in recommending changes to parental leave.
32. OCBCC 1981: 10.
33. While a majority of Canadians believe that child care services should be available to anyone who wants them, they are more ambivalent as to the amount of money governments should contribute vis-à-vis parents. For public opinion polling results over time see Michalski 1999.
34. See Teghtsoonian 1996b.
35. Teghtsoonian 1996a: 125 quotes Perrin Beatty, then-Minister of Health and Welfare under the Mulroney government, as stating in 1990 that Canadians do not "want to pay for the yuppie couple."
36. Some women have rejuvenated the campaign for societal recognition and the attachment of worth to work done in the home. See, for example, Beverley Smith's homepage at http://www.agt.net/public/bvgsmith and Mothers are Women at http://www.cyberus.ca/~maw/.
37. See, for example, Childhood and Youth Division, Health Canada 1999; Government of Canada, Governor General 1999; National Children's Agenda 1999.
38. See, for example, OCBCC 1999a.
39. Interview with Dianne Bascombe, former Executive Director of the Canadian Child Care Federation and current Director of the Centre for Voluntary Sector Research and Development, Ottawa, Ontario, May 19, 2000.
40. See, for example, Cleveland and Krashinsky 1998; McCain and Mustard

1999; and the National Center for Early Development and Learning 1999.

41. The Canadian Institute for Advanced Research has been sponsoring research on the determinants of health for many years, and the former head of that organization, Fraser Mustard, has published a number of research reports on the importance of early years, including the McCain-Mustard report 1999. See also Jenson and Stroick 1999a and b.

42. See, for example, NCW 1999 and the Invest in Kids Foundation website at http://www.investinkids.ca.

43. Osborne and Gaebler 1992.

44. White 2001.

Chapter 6

Working with Parties
Success and Failure of Child Care Advocates in British Columbia and Ontario in the 1990s[1]

Cheryl Collier

This chapter seeks to explain the sometimes stark differences in child care policy in two very similar provinces just prior to and throughout the 1990s. Both British Columbia and Ontario are large, relatively rich provinces that have elected both right- and left-wing governments during this decade. However, these provincial governments have reacted differently to very similar demands from provincial child care advocates. These diverging policy agendas are evident when we look at each province's actions in the child care arena.

In July 1996, the B.C. New Democratic government of Glen Clark introduced the *B.C. Benefits (Child Care) Act*. This comprehensive child care plan essentially redefined child care delivery as a labour matter, rather than a welfare issue, by widening the criteria used to entitle families to child care subsidies. Although it was not a textbook response, provincial child care advocates welcomed the policy announcement, especially since it dealt with a longstanding demand to remove the welfare designation from child care delivery. A few thousand miles away, the Ontario Progressive Conservative government of Mike Harris was releasing a review of its existing child care policy, *Improving Ontario's Childcare System* (the Ecker report). Even though the Ecker report was not fully implemented, it clearly demonstrated the Conservative philosophy regarding child care delivery in the province. Among other things, it outlined a willingness to decrease subsidies for non-profit centres while elevating those to commercial centres, and it advanced less frequent centre monitoring and a decrease in the preschool staff-to-child ratios.[2] Ontario child care advocates reacted negatively to the Ecker report because it demonstrated an unwillingness to support quality, non-profit care over child care that put profit first.

This brief sketch raises the core questions that will be explored in this chapter: Why has there been such divergence in these two similar provinces responding to similar pressures from provincial advocacy groups? What factors can explain differences in government policy responses in the child care arena? As these examples and further evidence will show, the ideas held by the party in power have a striking effect on that party's response to provincial child care advocates. Specifically, parties of the left are much more willing to enact child care policy that more closely mirrors the lobbying efforts of child care advocates than are parties of the right. It is the purpose of this chapter to demonstrate this trend in these two provinces during the 1990s.

Drawing on a variety of sources including confidential interviews with child care advocates and government actors, archival sources and internal advocacy documents, I argue that advocates must pay close attention to the type of party in power in order to maximize their lobbying efforts. However, I also argue that unfavourable ideas held by a party in power can be at least temporarily overcome if a strong child care lobby and women's movement can exert leverage around an upcoming election. To illustrate this conclusion, I will first briefly outline the partisan theory of public policy that argues party ideas have an important impact on policy diversity in similar jurisdictions. I will then briefly outline the history of child care advocacy demands and corresponding policy responses for each province in the 1990s.

Partisan Theory of Public Policy

In political science, the concept that party ideas have a marked impact on policy differentiation is widely held. D.A. Hibbs Jr. states that the party composition of government is often the main cause of variation in policy outputs and choice in constitutional democracies.[3] According to this theory, a governing party's ideas or ideology will best explain why it makes certain policy decisions even in the face of outside constraints including external global pressures, prior commitments resulting from previous policy decisions and demands made by changing social and economic forces in society.[4]

The idea that party ideology/ideas makes a difference to policy outcomes is also supported by feminist scholars. Many suggest that parties on the left would be more open to enact policy deemed favourable to women's movements than would parties on the right.[5] Left-wing parties are often characterized as being more willing to use the power of the state to intervene in the economy and to support the welfare state, while right-wing parties prefer the principles of free enterprise and less state involvement overall. Child care researchers have also started to point to ideology as a key factor in explaining the growing differences in child care policy across Canada. Gillian Doherty, Martha Friendly and Mab Oloman note that variations in child care policy are largely due to "provincial fiscal capabilities and provincial governments' ideologies."[6] Jane Jenson and Sherry Thompson support this assertion, arguing that "provinces have exhibited a capacity to innovate that belies any analysis in terms of 'path dependency.'"[7]

Comparing B.C. and Ontario

While party ideology/ideas may not explain all of the differences in child care policy between the provincial governments,[8] it can and will be argued that party is an essential ingredient in accounting for that difference. The cases of B.C. and Ontario in the 1990s demonstrate this quite clearly. Both the left-wing NDP and right-wing Progressive Conservative governments have held power in the 1990s in Ontario and the right-wing Social Credit and left-wing NDP have held power in B.C.

In order to illustrate how party impacts on the lobbying efforts of provincial activists in both B.C. and Ontario, I will briefly explore the history of child care advocate demands in each setting. Then, I will briefly touch on the child care policy history of each province. I conclude by showing that almost all pro-child care advocate policy has been enacted by left-wing governments during this decade, with one notable exception in each case where the electoral sway of the women's movement was able to cause a shift in right-wing government policy away from its traditional position.

Child Care Advocacy in British Columbia

Overall, child care advocates in British Columbia have traditionally lobbied government for many of the same policy outcomes as have child care advocates in other parts of the country, including Ontario. The B.C. movement has demanded a high-quality child care system that is universally available, affordable, accessible and that is responsive to the needs of parents, children and communities. The movement differs from that in Ontario, though, by not engaging in a debate over the merits of non-profit or commercial care. This issue never really materialized in B.C. due, in part, to the relatively low numbers of big chain commercial child care centres in that province.[9]

B.C. child care advocacy can be traced back to the WWII when governments partially funded licensed daycare institutions, to allow women to work and support the war effort while their husbands were away fighting. Individuals and groups lobbying government during this time period were advocating proper training for early childhood educators in these licensed institutions. This type of advocacy, called the "preschool movement," can be traced from the war into the 1950s when groups such as the Association of Co-operative Play Groups of Greater Vancouver pushed for more communities to open child care centres licensed under the *Welfare Institutions Licensing Act* (1937). As more and more women entered the work force, calls for full-time child care became more frequent.

Funding for preschool services, including child care, was virtually non-existent from the end of WWII until the introduction of federal cost-sharing grants under the Canada Assistance Plan (CAP) in 1966.[10] It was also during the late 1960s and early 1970s that child care advocacy blossomed in B.C. Yet, child care advocates refused to see child care as a welfare service even though funding came from the welfare provisions of the Canada Assistance Plan:

> Day care advocates in B.C. objected to basing eligibility on income level because, they argued, such a system helped to "perpetuate the notion that day care exists [only] for parents who have in some way failed in their family responsibility."[11]

This position was strongly supported by radical child care groups active in the early 1970s, particularly the Day Care Occupation Forces.[12]

Advocacy continued through the 1970s, and it remained radical and grassroots during this period. In 1981, however, some advocates joined together to form the more liberal nonpartisan B.C. Day Care Action Coalition (BCDCAC) which was established following a provincial conference called "Day Care: A Look to the Future." Its platform included many of the items advocates continued to lobby for into the 1990s:

- improved standards and support staff to enforce those standards (i.e., licensing officials, etc.),
- parent involvement in all aspects of child care operations,
- greater recognition of the work of care providers (i.e., im-

proved wages and working conditions,
- a variety of child care models to meet a variety of needs,
- adequate government financial support to ensure affordable services (daycare must be viewed not as a welfare service but as a basic community support service),
- the establishment of one government ministry mandated to formulate legislation and monitor all aspects of child care services.[13]

The BCDCAC, despite calling itself a coalition of provincial child care advocates, was not able to grow beyond a core group of individuals until the1990s. Advocates interviewed were unclear as to why lobbying was largely unorganized during the 1980s, explaining simply that, "they never really had a position" to collectively rally around.[14] It is possible that advocates were discouraged by the nonresponsiveness of the Bill Bennett Social Credit government during the early part of the decade.

However, things started to turn around in the late 1980s when seven child care member organizations amalgamating and sharing rent and resources formed the Westcoast Child Care Resource Centre in 1988. While not solely an advocacy organization, Westcoast marked a new cooperative trend among provincial advocates. In 1995, the Coalition of Child Care Advocates of B.C. (CCCABC) was formed and included Westcoast, the BCDCAC, along with other provincial organizations. The 1999 Child Care Advocacy Forum was formed by the CCCABC to bring groups even closer together. In June 1999, the forum released *A Common Agenda and Vision* that recognized "the importance of working on our own priorities" while agreeing, "that without a common vision for child care, few of our long-term goals are achievable"[15] These goals remained largely unchanged from the BCDCAC's advocacy agenda in the early 1980s.

Child Care Policy and Party Government in British Columbia

In 1942, British Columbia was the first province in the country to introduce licensing legislation for daycare. However, this "first" was tarnished when the province decided to put that licensing legislation under the *Welfare Institutions Licensing Act* (1937) branding child care as a welfare service well before the Canada Assistance Plan opened the door for other provinces (including Ontario) to do the same. Provincial funding was scarce until CAP funding was introduced in 1966, at which time the province could cost-share child care funds for working-poor mothers.

The Social Credit government continued to classify child care as a welfare issue into the mid-1970s, until it shifted responsibility for subsidies in 1976. Funding levels for child care centres and training remained low during the 1970s and into the 1980s, despite some promising expansion in the early 1970s under the Barrett NDP government. However, what little gains made under Barrett were cut during the mid-1980s under the fiscally conservative Bill Bennett Social Credit regime.

When new Social Credit premier Bill Vander Zalm took office in 1986, his government continued the right-wing approach to child care. While his government refrained from large cuts to child care programs, it did little to improve conditions over its predecessor. This all changed in 1988 when Vander Zalm, motivated by his desire to win the next election and to lift his sagging popularity among women voters, started to pay more attention to women's policy, specifically child care.[16] He appointed a new minister responsible for women's programs, a sub-ministry of Government Services. Between 1988 and 1990, spending on child care rose 40 percent, with the maximum parent fees increasing by 15 percent in 1989 and an additional 4 percent in 1990.[17]

More importantly during the Vander Zalm reign, the government announced the 1990 launch of the B.C. Task Force on Child Care to review its existing child care policies. The 1991 report outlined a number of recommendations in five key areas. These included recommendations to better coordinate government delivery of child care services, improve the level and types of child care funding, increase child care staff salaries, widen the array of ECE training programs, and, finally, simplify the licensing process.[18] Many of the task force recommendations reflected an understanding of the child care movement that was unparalleled by any previous B.C. government, especially a Social Credit one, as historically that party had done much damage. Whether or not the Vander Zalm Socreds would have responded positively to these recommendations remains a mystery, however, as they were defeated in 1991 after Vander Zalm resigned over conflict of interest charges.

The Mike Harcourt NDP government that replaced the Socreds responded very sympathetically to the task force recommendations and enacted many positive child care initiatives. After establishing the country's first free-standing ministry for women, the Ministry of Women's Equality (MWE) and in 1993 devoting over 80 percent of the well-funded ministry's budget to child care, the government released a barrage of pro-child care policies. Over the next three and a half years, the NDP increased child care spending fourfold from $41 million to over $200 million.[19]

Some of this spending went to government grant and subsidy programs, with a number of new grants being created. The 1992 B.C. 21 Child Care Expansion Initiative provided $32.3 million to support the expansion of community-based child care programs in schools, health centres, hospitals, government office buildings and post-secondary institutions.[20] The 1994/95 Wage Supplement Initiative addressed advocates' call to increase the meagre wages of child care workers in the province.[21] The government delivery of child care services was also streamlined, with the MWE becoming the lead coordinating ministry working with the ministries of Health and Education. Communication between government and child care actors and advocates further increased with the establishment of the Provincial Child Care Council in 1993. These last two improvements also addressed the main recommendations of the 1991 task force report.

After NDP premier Mike Harcourt left office in 1996, following another political scandal, Glen Clark captured another victory for the NDP. Many of the programs introduced by Harcourt were continued by Clark's government. Plus, in 1996, the Clark NDP added $13.7 million to the child care budget under the 1996 *B.C. Benefits (Child Care) Act.* This new subsidy legislation removed the "welfare" label from child care—something the child care lobby had fought for since the 1950s. However, even though many child care funding arrangements continued under Clark, the pace of child care expansion certainly slowed. After the auditor general released its review of the MWE child care programs, *Management of Child Care Grants*, responsibility for the programs was moved from the MWE to the newly created Ministry for Children and Families in 1996/97. Child care was not as prominent a focus in the new ministry, which concentrated more on issues of child welfare and child protection. In 1999, the responsibility for child care was moved again, this time to the newly created Ministry of Social Development and Economic Security.

After Glen Clark became the third B.C. premier in a row to succumb to scandal and resign, the NDP promoted Ujjal Dosanjh to lead the party and the government. With Dosanjh's NDP at a low point in the polls, the government announced the most progressive child care policy in the history of British Columbia. In June 2000, the B.C. NDP introduced a publicly-funded, after-school program for children from grade one to the age of twelve. This seven-dollar-a-day program was only the second publicly funded child care program to be launched in North America and was praised by provincial advocates.[22]

The comparison of the demands of child care advocates in B.C. with the policy enacted by different governing parties supports the thesis that left-wing governments do more for child care advocates than right-wing governments. The only real exception to this rule is the advocate-friendly child care policies of the right-wing Vander Zalm government during the latter half of his term. However, the fact that Vander Zalm was appealing to the province's disaffected women voters largely explains this shift.[23] It is hard to say definitively if the shift went beyond a simple willingness to buy votes for the next election, as Vander Zalm and the Socreds were not re-elected.

Key policy initiatives achieved by advocates during the Harcourt NDP reign—huge increases in funding to improve service delivery, streamlining of the governmental process and growing communication with advocates—further support the above thesis. Even Glen Clark's government was able to introduce favourable legislation while dealing with huge budget deficits and cuts to federal funding under CAP.[24] Indeed, the fact that the NDP resisted cutting more from the child care expansion agenda of the previous Harcourt regime indicates a willingness to protect the child care lobby's hard-fought gains. The announcement of the publicly funded child care program under the Dosanjh NDP during a continually tough economic climate goes even further to illustrate the close ideological fit between the left-wing NDP and B.C. child care advocates.

Child Care Advocacy in Ontario

Just as in B.C., in Ontario, child care advocates have traditionally lobbied governments for universally affordable, available, accessible and responsive high-quality child care. However, the Ontario groups differ from their B.C. counterparts in two ways. First, child care advocates must lobby three levels of government—federal, provincial and municipal—due to the formal involvement of Ontario municipalities in service delivery and funding; such municipal involvement does not exist in B.C.[25] Second, the existence of a large number of commercial centres tied to a strong commercial lobby has forced Ontario advocates, in order to protect child care quality, to lobby against government support of for-profit care.

As is the case for British Columbia, child care advocacy in Ontario can be traced back to WWII.[26] Similarly, advocacy continued to expand during the 1960s and 1970s due to the growing number of mothers entering the workforce. As in B.C., many of these early advocacy groups were feminist and radical in orientation. These included groups like the Day Care Organizing Committee (DCOC), established in 1972 to expand "parent-controlled" child care services.[27] In 1974, the DCOC helped form the Group for Day Care Reform, a network of groups advocating non-profit child care.

Also in 1974, the governing Tories released the *Birch White Paper*. This was the first public statement about daycare to come from the province. But, the report's rejection of free, universal daycare and support for the commercial sector angered many child care advocates and resulted in the formation of the Day Care Reform Action Alliance. A loosely based coalition of child care advocates including feminists, parents and daycare workers, the alliance lobbied successfully to stop a good majority of the report's proposals.[28] The alliance's demonstrations, pickets and actions in the legislature united the daycare community and helped "clarify common principles and concerns" among activists:

> Many of the views that have characterized child care advocacy in Ontario over the last two decades—the insistence on quality child care, the demands for better, more extensive public funding, and the concern that making profits on child care was a disincentive to quality—had their beginnings in the advocacy efforts of this period.[29]

In 1980, a new daycare advocacy organization, Action Day Care, came on the scene. It was one of the first groups to advocate the creation of a comprehensive child care system under the "neighbourhood hub model" and supported free, universal, high-quality, accessible, non-profit daycare, as well as the unionization of daycare workers.[30] Unlike most other advocacy groups, Action Day Care was not nonpartisan since its director campaigned for, and participated in, Ontario NDP conventions.[31] In 1981, Action Day Care members, along with members from other provincial child care and labour organizations, founded the Ontario Coalition for Better Day Care. The coalition's establishment followed a series of public forums on daycare in eight Ontario communities. In 1986, the coalition changed its name to the Ontario Coalition for Better Child Care (OCBCC) and widened its network to broadly represent groups across the whole province.[32] The coalition has remained the main provincial child care advocacy group throughout the 1990s, advocating for universal, non-profit child care as well as improved wages and working conditions for child care workers.

Child Care Policy and Party Government in Ontario

While in 1942 B.C. was the first province to introduce licensing legislation in Canada, Ontario has the distinction of being the first province in the country to introduce child care legislation. The 1946 *Day Nurseries Act* was implemented after intense lobbying from groups such as the Toronto Day Nursery and Day Care Parents' Association. Unlike B.C., Ontario and Quebec qualified for federal money to run wartime daycares, but when the war ended, so did the federal, and hence the provincial, assistance. The *Day Nurseries Act* re-established provincial funding on a 50-50 cost-shared basis with provincial municipalities.

The 1966 federal Canada Assistance Plan made funds available to assist working-poor mothers who used daycare, and just as in B.C., CAP funding painted daycare provision as a welfare service. The Ontario government assumed 30 percent of the cost of daycare, with the federal government paying 50 percent and municipalities picking up the remaining 20 percent. The Ministry of Community and Social Services was created in 1972 and child care came under its jurisdiction. Gradual expansion of child care services occurred in the 1970s along with a corresponding increase in demand for spaces and availability of CAP funding.[33] However, government expansion in the field did not keep up with demand.

The Bill Davis Progressive Conservatives released the 1974 *Birch White Paper*, which was hotly criticized by advocates. Even though lobbying stopped many of the specific proposals in the White Paper, much of the ideology behind that paper remained. Davis's successor, Frank Miller—on the advice of election advisors, in an effort to appeal to female voters—tried to address some of the concerns of child care advocates in the 1985 pre-election package, Enterprise Ontario.[34]

When Miller lost power shortly after the 1985 election, the succeeding Liberal-NDP Accord government went beyond Enterprise Ontario, further increasing child care funding.[35] The David Peterson Liberals went on to win a majority government in 1987. They continued to pursue a pro-advocacy child care agenda, no doubt influenced by the popularity of past NDP policies. Particularly, in 1987, the Liberals released *New Directions for Child Care,* which promised to move child care "from a welfare connotation toward one of public service."[36] It also included a promised $325 million (gross: federal, provincial and municipal shares) increase in funding over the next three years. Although this promised funding was scaled back with the announcement of federal limits to CAP payments in 1990, *New Directions for Child Care* represented an important move addressing the concerns of provincial child care advocates.

The Liberals lost the 1990 election, giving rise to the first NDP government in Ontario's history. Bob Rae's NDP made a strong commitment to child care in its election platform, which the party only partly addressed upon taking office. Particularly, the NDP promised to revive the issue of moving child care into the Ministry of Education and hence out of the welfare shadow of the Ministry of Community and Social Services; in the end, this promise was left unfulfilled.[37] Conversely, despite the beginning of federal spending cuts and a recession that hit Ontario harder than any other province, the NDP increased funding for child care under the Jobs Ontario program.[38] Along with this, the Rae NDP announced a $105 million conversion program that provided financial incentives for commercial centres to convert to non-profit status. As part of this program, in 1991 the Wage Enhancement Grant was introduced to increase salaries of child care workers in not-for-profit centres. Both of these policy initiatives reflected an ideological symbiosis with the child care movement, as both favoured non-profit over for-profit care. Although increases in child care subsidies were not as high as child care advocates had hoped for, groups initially reacted positively to the NDP's actions, blaming any timidity in the government's spending agenda on cutbacks to federal transfer payments.[39] However, the OCBCC was later critical of the NDP's failure to fund a promised free, universal child care program, which would have been the most progressive child care policy in Canada to date.[40]

Rae lost the 1995 election to the Mike Harris Tories and his Common Sense Revolution (CSR). As was mentioned above, the CSR election platform promised a revamped child care system, along with reduced government spending and a balanced budget by 2000. In short, these promises did not spell good news for the child care lobby. During their first year in power, the Harris Tories systematically cancelled much of the legislation introduced by the NDP, including the conversion program, Jobs Ontario, funding that supported the inclusion of child care into new school sites and policy that limited new funding exclusively to non-profit child care centres. The sheer magnitude of the 1995 cuts prompted OCBCC director Kerry McCuaig to describe the actions as, "an all-out attack on the quality of daycare in Ontario."[41] In 1996, the Tories outlined their approach to child care in the Ecker policy review. As was mentioned, even though this report was largely unimplemented, the ideology behind it continued to be embraced.[42] The 1997 Ontario Child Care Tax Credit allowed some families to claim child care expenses and the 1998 Workplace Child Care Tax Deduction encouraged companies to provide on-site child care in exchange for tax breaks. Both of these policies were criticized by advocates for being restrictive, inadequate and unfair to many families.[43] Also in 1998, the province amended the *Day Nurseries Act* to download more responsibility for service delivery to municipalities. Advocates had argued against downloading, as it produced disparate service delivery across the province and was contrary to movement calls for universality.[44] After the 1999 release of the Fraser Mustard *Report of the Early Years Study*, the Tories "embraced an integrated approach" to early childhood development under the newly formed Integrated Children's Services Division.[45] However, enacting new child care programs or improving child care service delivery was not a concerted part of this integrated approach.

In the end, it seems clear that as in the case of B.C., so too in Ontario, left-wing governments (or left-influenced governments such as the 1985 Liberal-NDP Accord) enact pro-child care policy more willingly than right-wing governments—the only practical exception to this rule occurring in 1985 during the lead up to another provincial election, when the right-wing Tories under Frank Miller reached out to women's movements and the child care lobby. Similarly, as was the case with the B.C. Vander Zalm Socreds, it is impossible to know if the Miller Tories' commitment went beyond a simple pre-election appeal for votes, because Miller was forced from office shortly following that election. As well, the stark contrast in gains made during both the Liberal-NDP Accord (and subsequent Liberal majority government) along with the NDP government in the early 1990s, versus the huge losses later suffered under the Harris Tories, clearly shows that party does indeed matter to the child care lobby in Ontario. In retrospect, advocacy criticism that the NDP government did not go far enough during its stay at Queen's Park appears hollow in light of all that the NDP was willing to protect in an era of fiscal restructuring and federal downloading. NDP initiatives seem much more clear in contrast with the willingness of the subsequent Tory government to sacrifice many of these gains on the altar of fiscal conservatism.

Conclusion

In the twenty-first century, it seems more and more likely that B.C.'s and Ontario's responsibilities for the delivery of child care services will continue to grow. The federal government has failed to enact a national child care program, and despite its September 2000 announcement of $2.2 billion over the next five years for early childhood development, the future of a national program hardly looks promising.[46] Because of this, child care advocates need to focus more of their lobbying efforts on the subnational level of government. As well, the evidence presented in this chapter strongly suggests that those lobbying efforts take party into account as a strong indicator of government's receptivity to child care advocates. Some provincial advocates have supported provincial New Democratic parties because the ideological fit between the two groups is quite strong. However, discernible differences in vision and ideology do exist and advocates would do well to reckon with these. Whether party support is the best tactic may be examined in light of the evidence presented above.

In conclusion, the question of why policy has differed so much over the years in B.C. and Ontario may largely be explained by the fact that left- and right-wing governments, with their opposing predispositions toward child care lobbyists' demands, have both held power in each province. Party ideas clearly do matter to provincial child care activists and affect provincial child care policy. However, a strong women's movement seems capable of swaying in its favour the pre-election strategies of right-wing governments. Whether or not such effects would last past an election is yet another question.

Notes

1. I wish to thank Elizabeth Moore for commenting on an earlier draft of this chapter.
2. Child Care Resource and Research Unit 2000a: 45.
3. Quoted in Schmidt 1996: 155. For more on this see Castles 1982; Hicks and Swank 1992; Klingemann et al. 1996.
4. Others question the amount of autonomy governments actually have to make policy decisions and have argued that these constraints will equally be able to explain the variance in public policy decisions. These include Blais et al. 1993 and Rose and Davies 1994.
5. For more, see Katzenstein and Mueller 1987 and Bashevkin 1998.
6. Doherty, Friendly and Oloman 1998: 17.
7. Jenson and Thompson 1999: 2.
8. Other variables can include: strength of the women's movement, economic health of a province, political culture, policy inheritance and policy diffusion. It is beyond the scope of this study to test these variables in any depth.
9. Personal interviews 1999 and 2000.
10. The Canada Assistance Plan provided federal cost-sharing on a 50/50 basis with the provinces for social programs, including child care.
11. Griffin et al. 1991: 27.
12. For more on this group see Cohen, Duggan, Sayre, Todd and Wright 1973.
13. Griffin et al. 1991: 30–31.
14. Personal interview 2000.
15. CCCABC 1999a: 2.

16. Personal interviews 1999.
17. Griffin et al. 1991:95.
18. B.C. Task Force on Child Care Summary Report 1991.
19. Personal interview 1999.
20. MWE 1995.
21. More than 4,435 child care workers had salary increases of approximately $2 per hour by 1996/97. See MWE 1998.
22. The first was a five-dollar-a-day program introduced in Quebec in the 1990s; Mickleburgh 2000.
23. Vander Zalm's personal attitude toward women and high profile anti-abortion views alienated women voters.
24. In 1989, the federal government capped increases in CAP payments to the three "have" provinces (B.C., Alberta and Ontario) at 5 percent and later froze increases altogether. In 1996 the federal government replaced CAP, along with other transfer payments, with the Canada Health and Social Transfer. The CHST represented a substantial decrease in block funding for health, post-secondary education and social services.
25. For more on this see Doherty, Friendly and Oloman 1998 and Child Care Resource and Research Unit 2000.
26. The Toronto Day Nursery and Day Care Parents' Association was formed in 1946 to protest the closing of war-time day nurseries after federal funding for the programs was halted at the end of WWII.
27. Women's Movement Archives, University of Ottawa, Day Care Organizing Committee, Toronto file 1972, Box 27.
28. Women's Movement Archives, University of Ottawa, Day Care Reform Action Alliance file, Box 27.
29. Kyle et al. 1991: 374.
30. This was a community-based daycare system designed to meet the specific needs of the local community. See Kyle et al. 1991: 377.
31. Women's Movement Archives, University of Ottawa, Action Day Care Toronto file 1979–1983, Box 1.
32. Women's Movement Archives, University of Ottawa, Ontario Coalition for Better Child Care file, Box 87.
33. The 1966 Canada Assistance Plan "was not really operational until 1970" as legislative regulations were being finalized. See Doherty, Friendly, and Oloman 1998: 8.
34. *Enterprise Ontario* included a proposed $30 million to provide for 7,500 new child care spaces over 2 years along with $22 million for six Child Care Initiatives aimed at helping mothers obtain job training. For more, see Speirs 1986.
35. The minority Miller government was forced to resign in 1985 after it lost the confidence of the legislature and instead of holding another election, the Liberals entered into an accord arrangement with the NDP in order to obtain power.

36. Quoted in Kyle et al. 1991: 382.
37. Child Care Resource and Research Unit 2000.
38. 8,200 new spaces were created under the program.
39. Women's Movement Archives, University of Ottawa, Ontario Coalition for Better Child Care file, Box 87.
40. Personal interview 2000. Also see Rankin 1997: 171, note 65.
41. Quoted in Lightman and Baines 1996: 149.
42. See Child Care Resource and Research Unit 2000.
43. Ontario Coalition for Better Child Care, "Presentation to the Standing Committee on Finance." November 9, 1999, Toronto: OCBCC. (Available at http://www.web.net/~ocbcc/fbud200/budbrf.htm.)
44. Doherty, Friendly and Oloman 1998.
45. Personal interview 2000.
46. The federal Progressive Conservatives introduced Bill C-144, *A National Child Care Act* in 1988 but the Act died on the order paper just before the 1988 election and was never revived. The 1993 federal Liberal Party *Red Book* platform promised to enact a replacement national child care act but to date has not done so. Linda White discusses Bill C-144 in her chapter in this anthology.

Chapter 7

Advocacy Ignored
Child Care Policy in Ontario in the 1990s[1]

Vappu Tyyskä

Introduction

For three decades now, beginning with the recommendations of the *Report of the Royal Commission on the Status of Women*, there has been pressure from advocates to create a comprehensive, national daycare system in Canada. The 1980s witnessed a particularly active child care advocacy movement across the nation that effectively catalyzed the federal Liberal and Conservative governments to initiate child daycare policy processes.[2] After three decades of advocating a publicly funded child care system, there has been an increase in public awareness but no real relief for the vast majority (approximately 90 percent) of Canadian families who require publicly funded child care while parent(s) engage in waged work or studies.[3] In July of 1999, yet another set of reports by Canadian think-tanks and federal government bodies affirmed the need for "a new system of care for children," but deemed that "it seems unlikely that a universal day-care system [will] be part of the picture."[4]

This chapter will examine how the development of Canada's child care system was stalled. In my discussion, I take into consideration the following elements that contributed to the development of child care policy in the 1990s: (1) the division of power between the federal, provincial and municipal governments; (2) the role of child care advocacy associations and their strategies for engaging with governments (insider versus outsider, and conflict versus consensus models); and (3) the neo-conservative and neo-liberal political climate of the 1990s.

To begin with, the complexities of the Canadian federalist structure (i.e., the division of power between the federal, provincial and municipal levels) affect the uneven development of the social-service sector generally and the child care sector particularly. Therefore, I will first give a brief

overview of federal child care policy developments. I will then outline
the trends in child care policy in the province of Ontario. Further details
are provided about the municipal level, in relation to child care policy and
advocacy in two municipalities in Ontario: the city of Toronto and the
regional municipality of Peel.[5]

Second, one part of the landscape of policy development is social
movements and organizations that press for changes. In Canada, the input
of social movements, including advocacy associations, on policy development is seriously limited. Advanced by the women's movement, child care
is historically considered one of a range of "women's issues"—a designation which immediately reduces it in the order of priorities. Thus, given
women's poor representation in official politics,[6] child care advocates are
left "outsiders" in relation to the state and government. Nor do their
alliances with other relatively weak outsider organizations, such as
women's organizations or labour unions, enhance their position.[7]

Views on child care are also subject to partisan political and ideological
divisions. Advocates for universal, publicly funded, not-for-profit child
care clash with those who promote child care as a for-profit activity.
Representatives of the former view have supporters among the Liberals
and the New Democratic Party (NDP), while the latter have Conservative
allies. Overall, advocates of public, not-for-profit child care are traditionally in a weak position due to the relative or total absence of their strongest
electoral ally, the NDP, from provincial and federal politics.[8]

Meanwhile, child care advocates adopt different strategies to achieve
their goals. Some of this difference is exemplified in the opposing
"conflict" and "consensus" models. In the conflict model, advocacy is of
a more assertive variety, involving extensive lobbys, demonstrations and
confrontational tactics. This conflict model is typical of advocacy in
Ontario in general, and in Toronto in particular, where the main
organizations are the Ontario Coalition for Better Child Care (OCBCC)
and the Metro Toronto Coalition for Better Child Care. These groups'
conflict orientation to advocacy is evident, first, in their traditional
lobbying tactics and alliances with organized labour and the political
left.[9] Second, their insistence on publicly funded, not-for-profit child
care is on palpable conflict with organizations such as the Association of
Day Care Operators of Ontario (ADCO), an agency of for-profit daycare
operators, favoured by the Mike Harris Conservative government.

In contrast to the conflict model, the consensus model of child care
advocacy promotes an approach based on negotiation, accommodation
and compromises between stakeholders, with less emphasis on lobbying

or demonstrations. This is exemplified by the Region of Peel Child Care Committee, a loose coalition of citizens, advocates and service organizations founded in 1993 to provide consultation to the local office of the Ministry of Community and Social Services.

The third element in my discussion argues that the political climate of the 1990s at the federal and provincial levels has made advocacy increasingly difficult. Advocacy strategies seem to make little difference for outcomes. Advocates for accessible, not-for-profit child care are struggling to hold onto existing levels of service and funding amidst a climate of cutbacks on the one hand and rising demand for child care on the other. Consequently, there has been a taming of the not-for-profit advocates in Ontario. They are labeled "special interest groups," while the Ontario government, buoyed by the legacy of federal neo-conservatism and neo-liberalism, turns its ear toward for-profit organizations that support cutting back and privatizing services.

Federal Neo-Conservatism and Neo-Liberalism

From the mid-1980s onward, a vocabulary of "reducing welfare dependency" entered into Canadian public policy debates, reflecting a general neo-conservative and neo-liberal shift in the federal government's approach to social policy and family policy.[10] In line with this ideology, in 1990 the federal Conservative government abandoned its Canada Assistance Plan involvement (the open-ended social services cost-sharing agreement, also known as CAP) with the three "have" provinces— Ontario, British Columbia and Alberta[11]—by capping shared costs, including those for child care. Soon thereafter, it formally abandoned its promised national child care plan.[12]

When the Liberals won the 1993 federal election, they began their term by breaking promises to improve the child care system.[13] Intent on reducing federal government expenditures, they initiated a Social Security Review in 1994, which ushered in the Canada Health and Social Transfer (CHST). Taking effect on April 1, 1996, this program rolled together into a single block fund social services cost-sharing programs under the CAP and health and post-secondary education funding initiatives under the Established Programs Financing (EPF).

Due to its generally reduced level of funding compared with the CAP, the CHST caused a lot of concern among advocates for universal child care.[14] Under the CHST, child care was not guaranteed any share of funds by the provinces and territories, which were responsible for distributing the dollars to a wide variety of social transfer areas, including health.[15]

In response to this new insecurity, negotiations for a new cost-sharing plan with the provinces began in 1995. The talks were abandoned the following year.[16]

Interestingly, recent examinations of annual provincial allocations for regulated child care show that funding levels were either maintained or increased slightly between 1996 and 1998 in seven of the ten provinces. Manitoba, Alberta and Ontario were the only provinces where funding was cut back. In Ontario, funding decreased from close to $520 million in 1996 to approximately $432 million in 1998.[17]

Thus, the feared funding cuts in child care have not materialized. However, the CHST reduces the federal role in areas of exclusive provincial jurisdiction.[18] This opens the door to a gradual erosion of child care service, as future funding levels are projected to fall far short of increased demand for service. Most significantly, the watering down of federal responsibility makes the struggle for publicly funded, not-for-profit child care extremely difficult in provinces with governments that actively promote a political agenda based on "family values" and self-reliance. This is evident in Ontario.[19]

Child Care in the Province of Ontario

Ontario's publicly funded, licensed child care system provides spaces for approximately 10 percent of children in need of care, a fraction equal to the national average.[20] Fee subsidies are given for children in financial need. Since 1989, additional child care funds in the form of a net-earning deduction have been provided under the Support to Employment Program (STEP) to welfare recipients and the working poor.[21] Significant changes to child care took place in the 1990s, as two totally different governments, the New Democrats (1990–1995) and the Progressive Conservatives (1995–present), each tried their hand at running the province.

The NDP Era (1990–1995): Where Are the Spaces?

The Ontario government, that had a short term in power under Premier Bob Rae, has been a traditional ally of the Ontario Coalition for Better Child Care and has maintained a long-term commitment to publicly funded, non-profit child care. Elected in 1990, the NDP began its term in office by including child care workers under the *Pay Equity Act*. The pay equity increase (approximately $2,000), added to the wage enhancement grant for staff in Ontario's not-for-profit child care facilities,[22] resulted in the field's second-highest staff salaries in all of Canada.[23]

After initially adding 5,000 subsidized child care spaces,[24] the NDP government announced in 1992 its major plan to convert for-profit child care spaces into not-for-profit spaces.[25] While continuing funding under the STEP program,[26] the NDP government also introduced a Jobs Ontario Training Fund, subsidizing 100 percent of the fees for 14,000 participants in training programs, students in secondary and post-secondary education, and social assistance recipients who entered the paid labour force. The NDP government also required school boards to provide junior kindergarten programs, as part of a comprehensive plan providing care and early childhood education to preschool age children.[27] Consequently, by 1995, Ontario's child care expenditures were 80 percent higher than in 1989,[28] with the per capita child care expenditures ranked third highest among the provinces and territories.[29]

In the end, however, the NDP government measures did not add new daycare spaces. While there was a gradual but minimal reduction in the number of for-profit child care centres and agencies in 1993–1994, growth in the not-for-profit child care sector was minimal.[30]

Caught in the middle of a rising global neo-conservative tide, the Bob Rae government embarked on a series of unpopular cost-cutting measures, curtailing government expenditure. Having irked traditional NDP allies and having eroded electoral support, the government was headed for a massive election loss.

The Tories, 1995 and Beyond: Cut Costs!
On June 8, 1995, the NDP was replaced in a landslide victory by the Conservative party, headed by Mike Harris. This initiated a series of rapid general budget cuts to social service agencies, school boards and post-secondary institutions. These measures were put in place so quickly that no social organization, child care advocates included, had time to do anything but "cry foul" after the deed was done.

In the child care sector, the Conservatives canceled the planned conversion of for-profit child care spaces into not-for-profit spaces and permitted municipalities to subsidize spaces within for-profit centres. Conservatives also tried to reverse the previous government's inclusion of child care workers under the *Pay Equity Act*.[31] Other clawbacks included the elimination of capital funding to not-for-profit child care centres and cuts to special needs integration programs.[32]

Further, in 1995, there were reductions in the Jobs Ontario child care subsidies and the STEP program; the costing formula for both was changed from 100 percent provincial contribution to a new 80 percent/20 percent provincial/municipal cost-sharing formula. This new formula resulted in a $65 million reduction in available child care funds in the province.[33] The OCBCC fought back, presenting well-founded but ineffective arguments that the reduction of Jobs Ontario child care spaces had particularly ill effects on the most vulnerable segments of the population, including children at risk from poverty.[34]

In its economic statement of July 21, 1995, the government canceled financial support to child care centres in schools and put a stop to new child care centres planned for schools. This seriously reduced child care spaces, since at the time, 40 percent of licensed child care spaces were located in schools.[35] Junior kindergarten programs, attended by 85 percent of the province's 4-year-old children, suffered a 9 percent funding cut.[36] By early 1998 these programs were canceled in twenty-two Ontario school boards, disrupting the care of approximately 60,000 children.[37]

Advocacy Contained and Redefined

Amidst Harris government support for unregulated child care and the cancellation of junior kindergarten programs, in the fall of 1995 the OCBCC and the Ontario NDP (ONDP) called for public hearings.[38] These efforts were ineffective, as were the OCBCC and ONDP hearings held in 1995 and 1996, respectively,[39] and the OCBCC campaign promoting the 1995 child care cost-sharing negotiations, discussed above.[40]

These developments reflect the Conservative preference to marginalize large advocacy associations, relegating them to the status of just one of many "special interest groups." While the minister of Social Services, Janet Ecker, dismissed the OCBCC as "one of the groups" concerned with child care,[41] there was a concurrent increase in the advocacy influence of the Association of Day Care Operators of Ontario (ADCO), the lobby of for-profit daycare operators.

The Conservative government's partiality to the ADCO, rather than the wider child care lobby, is evident in the named parties' agreement on general policy principles; the ADCO publicly supported the Conservative party's child care platform prior to the election.[42] The for-profit child care lobby's own agenda supports eliminating the wage subsidy grant and pay equity; lowering the amount paid for child care subsidies and restricting subsidies to the "most needy"; decreasing the staff-to-child ratio; decreasing *Day Nurseries Act* requirements for space, toilets and sinks per child; and reducing licensing enforcement and the frequency of fire and health inspections.[43] At the core of the ADCO recommendations is the notion of "parental choice" for child care. In the name of choice, they argue, any licensed care situation should be eligible for accepting fee-assisted children.[44] As will yet be seen, all of the above elements were incorporated in the Conservative government's child care review.

The Ecker Report: Child Care Workers Under Fire
Janet Ecker, Minister of Community and Social Services, was targeted for demonstrations by not-for-profit child care advocates after her child care review report, *Improving Ontario's Child Care System,* was unveiled in August of 1996.[45] The report proposed that Ontario's child care should include "as many different kinds of quality care as possible." In line with the ADCO proposals, the report recommended reduced access to government-regulated and funded child care; an upward adjustment in the child-to-staff ratio for preschool children; a broader range of qualifications for staff (e.g., a recreation certificate); and the use of volunteers. Home care providers would be allowed two more children for after-school care spaces. And, for-profit child care operators would be given a program stabilization grant on par with not-for-profit providers.[46]

Most significantly, the Ecker report recommended that some of the provincial funding invested in wage subsidies for child care workers should be redirected into new fee subsidies to assist low-income families.[47] This measure resulted in wage reductions of up to 25 percent for approximately 83 percent of Ontario's child care workers. It was estimated by the OCBCC that the Tory plan would cut the wage subsidy (estimated at $4,000–$4,500)[48] of about 14,000 child care workers in the not-for-profit sector. Even including provincial wage subsidies, Ontario child care workers receive an extremely low average wage of approximately $19,000 per year.[49]

In exchange for this wage cut, the minister promised 12,800 new subsidized spaces.[50] This promise was described as a "cruel hoax" by the OCBCC, as by December 1996, approximately 9,000 spaces were cut by municipalities, due to reduced provincial funding.[51] Additionally, the elimination of the wage subsidy was projected to amount to an increase in parent fees, to offset the clawback's impact.[52] Thus, the cost of child care was transferred from the provincial government onto child care providers and parents.

Downloading of Social Services
A further blow to child care came from the general downloading of welfare, daycare, social housing and health care services from the province to the municipalities, as of January 1, 1998.[53] The downloading of child

care resulted in a fourfold increase in the municipal funding commitment.

Up to this point, the participation of municipalities in child care provision had been discretionary, and they could opt out of it completely Notably, the Conservative government's downloading of social services was accompanied with an obligation on each municipality to bankroll child care within its boundaries, making it near impossible for municipalities to make ends meet. In January 1997, it was also revealed that in order to retain their user fees, municipalities would be required to maintain their user levels. However, municipalities could now opt to subsidize informal care, with its lack of wage grants, smaller overhead and all round lower cost. The OCBCC described this as "the birth of the voucher system and the collapse of regulated child care."[54]

In Ontario, the arrangement since World War II was to cost-share social services, including child care, based on a 80 percent provincial/20 percent municipal cost-sharing formula. This was now radically redesigned by the Tories into a 50/50 arrangement in the areas of wage grants, resource centre supports, special needs provisions, and minor capital (program) commitments. Major capital expenditures were eliminated, and the previously provincial responsibility for licensing, under the *Day Nurseries Act* (1946), was slated to be transferred onto municipalities,[55] that would also carry the total cost.[56] This move was met with objections from all the main child care associations, including OCBCC, ADCO, and the Association of Early Childhood Educators of Ontario.[57] To date this measure has not been carried.

From a Child Development Model to a Needy Family Model

In May 1997, Finance Minister Ernie Eves announced a new tax credit to approximately 90,000 families and 125,000 children, amounting to $40 million. These funds would subsidize the child care expenses of the working poor and full-time adult students with children under seven years of age. Kerry McQuaig of the OCBCC responded that this measure would not help in any way the thousands of children, 18,500 in Metro Toronto alone, still waiting for a child care space.[58] Nevertheless, this program was expanded and formalized in the 1998 budget as the Ontario Child Care Supplement (OCCS).[59]

The OCBCC charges that the Ontario Child Care Supplement relies on "money taken from the poorest children—children on welfare"[60]— in that it makes them dependent on their parents' employment status for receipt of money.[61] In reality, the program is an income supplement to families where at least one parent is employed. However, based on a federal-provincial agreement, the provinces are allowed to clawback an amount equivalent to that expended on the OCCS from people on social assistance and use it, presumably, on children's programs. In Ontario, as well as in most other provinces, the clawback monies are redirected to the working poor, through the child care supplement. Hence, it is not really a child care expenditure.[62]

Launched in 1999, another initiative aimed at "families in need" required that young parents enrol in school in order to receive social assistance. This is extremely difficult because of the scarcity of child care spaces, and, in turn, it provides further stress to young mothers.[63] Prior austere measures include a policy from 1997, whereby child care bursaries were made no longer available to sole-support parents attending post-secondary institutions, unless they had three or more children. These expenses will now be temporarily covered by the Ontario Student Assistance Plan loans.[64] Together, these two measures amount to a blatant assault on and stigmatization of sole-support parents, most of whom are women.

As of January 1998, a workfare program was put in place. Called Ontario Works, Bill 142 requires able-bodied persons who receive social assistance to work, take training or engage in community placement tasks.[65] There is now a 80/20 (provincial/municipal) cost-sharing of child care for participants, whether it be in informal or regulated care, where previously only costs of regulated care were covered.[66]

These conservative measures conceptualize "child care not as early childhood education or child development, but solely as an employment support for low income families."[67] This departs from the past tendency in Ontario to also develop child care as a means toward child development and education.[68]

The provincial government's cost-cutting measures resulted in longer waiting lists and reduced budgets for licensed child care in Ontario. As of June 1996, 30,000 eligible families were waiting for access to child care services.[69] It was estimated that in March 1999 there had already been a 40 percent reduction in direct funding for licensed child care since the Conservative government took office.[70] This was counted in thousands of spaces lost due to elimination of Jobs Ontario funding alone, even as some municipalities opted to carry the costs.[71] It was also estimated in 1997 that 9,500 child care spaces and 26,000 junior kindergarten spaces were lost in Ontario since 1995.[72]

In summary, the 1990s in Ontario have seen a stalling of the publicly regulated and funded child care system. Whereas the NDP era did not live up to the rhetoric, the Tory government era has seen a marked deterioration in the quality and quantity of child care services in Ontario. There has been a gradual transfer of the increased costs of child care to parents and child care providers. The voices of advocates are rarely heard, and the municipalities are left to cope with the fallout from the draconian top-down measures.

Municipal Child Care Problems: Toronto

Toronto is the largest city in Canada, and it experienced further growth in the 1990s, particularly among the youngest age groups. In 1997, there were approximately 37,000 children in formal child care programs, 35,000 of whom are in licensed group centres. In 1996, the municipality subsidized the cost of care for 22,916 children. There are 265 child care programs in schools, of which 245 offer school-age programs. An additional 126 school-age programs are located outside of schools.[73] Nevertheless, there are over 10,000 children on the waiting list for subsidized child care in centres—many of them may have to wait over a year for spaces. An additional 759 children under the age of four are waiting for home child care, while 1,584 wait for nursery school spaces.[74]

The Municipality of Metropolitan Toronto is the largest and the longest running municipal child care delivery system in Canada. Historically, the city of Toronto has had a unique role in the area of daycare and has taken initiative in promoting national child care standards. This has been a direct reflection of long-term advocacy for not-for-profit child care in Toronto.[75]

The NDP Era in Toronto: Fighting for Fair Cost Sharing

Toronto has traditionally exceeded its required municipal contribution in times of provincial funding shortfalls. From the 1980s onward, the municipal burden of cost sharing increased to 30 percent, representing a 10 percent increase over the traditional 20/30/50 (municipal/provincial/federal) formula.[76] In 1988, supported by not-for-profit child care advocates, the city began to refuse requests to create additional subsidized spaces and began a fight for a return to the traditional cost-sharing pattern.[77] This fight intensified with the election of the new NDP government, a traditional ally of the not-for-profit child care lobby. A review cosponsored by the two levels of government found a serious funding shortfall, which was not covered by the provincial NDP government.[78] The municipal government persevered and returned to its 20 percent cost-sharing responsibility by 1993. However, the resultant funding shortfall was manifested in a decline in the quantity and quality of services, an increase of parent fees from 6 or 7 percent of total cost to approximately 12 percent of costs[79] and a skyrocketing of subsidy waiting lists.[80]

Amidst this serious crisis in child care, the Metro Council entered into consultations with the NDP government and the child care community in January 1993.[81] This process was interrupted as there was a change from the NDP to the Conservative government.

Reactions to the Harris Government's Measures

The first sign of things to come was the shelving of municipal efforts to develop a strategy for school-age child care within Metro Toronto.[82] The cuts that followed spelled serious consequences for the municipalities' ability to maintain service levels.

Cost analyses of the Conservative government's downloading of services from the province to the municipalities project millions of dollars of increase in the municipal funding load.[83] In the area of child care, spaces will be lost in the long run.[84] The only way to fund child care services is by lowering standards and wages and by opting for unregulated child care.[85] The 1997 annual report of the United Way[86] notes the need for 77,000 licensed spaces, 48,500 of which should be subsidized.[87] The report expresses concern over the Ontario government's plans to privatize child care and reduce child care quality:

> There is concern that a two-tier system of child care will evolve. As the public system loses funding and minimum standards are reduced, middle-income parents are likely to leave and pay privately for high quality care. This will result in further erosion of the public system, leaving lower-income working families with substandard or unaffordable child care and creating a downward cycle of erosion.[88]

Municipal Problems: Peel

The Region of Peel is composed of three municipalities: City of Brampton, Town of Caledon and City of Mississauga. In 1994, the majority of the population, about 64 percent, lived in Mississauga, while 31 percent lived in Brampton and 5 percent lived in Caledon. About 30 percent of Peel residents are young people, nineteen years of age or younger. Together, these three communities form the second-fastest-growing municipality in Ontario;[89] the region's population grew from 260,000 to over 850,000 from the mid-1970s to the mid-1990s.[90]

In Peel, there is urgent need for child care services. Local Children's Services operates only eleven licensed child care centres in Brampton and Mississauga and provides subsidized access to centre- and home-based child care in approximately 250 licensed programs. There are 761 directly operated licensed spaces and 1225 subsidized spaces.[91]

Despite the rapidly growing need for child care, Peel's Child and Family Services have been underfunded for years, and money annually spent per capita on child care is much lower than the provincial average. The Fair Share for Peel Task Force was established to work with the provincial government to redress the inequities.[92]

The NDP Era: Peel Child Care Committee

In 1993, in the new atmosphere of consultation initiated by the provincial NDP government, the Peel Child Care Committee (PCCC) was established at the request of the Ministry of Community and Social Services (MCSS), Mississauga Area Office. The purpose of this volunteer committee is to provide advice and consultation to the regional office.[93]

Initially, the PCCC was composed of forty members, representing local communities, child care providers, and community organizations.[94] The initial eight planning committee members included representatives from the MCSS, school boards, the Parks and Recreation Department, and Family Day Care Services, as well as one "community representative." The general committee membership has since shrunk to seventeen from forty.[95]

The PCCC attempted to create a consensus among the different interest groups represented in the child care community, and in 1994 it identified six regionwide priorities:[96] local child care planning (its main mandate); child care information accessibility; child care affordability; flexible child care programs; child care training and professional development coordination; and parents' and informal child care provider support.[97]

This original mandate has gradually narrowed. Telephone interviews conducted with nine members of the PCCC show that the group is now seen primarily as a consumer-oriented service organization whose work includes training, providing an information line, and educating people about the services available.[98] A few members interviewed identified making local politicians aware of what is needed in child care and what clients are looking for as main goals.[99] The active members seem to have little interest in lobbying but instead opt for a "support service" approach. Further, the PCCC policies are also reflective of organizations either in agreement with, or compliant with, the Tory government policies.

The Impact of the Cuts by the Provincial Conservative Government
Under the mandate of making child care affordable, the PCCC recommended that those services that are purchased rather than directly operated should be included in subsidy provision.[100] Because of a lack of funding, there was a doubling of the number of for-profit service arrangements between 1997 and 1998, and there was a significant drop in the not-for-profit spaces.[101] This exacerbated the problems created by the province's withdrawal from junior kindergarten programs, which added 82 percent to the municipal funding load.[102]

As in Toronto, so in Peel, there has been a gradual lengthening of the waiting list for subsidized child care—in the latter estimated as including 5,700 children.[103] There was a significant drop, of more than 50 percent, in the number of subsidized spaces under the Jobs Ontario program, reflecting a tightening of eligibility requirements. As the Ontario Works requirements take full effect, more pressure is expected on the waiting list,[104] which will grow to an estimated 15,000 children.[105]

The PCCC needs to raise money for its own operations as well, after municipal funding was withdrawn and as the member organizations are unable to grant monetary support.[106] These obstacles have had a negative impact on the size and composition of the Peel Child Care Committee. Although the committee meets regularly, it focuses on the existing services, rather than looking forward and striving for more and better services. This mentality is reflective of a political climate unreceptive to the needs of contemporary families.

Conclusions
Child care policy developments of the 1990s show a general pressure toward downsizing and privatization of services. This is the primary hallmark of the neo-conservative and neo-liberal trends that are evident on the national level and in Ontario. The prevailing political climate is also reflected in the return to the rhetoric of the "needy child." This stands in contrast with the 1970s and early 1980s when advocacy associations pressured for universal, publicly funded child care, as necessary for both child development and parental (especially maternal) self-actualization and economic contribution. Although building alliances with different social movements is an important part of child care advocacy, there is a

risk of muting or shifting the core principles of the movement away from support of universal, publicly funded and regulated child care. At the same time, the message regarding child care as a women's issue needs to be maintained more strongly.

To some degree, public child care advocates have been compelled to join their efforts with those of anti-poverty advocates.[107] They fear that they would otherwise be completely isolated, through another hallmark of neo-conservatism, the reduction of consultations with the public. As illustrated, this fear is well founded, as advocates, whether conflict or consensus oriented, must struggle to make their voices heard. Despite their sustained outsider status, advocates' presence was more visible two decades ago. In the neo-conservative 1990s, their voices are being muted and their efforts have been tamed. On the civic level, as illustrated in the case studies of Toronto and Peel, municipalities are able at best to hold onto existing funding, which does nothing to solve the problem of increasing need—witness the ever-lengthening lists of those who wait for a child care space. Meanwhile, the pressure toward using for-profit solutions is increasing and is more evident in Peel where the advocates have more readily embraced a consensus- and service-based strategy in relating to the provincial government.

There is a sense that social activists need to renew or reinvent themselves in order to capture more of the attention of politicians, the public and the media. There is a real need for an integrated approach to child care solutions as a part of the larger plan to combat child and family poverty. Such an approach would make alliances between child care and anti-poverty movements a logical affinity. At the same time, the message of "families in need" is certainly more appealing to neo-conservatives than is the notion of child care as an issue of women's rights.

In the end, the research results I have outlined, point toward a few recommendations for advocacy and policy. It is unavoidable that advocacy organizations experience ups and downs throughout many decades of effort. From the more promising 1970s and 1980s, we moved into the depressing 1990s. These days, simply sustaining a basic level of service and organization requires all available energy. In the current corrosive political climate, it is more important than ever to continue on the path of developing strong platforms and alliances. However, currently, community organizations have less chance of being heard, regardless of their tactics, vocabulary or alliances than in previous years. Thus, it is all the more important to get out the strongest possible message. This includes advocating the long-standing vision of child care as a universal service that promotes equality.

Ultimately, the question is: What do we think would happen if organizations acted as if they had a chance to get through to the media, the public and the politicians? In the worst case scenario, they would continue to be ignored. At best, they would sustain a level of political effort that is likely to produce minor shifts now and much more positive outcomes upon the long-awaited turn of the political tide.

Notes

1. This paper is a result of research funded by the Social Sciences and Humanities Research Council of Canada, through the Ryerson Polytechnic University. I thank my two research assistants, Anna Blaszcyk, and especially Fiona Whittington-Walsh. I am appreciative of the support and editorial comments of Allen Tyyskä. Previous versions of this study were presented at the Annual Meetings of the Canadian Sociology and Anthropology Association, Sherbrooke, Quebec, June 7, 1999; and at the Women's Worlds '99 Conference in Tromsø, Norway, June 21, 1999.
2. Tyyskä 1995.
3. Tyyskä 1995; Doherty et al. 1998: 1–2.
4. McIlroy 1999.
5. I relied on several sources of information: government documents, newspaper articles, advocacy materials, and interviews. Getting access to data on this topic is made difficult by the division of powers between different levels of government. I experienced difficulties in obtaining relevant information from the numerous government departments and offices. A further problem arose in that there were discrepancies between information obtained from different levels of government. Yet another complicating factor is that advocates operate with limited resources, making access to information and people a complicated enterprise. I used the time and efforts of two research assistants and myself, but there are still qualitative and quantitative discrepancies in the data obtained for the two municipalities. There is a lot more information available from all sources from the City of Toronto than the Peel Region. In order to compensate for this, I relied on over-the-phone key informant interviews in Peel. In the end, the picture that emerges from Toronto is more complete than that from Peel.
6. MacIvor 1996.
7. Tyyskä 1995; 1998.
8. Tyyskä 1995; 1998.
9. Colley 1983; Prentice 1988a.
10. Cohen 1993: 271; Myles and Pierson 1997.
11. Mab Oloman, "Child Care Funding. A Child Care Agenda for the 90s: Putting the Pieces Together," Ottawa: National Child Care Conference and Lobby, October 15–19, 1992.

12. Lero and Johnson 1994.
13. Bach and Phillips 1998: 235.
14. Doherty et al. 1995; Bach and Phillips 1998: 241–46.
15. Doherty et al. 1995; Torjman and Battle 1995.
16. Bach and Phillips 1998: 243–45.
17. Childcare Resource and Research Unit 2000b.
18. Bach and Phillips 1998: 245.
19. Olivia Chow, "Irresponsible Provincial Budget's Child Care Program has Roots in Federal Liberal Policies, Charges Metro Concillor Olivia Chow," press release, May 6, 1997.
20. Childcare Resource and Research Unit 2000.
21. City of Toronto, Planning and Development Department 1991: 30–31.
22. Marion Boyd, "Statement in the Legislature by the Honourable Marion Boyd, Minister of Community and Social Services," December 2, 1991; Metro Toronto Coalition for Better Child Care, "Making the Connections. Child Care in Metropolitan Toronto," August 1992.
23. Childcare Resource and Research Unit 1995.
24. Ontario Coalition for Better Child Care 1993.
25. Ministry of Community and Social Services 1992; Metro Toronto Coalition for Better Child Care, "Making the Connections. Child Care in Metropolitan Toronto," August 1992.
26. Ontario Coalition for Better Child Care 1995a.
27. Ontario Coalition for Better Child Care 1997a.
28. Office of the Provincial Auditor, Ontario 1995: 39.
29. Childcare Resource and Research Unit 1995.
30. Ministry of Community and Social Services 1993; 1994a; 1994b.
31. Ernie Eves, "Ontario Fiscal Overview and Spending Cuts," July 21, 1995, (Toronto Department of Finance).
32. Ernie Eves, "Fiscal and Economic Statement," November, 1995, (Toronto Department of Finance).
33. Ernie Eves, "Ontario Fiscal Overview and Spending Cuts," July 21, 1995, (Toronto Department of Finance).
34. Ontario Coalition for Better Child Care 1995a.
35. Ontario Coalition for Better Child Care 1997b
36. Ontario Coalition for Better Child Care 1995a.
37. McQuinty 1998: 15.
38. Ontario New Democrats 1996.
39. Ontario Coalition for Better Child Care 1995b; Marilyn Churley, City Councillor, "Letter to the Public," press release October, 1996.
40. Ontario Coalition for Better Child Care 1995a; 1996a.
41. Hansard, Ontario Legislature, Ms. Frances Lankin's (Beaches-Woodbine) Question to the Minister of Community and Social Services on Child Care, October 2, 1996.
42. Association of Day Care Operators of Ontario (ADCO) "ADCO's 1995

Ontario Pre-Election Child Care Issue Challenge," 1995 (Toronto: ADCO); Association of Day Care Operators of Ontario (ADCO) "Child Care in Ontario. The Common Sense Approach," July, 1995 (Toronto: ADCO).

43. Ontario Coalition for Better Child Care 1995a.
44. Association of Day Care Operators of Ontario (ADCO) "Child Care in Ontario. The Common Sense Approach," July, 1995 (Toronto: ADCO).
45. Ministry of Community and Social Services 1996a.
46. Ministry of Community and Social Services 1996b; Ontario Coalition for Better Child Care 1996b.
47. Metro Toronto Community Services 1996.
48. *Ottawa Citizen* 1996.
49. Ministry of Community and Social Services 1996b; Ontario Coalition for Better Child Care 1996b.
50. Ministry of Community and Social Services 1996a; Rusk 1996; *Toronto Star* 1996.
51. Ontario Coalition for Better Child Care 1996b.
52. Ontario Coalition for Better Child Care 1997b.
53. Janet Ecker, speech by the Honourable Janet Ecker, Minister for Community and Social Services, Halton, Ontario, January 14, 1997.
54. Ontario Coalition for Better Child Care 1997c.
55. Janet Ecker, speech by the Honourable Janet Ecker, Minister for Community and Social Services, Halton, Ontario, January 14, 1997; *Toronto Star* 1997.
56. Ontario Coalition for Better Child Care 1997b.
57. *Toronto Star* 1997.
58. Mallan 1997.
59. Ernie Eves, "1998 Ontario Budget. Budget Papers. Jobs for the Future, Today," May 5, 1998 (Toronto Department of Finance).
60. Ontario Campaign 2000 and Ontario Coalition for Better Child Care, 1999, "Ontario Conservative Party 1999 Pre-Budget Consultation." Toronto: OCBCC.
61. Ontario Coalition for Better Child Care 1999a.
62. I thank Martha Friendly, Child Care Resource and Research Unit, University of Toronto, for clarifying the links between the provincial and federal measures.
63. Ontario Coalition for Better Child Care 1999a.
64. Ontario Students Advocacy Group for Sole Support Parents, "Facts About the Cuts to Social Assistance for Sole-Support Parents Attending Post-Secondary Institutions," February 14, 1997.
65. Ontario Coalition for Better Child Care 1997d.
66. Ontario Coalition for Better Child Care 1998.
67. Ontario Coalition for Better Child Care 1999a: 3.
68. Ontario Campaign 2000 and Ontario Coalition for Better Child Care, 1999, "Ontario Conservative Party 1999 Pre-Budget Consultation." Toronto:

OCBCC.

69. Ontario Coalition for Better Child Care 1997b.
70. Ontario Coalition for Better Child Care 1999a: 1.
71. Legislative Assembly of Ontario, Standing Committee on Social Development 1997: 17.
72. Olivia Chow, "Irresponsible Provincial Budget's Child Care Program has Roots in Federal Liberal Policies, Charges Metro Concillor Olivia Chow," press release, May 6, 1997.
73. Metro Task Force on Services to Young Children and Families, "The First Duty. Report of the Metro Task Force on Services to Young Children and Families. Working Version," May 1997.
74. Children and Youth Action Committee, "The Status of Child Care and Children's Services. Conference Summary," February 15, 1999. Available at www.torontochildren.com/research.
75. Colley 1983; Prentice 1988a; City of Toronto, Planning and Development Department, "Cityplan '91. Planning for Daycare in the City of Toronto. Past and Future Initiatives," June 1991.
76. Metro Community Services (MCS), "Face of the Future. Comprehensive Review of Child Care. Report," 1990.
77. City of Toronto, Planning and Development Department, "Cityplan '91. Planning for Daycare in the City of Toronto. Past and Future Initiatives," June 1991.
78. City of Toronto, Planning and Development Department, "Cityplan '91. Planning for Daycare in the City of Toronto. Past and Future Initiatives," June, 1991; Ontario Coalition for Better Child Care 1993.
79. Ontario Coalition for Better Child Care 1993.
80. Metro Community Services (MCS), Children's Services Division, "Infosheet," July, 1993; Metro Community Services (MCS), Children's Services Division, "Business Case for Child Care," February 9, 1995.
81. Metro Community Services (MCS), "Focus on Child Care in Metro," November 1993.
82. Metro Task Force on Services to Young Children and Families, "Proposal. Pilot Projects for Restructuring School-Age Child Care in Metro Toronto. Submission of the Metro Task Force on Services to Young Children and Families to the Ministry of Community and Social Services," June 1996.
83. Metro Community Services (MCS), "Implications for Metro of Recommendations in Ontario's Child Care Review," September 16, 1996; Ontario Campaign 2000 and Ontario Coalition for Better Child Care, 1999, "Ontario Conservative Party 1999 Pre-Budget Consultation." Toronto: OCBCC.
84. Olivia Chow, "Irresponsible Provincial Budget's Child Care Program has Roots in Federal Liberal Policies, Charges Metro Concillor Olivia Chow," press release, May 6, 1997; *Toronto Star* 1997.
85. Ontario Coalition for Better Child Care 1999a.

86. United Way of Greater Toronto, "Metro Toronto: A Community at Risk. Demographic, Economic, Social, and Funding Trends in Metropolitan Toronto," 1997 Toronto: United Way of Greater Toronto.
87. According to other earlier estimates, an additional 25,000 subsidies and 45,000 spaces are required to meet the need (Metro Community Services (MCS), Children's Services Division, "Business Case for Child Care," February 9, 1995).
88. United Way of Greater Toronto, "Metro Toronto: A Community at Risk. Demographic, Economic, Social, and Funding Trends in Metropolitan Toronto," 1997 Toronto: United Way of Greater Toronto.
89. Social Planning Council of Peel, "The Social Profile of Peel 1994," 1997. Available at www.netrover.com/-spcpeel/profile.
90. Peel Children's Centre, "Fair Share for Peel Children and Families," 1996. Available at www.peelcc.org/fair.
91. Region of Peel. 1999. "Children's Services." Available at www.region.peel.on.ca/childcar.
92. Peel Children's Centre, "Fair Share for Peel Children and Families," 1996. Available at www.peelcc.org/fair.
93. Peel Child Care Committee, "A Community Child Care Plan for Peel," September, 1995 Mississauga, Ontario.
94. Peel Child Care Committee, "A Community Child Care Plan for Peel," September, 1995 Mississauga, Ontario.
95. Interview with Jane VanBerkel, Member, Peel Child Care Committee (Private Consultant), February 17, 1999.
96. Later reduced to three (interview with Jane VanBerkel, Member, Peel Child Care Committee (Private Consultant), February 17, 1999.)
97. Peel Child Care Committee, "A Community Child Care Plan for Peel," September, 1995 Mississauga, Ontario; Peel Child Care Committee, "Executive Summary. A Community Child Care Plan for Peel," 1995 Mississauga, Ontario.
98. Interview with Cheryl Rogers, Member, Peel Child Care Committee (Family Daycare Services), March 8, 1999.
99. Interview with Sylvia Leal, member of the Peel Child Care Committee (Plus Child Care Services), March 12, 1999.
100. Peel Child Care Committee, "A Community Child Care Plan for Peel," September, 1995 Mississauga, Ontario.
101. Region of Peel, Children's Services, "1998 Budget—Draft Budget Ad Hoc Committee Review," February 2, 1998 Mississauga, Ontario.
102. Ontario Coalition for Better Child Care 1995a: 4.
103. Region of Peel. 1996. Annual Financial Report. Available at www.region.peel.on.ca/finance/ar.1996.
104. Region of Peel. 1996. Annual Financial Report. Available at www.region.peel.on.ca/finance/ar.1996.
105. Interview with Cheryl Rogers, Member, Peel Child Care Committee

(Family Daycare Services), March 8, 1999; interview with Lorna Montgomery, member of the Peel Child Care Committee (Peel Infant Development), March 16, 1999.

106. Interview with Cheryl Rogers, Member, Peel Child Care Committee (Family Daycare Services), March 8, 1999; interview with Sylvia Leal, member of the Peel Child Care Committee (Plus Child Care Services), March 12, 1999; interview with Jane VanBerkel, Member, Peel Child Care Committee (Private Consultant), February 17, 1999.

107. Doherty et al 1998: 47.

Chapter 8

In the Absence of Policy
Moving Toward Inclusion of Children with Special Needs in Canada's Child Care Centres

Sharon Hope Irwin and Donna S. Lero

Introduction

Despite the acknowledged benefits of child care to children with special needs and their families, licensed child care centres in Canada are not required to include children with special needs. Still, more and more centres choose to include these children. They include children with special needs in regular child care programs, despite the lack of public policy, supportive funding or adequate training for their staff.

In the late 1960s and early 1970s the inclusion of children with special needs in child care was not a pressing issue. Parents, physicians and organizations for the disabled tended to see specialized services as superior to inclusion in regular services. Most child care workers had no training in inclusion and thus did not have the skills to overcome their apprehensions regarding children with special needs. Furthermore, centres did not have the funds to train or otherwise enhance staff and reduce staff-to-child ratios. Nor did they provide for therapeutic assistance, equipment or physical modifications—essential elements for successful inclusion. Provincial child care legislation and regulations of the time were generally silent regarding children with special needs and lacked mention of terms such as "exceptional child" or "special needs child."[1]

Today, many more parents, early interventionists, researchers and consultants seek and recommend inclusive child care settings. Child care practice has developed considerably, with child care workers better trained and more accommodating toward children with special needs. Centres now receive modest funding to support inclusion though these sums are hardly adequate. Furthermore, provincial child care legislation and policy regarding children with special needs are somewhat less restrictive and, sometimes, even more encouraging than they were thirty years ago.[2]

This chapter outlines child care's move from exclusion to full inclusion of children with special needs and highlights some of the remaining vulnerabilities. It focuses on the role played by child care advocates, especially those who took on the issue of inclusion. Other child care advocates, while not considering inclusion their primary issue, have in fact increased the possibility of successful inclusion through their promotion of general policy changes to child care. Most of the inclusion work has been done by individuals, acting as pioneers, perhaps because the national and provincial child care organizations were not making it their issue. Although this is now changing, the bulk of the advocacy work on child care inclusion continues to be done by individuals in the field and individual parents. No child care organization in Canada has yet adopted a statement of principle regarding inclusion, although the example was set by the National Association for the Education of Young Children (NAEYC) in the United States in 1993.[3]

In all provinces the policy issue has moved from "Should we include children with special needs?" to "How can we best support child care for children with special needs, given available resources?" Policy formulation has not yet caught up with advocates who support the full inclusion in child care of all children with special needs.

No "Right" to Inclusive Child Care

On issues of social policy, Canada is usually seen as occupying the middle ground between the industrialized European countries, with their strong social safety nets, and the United States with its much weaker supports.[4] In comparison to United States programs, the *Canada Health Act*, Employment Insurance, tax-supported tuition in universities, and Old Age Insurance are stronger, more universally accessible programs. The American debate over proposals for a national health program serves as a reminder that 49 million Americans lack medical insurance. Americans also face a daunting unemployment insurance program, tuition that annually reaches or exceeds $US20,000 and very limited old-age insurance programs.

However, in the case of young children with special needs, Canada fails to match or surpass the U.S. standard that provides a much higher level of entitlements. Through the IDEA (*Individuals with Disabilities Education Act*, 1992), with its entitlements to "free and appropriate education in the least restrictive environment" for persons with disabilities ages three to twenty-one, and though the ADA (*Americans with Disabilities Act,* 1990), which prohibits discrimination on the basis of disability (even in child care centres and family daycare homes), the United States provides rights that do not exist in Canada.[5]

Even in the Canadian education system—another social program that lies within provincial jurisdiction and which is indisputably a more accepted public service than child care—no province has enshrined "free and appropriate education in the least restrictive environment" for persons with disabilities. All provinces now require public education for persons with disabilities,[6] but recent education-rights cases only confirm the weakness of those guarantees.[7] Since "free and appropriate education in the least restrictive setting" is not a legal imperative in Canada, it is not surprising that the issue of rights to inclusive child care for young children with special needs has been little addressed at the policy level. In Canada, even if a centre receives public funds, no antidiscrimination requirement is attached to those funds. Also, Canadian child care programs wanting to include children with special needs are often plagued with practical barriers such as low salaries, high staff turnover, minimal staff training, inadequate space and high child-to-staff ratios. Affordability to parents is yet another barrier.

However, many child care centres now include children with special needs, despite lack of legislation; lack of statutory entitlement to appropriate early childhood education for children with special needs; and the existence of many practical barriers.[8] According to a recent study, most Canadian child care workers believe that children with special needs should be included in regular child care programs.[9] Some early childhood educators draw this view from strong ethical or religious beliefs in nondiscrimination. Others still are familiar with research that suggests children with disabilities benefit from inclusion in programs with their typical peers.[10] Others say that their experience at including children with special needs has convinced them that inclusion is appropriate and doable.[11] Advocates (from child care workers to parents of typically developing children) often emphasize the value of inclusion for all children, that is, the benefits to typical peers as well as to children with special needs.[12] That said, without legislative entitlement and policy, the evidence suggests that full inclusion in Canadian child care is an improbability and that existing inclusion will probably not be maintained.[13] While Americans can look to the law for support of inclusion, in Canada there exists only the yet-untested promises of the Charter of Rights and provincial human rights codes that are not seen to apply to young children.

The movement toward inclusive child care in Canada is mainly a story of child care advocates. These inclusionary pioneers joined with parents of children with special needs, disability advocates and social service workers to push policy makers and politicians to support programs that their centres were already attempting. In this case, people started with "practice" and then used that "practice" as evidence to convince policy makers and politicians to provide appropriate funding and regulation. In turn, changes in government policy and funding were then used both to expand and improve inclusionary practice and as additional evidence to move policy and funding still further towards full inclusion.

These inclusionary pioneers draw upon a rich social justice tradition. A 1993 study of ten exemplary inclusive child care centres explored the centres' reasons for gravitating toward inclusion.[14] Seven of the ten directors had roots either in the women's movement or in other social justice movements. The study also noted that almost all of the ten leaders were "social entrepreneurs," deeply invested in their communities and aware of programs and services they might tap into. However, individuals' backgrounds alone were unable to completely shape the movement. Particular historical contexts strongly affected the potentials and outcomes of child care advocates' work to promote inclusion.

Pre-1960s

Prior to the 1960s, the care of children with special needs was usually seen as a family issue. The overarching theme was essentially "hopelessness," "shame and guilt" or "god's special child." Further, it was assumed that children with intellectual challenges could not learn and that children with physical challenges would die young. Upon the birth of a child with special needs, families usually had two choices: institutionalize the child ("It's better for her," or "He'll be happier with his own kind," the experts would say) or take on the total task without formal supports. Many provinces excluded children with special needs from schools and, of course, licensed child care was in its infancy. As Wolfensberger states:

> Families were deeply ashamed of having retarded children and often kept it a secret. Parents of that era had to cope not only with whatever challenges a handicapped child would present under the best of circumstances, and not only with the then prevailing lack of services, and not only with societal rejection of themselves and their handicapped child; they were also faced, in the vast majority

of instances, with their own negative attitudes, which quite understandably were those of their larger society.[15]

In the late 1950s, the dismal situation of people with disabilities started to change. It was at this time that the behaviourists demonstrated that everyone could learn tasks if they were they broken down into simple pieces, repeated many times and if participants were rewarded for success. This finding had a huge impact on people who were working with the intellectually challenged; techniques of behaviour modification were incorporated into training programs for mental retardation workers and into teaching methods for people with intellectual challenges. "Task analysis," "mastery learning" and "rewards" became hopeful motifs of institutions where many people with intellectual disabilities lived. As well, the new techniques gave parents both a feeling that their children could learn and a new cause worth fighting for.

Increasing use and sophistication of antibiotics meant children with physical disabilities, who might have died soon after birth, were living longer lives. As well, assistive technology and miniaturization offered new mobility and communicative possibilities. Furthermore, the concept of "rights" of disadvantaged populations, including persons with disabilities, gained advocates and media attention. In *Brown versus the Board of Education* (1954),[16] Thurgood Marshall (who later became a U.S. Supreme Court justice) argued, "We conclude that separate educational facilities are inherently unequal.... [They] generate a feeling of inferiority as to their status in the community that may affect their hearts and minds in a way unlikely ever to be undone." As to majority children, Dr. Kenneth Clark, a noted Black psychologist wrote:

> Those children who learn the prejudice of our society are also being taught to gain personal status in an unrealistic and nonadaptive way. The culture permits and at times encourages them to direct their feelings of hostility and aggression against whole groups of people perceived as weaker than themselves. Confusion, conflict, moral cynicism and disrespect for authority may arise.[17]

This case had tremendous influence on other disadvantaged groups (notably, people with disabilities and their advocates) who then argued that segregated schools and institutions had similarly negative effects on persons with disabilities and on nondisabled people.

1960s–1970s: Specialized Preschools

Throughout the 1960s and early 1970s, Canadian child care was characterized by both daycare centres and part-day nursery schools. The daycare
centres were primarily custodial environments for the children of the
working poor.[18] They provided a safe environment, nutritious meals and
adequate care. No one expected them to be much more. For middle-class
parents, on the other hand, the preschool/nursery school was the choice
care environment for three and four year olds. The child would attend a
social program for two hours in the morning or afternoon, spending the
rest of the day with his/her mother or housekeeper.

Influenced by the results that the behaviourists reported, parents and
advocates for young children with special needs were energized. If their
children could learn, then they, too, should have a formalized environment to foster that learning. Modeled on the emerging special-education
paradigm, a segregated program of specialized techniques and resources
was chosen by parents and researchers alike as the best learning system for
children with special needs. This parallel system of "developmental
preschools" for children with disabilities soon flourished.

Finding "regular preschools" inadequate or unwelcoming, parents of
children with special needs took matters into their own hands. Using the
Canadian Association for the Mentally Retarded (CAMR), now the
Canadian Association for Community Living (CACL), as a vehicle, they
developed a nationwide program of nursery schools and Child Development Centres (CDCs) for children with special needs. These programs
were characterized by specialization, segregation, and by strong parent
involvement (particularly in the case of the CAMR programs).[19] A
combination of modest public funding, incessant fundraising, low wages,
rent-free space and huge volunteer efforts by parents made these programs
accessible to most eligible children in areas where they existed: the
programs were usually free. Still, there were few, if any, full-day
programs for children with special needs, since the emphasis was strictly
on "development," not on maternal employment.

1980s: The Transitional Decade

With the growing workforce participation of middle-class mothers of
young children, the need to expand the length of preschool/nursery
school daily care was obvious. To accommodate children of working
parents, some preschools added a "bridge" program at lunchtime between their morning and afternoon programs. Some also added "wrap-
around" programs, before 9:00 A.M. and after 3:00 P.M. In addition, the

traditional daycare centres that had been seen primarily as custodial settings for low-income parents expanded their "developmental" or "educational" components.

In the 1980s, the group child care centre (daycare centre) became the characteristic nonparental setting for children ages two to five. In fact, many more families actually used nonlicensed out-of-home care or care-by-relative, but it can be argued that the licensed, group child care setting characterized the period. With the single exception of British Columbia, provinces allocated funds from subsidies cost-shared with the federal government almost entirely to centre-based care. Most training programs for early childhood educators were premised on the expectation that students would be employed in centre-based care. Quality measures were developed; training programs and qualifications were strengthened; provincial legislation began to reflect awareness that child care needed to enrich children, not just ensure they were "safe and fed."

Just as middle-income parents of typically developing children were pressing the system to provide high-quality experiences, parents of children with special needs were trying to get in. Mothers of children with special needs were in the workforce in greater and greater numbers, and just as other working mothers, they too needed child care. Individually and as part of advocacy groups such as CACL, parents were now looking for "normalized" or "least restrictive placements" for their children with special needs—placements such as community child care. The influence and popularization of Wolf Wolfensberger's normalization theory led people who previously believed in specialized services to advocate for inclusive and community-based services. A visiting scholar at the National Institute on Mental Retardation (NIMR) from 1971 to 1973, Wolfensberger challenged the NIMR, the Canadian Association for the Mentally Retarded (CAMR), provincial and regional affiliates, parents and service providers to move beyond the specialized, segregated programs that, he was convinced, were inherently dehumanizing. The 1978 publication of *Children with Special Needs: A Guide to Integration* by the National Institute on Mental Retardation[20] was a landmark—a statement to advocates for persons with retardation, advancing the view that children with special needs could, and should, be integrated into community child care. Funded and broadly disseminated by Health and Welfare Canada, this handbook became a resource book for child care providers and consultants struggling to develop integrated child care programs.

In line with such thinking, the CAMR nursery schools began to change form and function: first, they turned into "reverse integration" settings, where the totally segregated setting became one involving 50 percent typically developing children and 50 percent children with intellectual disabilities; then as their children moved into those settings, they adopted a support and consultation role for regular child care programs.

Generally, the child development centres changed more slowly. Often connected to rehabilitation centres or hospitals, with therapists on site, and often incorporating more accessible physical design features, these programs were usually more resistant to inclusion. And so, by the end of the 1980s, integrated child care for a child with a physical disability was often characterized by a sliced-up day. The child would go to a regular child care setting when his/her mother left for work, be picked up in the CDC van at 8:30, go to a two-hour therapeutic program for the morning and finally be taken by van back to the child care setting for the afternoon. Coordination between the two programs would range from non-existent to full. But between dressing for outdoors, waiting for the van, riding in the van, waiting to be undressed for indoors, being dressed again for the ride back, waiting for the ride, riding in the van and being undressed again for indoors—there was an enormous amount of very passive, wasted time.

Meanwhile, community child care centres were opening their doors to children with special needs. Often it happened one child at a time—a particularly persuasive mother or a particularly engaging child convincing centre directors to enroll that very first child. All across the country, child care directors such as Karen Thorpe in Toronto, Sister Ginger Patchen in Winnipeg, Dixie Van Raalte in Fredericton, Donna Michal in Edmonton, Monica Lysack in Regina, Trudy Norton in Coquitlam and Sharon Irwin in Cape Breton said yes to a child with special needs, rounding up the supports, training, resources and equipment afterwards.[21]

Trudy Norton is a good example of how this "advocacy from practice" worked:

> I just couldn't say no. Not only had the child attended a community child care centre in Calgary, but her three cousins were at our centre. But how were we to accommodate a child with a tracheostomy—a hole in her chest? All I could see was the rabbit and the sawdust, the sand table, the three- and four-year-old children who would find the "button" on the child's chest endlessly fascinating. But I couldn't say no. It was only after we all survived that year that I was able to think clearly about the implications—physical, legal, etc.—of what we had done. And I

decided to find out whether other child care centres in British Columbia were encountering what we then called "special health needs."[22]

Trudy took that incident and her inability to say no and erected a model training program, videos and an advocacy plan to ensure special health needs children the supports that would enable their inclusion in child care programs. After eight years of struggle, British Columbia adopted her plan, with many other provinces and regions moving to follow suit. To this day, Trudy's training manual and video remain the fundamental text on "special health care" in Canada.

In 1987, the Government of Ontario published *Integrating Children Experiencing Special Needs in Day Nurseries: A Background Report.*[23] This working document "was meant to provide information, offer some new insights and, in a general sense, identify policy and operational issues that would benefit from further consideration." Its descriptions of existing integrated programs demonstrate an almost unbelievable variability of program design, eligibility, geographic availability, staffing arrangements and ratios, and philosophy. Such diverse programs, all created in the name of integration, all supported by the provincial ministry, embody the rich form of services developed prior to policy. It is easy to see that many of these services were "advocacy driven." Funded within the discretionary budgets of regional, or even local, provincial government officials, or having received funding from charities, foundations, short-term grants or other ministries, these programs were shaped by their piecemeal funding.

At the end of the 1980s, despite the lack of legislated entitlement, many Canadian child care programs were beginning to include children with disabilities; the provinces were funding, in varying degrees, the extra costs of inclusion. Some of these costs were indirectly passed on to the federal government under the Canada Assistance Plan (CAP) agreements. Provincial policy direction remained unclear, and no federal policy required the cost-shared CAP funding for child care subsidies to be nondiscriminatory toward children with special needs.

The Early to Mid-1990s

By the beginning of the 1990s, child care began to look like a real service, that is, it had been on the agendas of all political parties in three elections and it had been the subject of a Liberal-led parliamentary task force (the Katie Cooke Task Force), as well as a Progressive Conservative parliamentary task force (the Shirley Martin Task Force). The public was beginning to understand child care as more than babysitting, and research was beginning to show positive outcomes from quality child care. Some provinces actually raised per diems and/or salary grids in recognition of levels of staff training. While salaries were still very low, there was a general sense that things were going to get better for child care service, for early childhood educators and for the quality of care; all provinces supported integrated child care to some extent. A 1990 "Summary of Provincial and Territorial Child Care Programs for Special Needs Children"[24] noted that six provinces (Alberta, Manitoba, Ontario, Quebec, New Brunswick and P.E.I.) specified available funds for integrated settings. Three other provinces (British Columbia, Saskatchewan and Nova Scotia) also provided some funding for integration in community-based child care. Although Newfoundland did not provide extra funding, it did allow daycare subsidies to be used for children with special needs, regardless of their parents' employment status. The summary provided no analysis of child care in the territories.

In 1992, with sponsorship from the Child Care Initiatives Fund, the SpeciaLink symposium in Cape Breton brought together over 200 child care directors, resource teachers, and early childhood educators, who had been identified by their peers as "experienced and influential" in practising and promoting inclusion. Outfitted in an army general's uniform, Dr. Karen Vander Ven, professor of child development and child care at the University of Pittsburgh, delivered a speech, "Military Strategy and the Economic Base of Child Care: A Radical Proposal for Our Future," that suggested military strategy as a metaphor and a plan of action for child care advocates.[25] The many "pioneers" in attendance, accustomed to being the only skilled inclusion practitioners in their area, quickly formed a support network that continues to this day. The basis was laid, in those four days in Cape Breton, for cross-province, as well as national, foci on advocacy—advocacy for regulations, training, supports, and techniques to promote inclusive practices.

Concurrently, many provinces (British Columbia, Saskatchewan, Ontario, Prince Edward Island, New Brunswick and Nova Scotia) were rewriting their child care legislation as it related to children with special needs. It was expected that the new legislation would dominantly feature clauses strengthening the inclusion of children with special needs in regular child care settings, rather than supporting a separate, segregated track.

In 1992, British Columbia began its move toward supported child care. Easily the most extensive special needs child care program review in

Canada, this effort began with a study of the actual child care situation of children with special needs in that province and included interviews with a large, random sample of parents, child care providers and child care consultants.[26] Based on the survey and on consultations during the following eighteen months, the reference committee reported to the province:

> This report represents a new vision and framework for Supported Child Care, which would replace the current Special Needs Day Care Program. The vision is rooted in a philosophy of inclusion, and suggests a principle-driven approach to working with families. The principles cover three broad areas—Family-centred Approach, Shared Responsibility, and Individual Planning for Children. Each is connected to a set of expected outcomes. The objective for the program reflects these principles and outcomes.[27]

The report was accepted by government as the basis of its new policy and seemed to provide a new beginning for inclusive child care in that province and a model for the rest of Canada. The province's economic downturn in the mid-1990s, with the subsequent elimination of both the non-needs-based preschool subsidy for all children with disabilities and the cap on spending for supports, provides a reminder that "enactment" is as necessary a step as "policy development."[28]

In late 1993, the federal Liberal government established a parliamentary task force to consider reforms to social security. An underlying assumption was that existing legislation kept many people on welfare when they wanted, and were able, to work. With coordination from SpeciaLink, inclusive child care advocates across Canada organized parents and child care providers to present briefs in every city where the task force met. Both the first copresenters in Whitehorse and the last copresenters in St. John's were paired teams of mothers of children with special needs and their child care providers. The mothers of children with special needs, each speaking of their individual experience, made it clear that child care was a matter of both employment and development. They cautioned the politicians that they, at least as much as other Canadian women, needed to be in the labour force. Without serious changes to child care policy and funding, they were destined for a special welfare ghetto — populated exclusively by mothers of children with special needs. They also explained that child care was the largest barrier they faced in maintaining employment. One mother appeared with her twin daughters with cerebral palsy (in their wheelchairs); she explained that her ability to stay employed and off of welfare was based on the most fragile of child care supports. Another mother displayed her cell phone (this was in 1993, when these devices were not yet common). She told the task force that she was not a yuppie but a cook and that she had to keep in touch with the caregivers of her severely handicapped child at all times. The cell phone, she explained, enabled her to leave the home to work.[29]

By the mid-1990s, despite the lack of legislated entitlement, more and more Canadian child care programs were including children with special needs. The quality as well as the quantity of inclusion in Canada had increased somewhat. Both preservice and in-service training were being redirected from an emphasis on exceptionality toward strategies for inclusion. The number of workshops on inclusion issues had increased significantly. Finally, programs that had formerly included only children with mild to moderate disabilities were beginning to include children with tougher challenges. Children with special needs were still disproportionately under-represented in child care, but the level of under-representation had decreased.[30]

The Mid-1990s: Debt, Deficit and Problems for Inclusive Child Care

The progress toward inclusive child care came to a crashing halt in the mid-1990s. The end of the Canada Assistance Plan and the increasing governmental obsession with debt, deficit and devolution made child care funding more precarious than ever. Child care programs were increasingly concerned about their own survival. Would provinces continue to allocate money to child care at the prior levels while more established programs (such as health, post-secondary education and welfare) vied for the same dollars? The obvious answer was no.

As always, the fate of inclusive child care was inextricably linked to the fortunes of child care in general. Within the context of decreasing support and without a legal mandate entitling equitable access, inclusive child care for children with special needs seemed in decline. Centres, with regret, in an attempt to keep their programs afloat, began to turn away children whose care was more costly. And thus, it appeared that children with special needs would be increasingly left out of child care. Their mothers would be increasingly less able to engage in training or employment. And nondisabled children would lose the advantages that early association with children with special needs can bring.

At the Millennium and Beyond

At the millennium, with federal and provincial debts and deficits giving way to surpluses, it appeared that there might be a chance that governments would readdress social issues such as child care and inclusion. The National Children's Agenda (NCA)[31] and the Early Childhood Development Accord (ECD)[32] may signal a willingness on the part of federal/provincial/territorial governments to address both child care and inclusion issues. However, it appears that the need for agreement by all provinces as well as by the federal government, under the Social Union Framework Agreement (SUFA), will seriously limit such commitments. The two federal/provincial/territorial-produced consultation documents for the NCA,[33] contained the word "child care" only once and words such as "special needs" and "disability" only twice.

There is now a growing awareness in advocacy groups that special needs are an issue that the movement should address. Child care and child care inclusion advocates mobilized quickly and effectively to make their position very clear at the regional round tables and focus groups, and through the internet, where the NCA vision questionnaire also appeared. Consequently, the public response document, *Public Dialogue on the National Children's Agenda: Developing a Shared Vision*,[34] was significantly different in emphasis from the consultation documents. It mentioned words such as "special needs" and "disability" eight times and expanded on early childhood health and development; it stressed "universal access" to early childhood programs and provided examples of services that should be accessible to everyone, including pre- and postnatal care, nutritional care, child care, and preschool and literacy programs. As well, it seemed to emphasize the inherent value of children as children, not just as future workers and taxpayers. It also added a value statement about compliance with the Canadian Charter of Rights and Freedoms and the U.N. Convention on the Rights of the Child. Even the news release from the Government of Canada stated that, "During the dialogue process, participants stressed the needs of children with disabilities and children from diverse cultural and linguistic backgrounds, no matter where they live in this country."[35]

Yet, it must be asked whether advocacy actions, such as the mobilization for the National Children's Agenda consultations, really make a difference. In the short run, they created a public document markedly different from the proposed one. Only time will tell how this document will be used. Perhaps the Early Childhood Development (ECD) Accord, which followed the NCA consultations, reflects the earlier public response, but this cannot be proven. Certainly this is not a decisive victory, as is illustrated by the statements of one aging advocate:

> I feel like an old fire dog now. When I was young and frisky, I'd respond to the bell right away—I'd jump right up on that fire truck. Now I'm still in the station and when I hear the bell ring, I hope it's a false alarm. Then it rings again, and I tell myself it probably isn't an important fire. Then it rings one more time, and I get myself up slowly and I just manage to climb on that fire truck to go to the fire. Maybe this one will really matter.[36]

Despite many years of hard work, advocates for inclusive child care still have their work cut out for them.

Next Steps

Policy has lagged behind the reality of inclusive child care. Many advocates created inclusive centres and then challenged governments to fund the services they had created. Short-term job creation initiatives—Local Initiatives Program (LIP), Canada Works and summer student grants such as SEED—often provided the additional human resources and social capital for innovation. But they left "self-sufficiency" to the lobbying efforts of the people who started the programs and to the constituencies that had benefited from them. Policy-relevant Canadian research, such as *You Bet I Care! A Matter of Urgency*, and work from the Roeher Institute's Child and Family Series began to provide evidence necessary to help child care inclusion advocates make their case to politicians and policy makers. Many centres continued to include children with special needs despite the costs that were ultimately downloaded on them. When finances became more difficult during the mid-to-late 1990s, centre directors feared that they would have to cut back on their level of inclusion and some actually did.[37]

At the millennium, the increased prosperity of the federal government and most provincial governments seems to have stopped clawbacks for a time. However this prosperity has yet to translate into substantial increases in funding or support for inclusion.

Strategic partnerships have become increasingly important. It appears that parents of and advocates for children with special needs are coming to understand that advocating for inclusion also means advocating for high-quality, accessible, affordable child care for all children.[38] Without this strong foundation, there is no appropriate program for their children to join. In a similar manner, child care advocates are coming to understand that the parents of and advocates for children with special needs can be powerful allies. This partnership not only widens the circle of people with an interest in child care or inclusion but it may also inform government officials, the public and politicians of the multiple roles that child care can play. Presentations about inclusive child care given at House of Commons subcommittee hearings—one on "Children at Risk" and another on "Status of Persons with Disabilities"—have since led to a combined hearing of the two committees as the subcommittee chairs recognize the interrelatedness of the two issues.[39]

Change has come slowly, regarding the inclusion issue, to child care organizations in Canada, with groups sometimes leading their member-ships and other times responding to them. The Early Childhood Educators of British Columbia (ECE-BC) has been active on the inclusion issue since the mid-1990s, always including a large number of workshops on inclusion at its annual conferences and including a regular column, "Moving Toward Inclusion," in its periodical. In Saskatchewan, not only have the annual conferences of the Saskatchewan Child Care Association featured inclusion issues, but the organization has gone so far as to partner with the Early Childhood Intervention Program (ECIP) for recent annual conferences, thus modeling the collaborative approach to early childhood intervention that inclusion advocates promote. In Manitoba and New Brunswick, the Associations for Community Living sponsor workshops at ECE conferences and have invited early childhood educators to speak at ACL conferences. In terms of representation, documents created by advocacy organizations now typically mention "inclusion of children with disabilities" and their visual imagery usually includes a child with a visible disability. In addition, the famous Keep the Promise poster depicting children holding up the Liberal Red Book (that included promises for child care) also includes the image of a child with a visible disability.[40]

In the interest of altering inclusive policy, the recent focus on "rights-based entitlements" for children may prove an option worth further exploring.[41] The focus on "needs-based services," the primary direction of inclusive child care advocates until now, may have exhausted its potential and there may be a more effective means to change policy at this time. Linking the rights to inclusion and child care to Canada's indelible signature on the U.N. Convention on the Rights of the Child might be a productive strategy. The upcoming U.N. special session on this conven-tion could provide opportunities to highlight Canada's weaknesses in these areas.

In closing, as illustrated throughout this chapter, achievements based on "discretion" rather than "mandate" are fragile and risk disappearing or shrinking in times of fiscal restraint and changing governmental priorities. It is essential that Canadian legislation—both federal and provincial—ensures that children with special needs are not excluded from community child care centres on the basis of their special needs. It is essential that public policy in all the provinces and territories go beyond "encouraging" inclusion to actually providing the leadership, funding and supports to make it viable for centres and valuable for children. Child care advocates must continue to work to ensure that their gains on the frontlines are no longer vulnerable to the whims and vicissitudes of governments. To be sure, operating in the absence of adequate legislation and policy relating to inclusion and child care proves dangerous time and again.

Notes

1. See for example, Nova Scotia, Department of Social Services 1971.
2. British Columbia, Ministry for Children and Families 1996.
3. Division of Early Childhood 1993. Endorsed by NAEYC in 1994.
4. McQuaig 1993.
5. *Individuals with Disabilities Education Act* 1975 mandates free and appropriate educational services in the least restrictive environment to individuals three to twenty-one, mandates transition services and assistive technology services to be included in a child's or youth's IEP, and adds autism and traumatic brain injuries to the list of categories of children and youth eligible for special education and related services. Part II refers to services for children 0-3 and their families. The *Americans with Disabilities Act* of 1990 is based on concepts of the *Rehabilitation Act* of 1973 and guarantees equal opportunity for individuals with disabilities in employment, public accommodation, transportation, state and local government services, and telecommunications. It specifically includes children of all ages, in group child care and family daycare.
6. Smith 1994.
7. See P.R. de Massy 1997; and C.S. Judd 1997.
8. Doherty et al. 1995.
9. Irwin, Lero, and Brophy 2000.
10. Strain 1999.
11. Irwin, Lero and Brophy 2000: 110.
12. Peck, Carlson, and Helmstetter 1992: 353–64.
13. Irwin, Lero and Brophy 2000: 163.
14. Irwin 1992.
15. Wolfensberger 1991: 1-15.
16. *Brown v. Board of Education,* 1954, see OYEZ Project at Northwestern University (available at www.oyez.nwu.edu/cases/cases).

17. Clark 1993: 38.
18. Friendly 1994: 139.
19. Roeher Institute 1993: 171.
20. National Institute on Mental Retardation 1977.
21. Irwin, 1993a: 131–48. All were invited to the 1992 SpeciaLink symposium after being identified by peers, advocacy organizations and child care agencies as "effective, experienced and influential" mainstream pioneers.
22. Irwin 1993a: 26–28.
23. Government of Ontario, Ministry of Community and Social Services, Child Care Branch 1988.
24. Government of British Columbia, Task Force on Child Care 1993: 101.
25. Vander Ven 1992: 69-85.
26. British Columbia 1992.
27. British Columbia. Special Needs Day Care Review Reference Committee 1993: iii.
28. Meisels 1988: 115–26.
29. House of Commons 1995. Copies of the briefs related to child care and children with special needs are available from SpeciaLink.
30. Irwin 1997. Updated bi-annually.
31. First Ministers, Prime Minister and Territorial Leaders 1997.
32. First Ministers 2000.
33. Federal/Provincial/Territorial Council of Ministers on Social Policy Renewal 1999.
34. Federal/Provincial/Territorial Council of Ministers on Social Policy Renewal 2000.
35. Government of Canada 2000.
36. This advocate oreferred to remain anonymous.
37. Irwin, Lero and Brophy 2000: 138–140.
38. Roeher Institute 1993: 172–74.
39. Brief from SpeciaLink to Human Resources and Development Canada Subcommittee on Children at Risk Hearings, re Readiness, 1999, (available from SpeciaLink, PO Box 775, Sydney, Nova Scotia, BlP 6J1) and Joint Hearings of Subcommittee on Children at Risk and Subcommittee on Persons with Disabilities, June 6, 2000, (available from SpeciaLink, PO Box 775, Sydney, Nova Scotia, B1P 6G1.)
40. "Keep the Promise: A National Child Care Program Now!" is a poster that was sponsored by the Child Care Advocacy Association of Canada, the Canadian Auto Workers, the Canadian Union of Postal Workers, the Ontario Coalition for Better Child Care, the Canadian Labour Congress, the United Food and Commercial Workers International Union, The Public Service Alliance of Canada, The Federation of Women Teachers' Association of Ontario, The United Steelworkers and the Canadian Teachers' Federation.
41. Canadian Coalition on the Rights of Children 1999.

Chapter 9

History, Lessons and a Case for Change in Child Care Advocacy[1]

Judith A. Martin

This chapter has a dual agenda. It will present an analysis of child care advocacy in Saskatchewan from 1971–2000, and it will provide a commentary on why and how I believe the vision and style of child care advocacy ought to change.

To begin, a little of my personal child care story to assist readers in appreciating the assumptions and experience that have influenced the views here expressed. I am the mother of several graduates of child care and, as a community developer, an academic, a citizen-activist and a senior manager, I have had a variety of roles in and around child care. I have been a full-time employed mother since 1978 who never had (nor wanted) the choice of abdicating the workplace. I have, however, had fairly good jobs and for some years was married, so I could afford good child care. I have not faced holding a bad job for bad pay while leaving children in bad care, as so many Canadian parents still must do.

While doing graduate work (including looking first-hand at Swedish policy and programs) on the special changes needed to allow mothers a chance at equality and an opportunity to enjoy parenting, I became committed to the struggle for child care and for change in the workplace to enable both fathers and mothers to spend more time with their children. Not personally subordinating "family life" to "work life," I thought it strange that some mothers would boast about being back at work just weeks after having a baby, as did some of my friends in the 1970s. As I said to the 1986 Parliamentary Task Force on Child Care:

> The more fundamental problem around the child care issue, is not really the question of non-parental care and universal funding... the more fundamental question is about the workplace. And why

should we expect the parents of young children to engage in the workplace in the same way that non-parents do?[2]

Child Care and Child Care Advocacy in Saskatchewan, 1971–1982

When the curtain opens on the child care situation in 1971 we see a dismal reality—there were licensed private centres, 636 licensed public spaces, and minimal standards—all juxtaposed with a sense of hope. Hope sprung from the commitment to child care shown by the newly elected NDP government in its promise of "child care centres and after-school programs for working parents."[3]

As 1972 drew to a close with yet no action on child care, leaders from a couple of centres foresaw that gaining further support for child care was going to be tough. Late in 1972, the Saskatoon Daycare Development Committee was formed and began a series of private meetings with MLAs and cabinet ministers.[4] While this seemed like a good strategy, given the government's pledge to child care, it was only after three publicly reported events (the establishment of a broadly based child care coalition which included labour and church activists; a media-covered public meeting; and a demonstration at the legislature) that the government reluctantly moved to bring in new child care policy in March 1974. It is telling that in the throne speech of 1973 there was no mention of child care. That advocacy had played a role in prompting action on child care is also suggested in a memo sent from the deputy minister in charge of child care to the Department of Finance:

> The government and department have been under considerable pressure, especially during the past year, to substantially increase their support for the day care of children in Saskatchewan in response to needs in the community and in fulfilment of political commitments. The existing very limited program is clearly inadequate.[5]

The 1974 budget saw an increase in funding to child care from $100,000 to $1.7 million. It raised subsidies, eligibility levels and start-up funds, made provision for family daycare homes and, very importantly, established non-profit, parent-controlled centres as the major delivery mechanism for child care. Most child care advocates saw this as a real victory. At this time there was very little critique of child care as a selectively subsidized user-pay service. Following this victory, there appears to have been little organized child care advocacy. There also was limited monitoring of the gap between the child care budget and actual spending. For fiscal years ending in 1975, 1976, 1977 and 1978, an average of only 39.5 percent of day care budgets was spent!

In 1979, the government decided to evaluate the 1974 reforms. Questionnaires were sent to centres. It was that questionnaire in my child's cubby that propelled me into child care advocacy. Our family had been appalled when, upon moving to Saskatchewan in 1979, we spent two days touring church basements of all places in search of child care. I was a community developer at a local college and upon being told that "the evaluation process will just consist of the parent users answering these questions," our college organized a community dialogue to help parents make an informed assessment as to what constituted high-quality child care. The Daycare Evaluation Coordinating Committee, which emerged out of this process, succeeded in pressuring the government to hold public hearings and vow that the report would be made public. Thus, a closed stakeholder process had become a public citizen process.

When the hearings finished, a small broadly based advocacy group called Action Child Care was formed, and again the child care community was hopeful—given the success of the hearings and the media's support for improvements in child care. When word got out that the budget for 1981/82 included a 10 percent increase for child care, Action Child Care organized a rally of 300 that converged on the NDP annual convention. Three demands were made at the rally: increased spaces, higher standards and significant direct funding. Child care was once again (as in 1973–1974) a hot public issue.

Things were also hot within the advocacy movement. User fees were going up and some parents were forced to switch to unlicensed care. An ongoing debate about pressing for money versus policy change came to a head when a copy of the evaluation report was leaked to Action Child Care. Instead of releasing it to the press, the group used it as a bargaining chip around the upcoming budget. The issue that united this diverse group was the need for more money. And few advocates were prepared to trade money for a new approach to child care which conceptualized it as a universal service, stripped of its social welfare origins. The government got the message and then released a budget, their last for the next decade, in which child care funding was doubled from the previous year. As in 1973–1974 the government had responded to child care as a genuine public issue.

Many activists felt that getting the budget doubled was a victory. It meant a great deal to those who could not afford child care. From a policy perspective, however, the victory was hollow. The "1981 changes served to further entrench the selectively-subsidized, user-fee approach to day care."[6]

Clearly, 1971–1982 saw significant child care advocacy in Saskatchewan. Further, a strong case can be made that without such advocacy, important improvements in child care would not have happened. Why such advocacy was necessary in the first place, and why it yielded only modest success in achieving progressive child care policy, given the legacy of radical policy reform by social democratic governments in Saskatchewan (medicare and occupational health and safety legislation come quickly to mind), are questions that merit consideration in any analysis of the struggle for child care in this province. Further, the failure of the NDP to take a social democratic approach to child care is particularly astonishing in respect to the Blakeney years (rather than to the Romanow term of 1991–2000), because in the 1970s, unlike two decades later, enhancements were still being made to the welfare state. In fact, the Blakeney government was willing to act on social democratic principle on some issues, even in the face of practical obstacles. The successful, but difficult, struggle to bring potash production under public ownership is a case in point. In contrast, my review of public accounts, orders-in-council, entries within Hansard and resolutions passed at NDP conventions, as well as my scrutiny of numerous internal documents, leads me to argue that there was much in place (including, of course, the structural prerequisite for child care, due to the increasing employment of mothers) to support a progressive approach to child care: there was money available—even some from the limited child care budget; there was significant support from within the bureaucracy—evident in papers, sponsored research and in the progressive recommendations of senior bureaucrats; and finally, there was consistent (if not always well thought out) support for child care from the NDP rank and file, as expressed at the annual conventions.

So why was child care such a hard sell to the NDP government of Allan Blakeney? What prevented the social democrats from taking on this issue which has many of the same inequities that marked premedicare health care? The record from Hansard suggests where the answer to this critical question likely lies. A prominent cabinet minister in the Blakeney inner circle addressed the legislature, saying, "the lowest priority [for public spending for child care] is where the parent has adequate income... but merely wants someone else to look after the children. In all possible cases people who have children should raise them too."[7] Shortly after this comment was made, another leading NDPer rose in the House to acknowledge the legitimacy of an opposition member's linkage of child care to abortion, summarily stating, "the mother's place is in the home." Despite the damning weight of this statement, the premier subsequently appointed this same member minister in charge of child care.[8] Further, the key planning document that informed the unprogressive 1974 child care reform also makes a bold claim about the assumed place of women. The striking similarity of these attitudes suggests that the NDP politicians generating the document were not out of sync with the dominant thinking of those within the NDP inner circle.[9] For the Blakeney government, the main issue in the child care debate was not simply money; rather at issue was a fixed notion about which mothers merited state support to work outside of the home. Universal funding for child care was rejected by the government due to a belief that public funding for child care should be limited, in the main, to instances where the mother's employment was necessary for the economic survival of her family.

Needless to say, politicians who argued that those who have families ought to stay home and care for them did not mean that all the fathers in Saskatchewan ought to quit their jobs! Researcher Mary Ruggie has documented a relationship between the ideological conception a society has about mothers' labour-force attachment and whether in the given society, programs such as child care are universally available. After a look at the evidence, Ruggie would likely agree that the main stumbling block to progressive child care in the NDP heartland in the 1970s was good-old-fashioned sexism.[10] My own research in this area has yielded ample evidence to support the claim that sexism was the culprit in the 1970s child care drama in Saskatchewan. Yet, it must also be said that the focus of child care advocacy during this period on a single material solution to the complex dilemmas faced by employed parents did little to foster a broad base of active support for child care and/or other progressive responses to the reality of the dual-income family particularly as that reality relates to the above culprit.

Child Care and Child Care Advocacy in Saskatchewan, 1982–1990

Almost at the very moment child care made it onto the national agenda, Saskatchewan advocates were preoccupied with resisting commercial child care. In 1982, the Canadian Day Care Advocacy Association (CDCAA) was formed at a conference in Winnipeg that was attended by more than sixty activists from Saskatchewan. The CDCAA was instrumental in putting child care on the national policy agenda. Federally linked venues that soon emerged provided high-profile platforms for advocacy in this province. Opportunities for advancing the child care cause with both Ottawa and Regina included the 1984 Ministerial Task Force; the 1984 federal election in which child care was, for the first time, an issue; the 1986 Parliamentary Task Force on Child Care; and the 1987 federal government response to child care.

A brief sketch of child care and child care advocacy in Saskatchewan at the close of the 1980s can be deceptive. In 1988 the child care budget was $13 million—twice that spent in 1982. Spaces had increased from 3,914 to 6,060, all of which were in non-profit centres or family-child care homes. And, on the advocacy side, the small, fiery coalition, Action Child Care, based primarily in Saskatoon, had evolved into a provincewide, membership-based association called the Saskatchewan Child Care Association (SCCA).

Unfortunately this sketch misses the real story. For while more spaces had been opened, subsidies were still at 1982 levels. This freezing of support had severe consequences for staff wages and the quality of care, but these issues got little attention as the 1980s proceeded, since advocates' energy was focused on the profit/non-profit debate. Soon after the 1982 election, child care supporters had to gear-up for another child care review. Once again, after being pressured, it was agreed that the 1983 review would involve public hearings. At these well-attended meetings child care supporters, church activists and labour organizers did an admirable job of identifying the strengths of the parent-controlled, non-profit model. It seemed that the minister in charge agreed that there was no place for commercial care in Saskatchewan. As such, in December 1983, he wrote the following to his Child Care Advisory Board:

> Among individuals and groups who have made submissions there has been no support for the introduction of private day care. This sentiment coupled with Ms. Zazalenchuk's personal research has led her to inform me she will not be recommending that private day care for profit be permitted to operate in Saskatchewan.[11]

A few weeks later, after confirming these sentiments at a public meeting, the minister told his same advisors that small commercial centres were, in fact, an option for the province. The majority of the advisory board members supported this option. However, I resigned. The 1984 report on the previous year's hearing said very little but did recommend "owner-operated child care mini-centres as one option and alternative for

Saskatchewan through the 80s and 90s."[12] Shortly after the release of this report, commercial child care became a public issue under the leadership of Action Child Care. At well-attended forums in Saskatoon and Regina, representatives from labour, children's services, women's groups, churches and child care centres spoke out against commercial care. Child care advocates from across Canada supported this struggle. Following these forums, the government appeared to lose interest in commercial child care, and no moves were made to change the non-profit policy. A letter from the Saskatchewan minister to MP Ray Hnatyshyn sent one year later suggests that the non-profit system was safe, even if the federal government offered cost-sharing dollars to commercial centres.

> Should a change in Federal legislation actually occur for this province, I do not foresee any significant shifts away from the predominately non-profit, parent controlled centres which presently exist.... In addition, little pressure exists from within the private sector at present to expand into the day care field....Nor do we foresee any significant shifts in the mode of delivering day care service in Saskatchewan should a reinterpretation or regulatory change be made to the Canada Assistance Plan which would eventually result in the cost sharing of commercial operation.[13]

The minister who wrote this letter was defeated in the 1986 election, and all was quiet on the front until, in 1987, the federal government announced their plan to extend public funding to users of commercial centres. In June 1988, a bill was introduced which included provision for commercial care. The Saskatchewan Child Care Association tried to fight this legislation, but the conditions for a successful fight did not exist: "Parents and staff were exhausted."[14] Further, the province was preoccupied with the threat of privatizing crown corporations.

So it came to be that in 1989 provincial legislation allowing the licensing of new commercial centres was passed. As it turned out, Saskatchewan did not get into commercial child care. The regulations which accompanied the new Act were not put in place until late 1990 and, barely ten months later, the NDP were back in government.

Although this period put a great deal of stress on Saskatchewan child care advocates, almost any review of this phase of the struggle for child care in Saskatchewan would credit citizen advocacy with preventing commercial child care from taking hold in the province. This was no small success.

Child Care Advocacy and Child Care in Saskatchewan, 1992–2000

Those who had hoped that child care would flourish upon the NDP's 1991 re-election have been disappointed. In 1998–1999, $19 million was spent on child care and there were 7,547 licensed spaces. The subsidy for preschool spaces remained at 1982 levels, although the subsidy for infants and toddlers increased. As well, the eligible income level for subsidy did not change. In 1992, 67 percent of users received subsidy, while in 1999, only 54 percent did so—meaning the child care system grew less income-mixed and more stratified. In fact, if the ratio of subsidy eligibility and median family income had remained constant from 1982, the income level for full subsidy today would be $28,000 not the actual $19,000. Still, more money than ever before is spent on child care, with average annual new dollars almost twice what they were in the preceding two decades. The bulk of new money spent in the last seven years has been allocated to improving specific features of child care services that had been badly neglected. Infant spaces and spaces for babies of teen parents more than doubled during this period. Grants for special needs programs more than doubled, while the average number of spaces opened per year was significantly lower than it was in previous decades. In 1996, a wage enhancement grant was implemented which saw the average hourly child care wage increase from $7.52 to $10.47. Meanwhile, the legislation that permits commercial care has not been struck down. This has avoided what almost everyone, including most advocates, feels would be a non-productive, politically charged battle. Because for-profit centres cannot access public funds, they soon close or are transformed into non-profit entities. Overall this crude snapshot suggests that, while the government has allocated new dollars for child care, the program has become less focused on affordable, high-quality care for children of employed families.

Child care was already on the provincial and national policy agendas when the Saskatchewan Child Care Association was formed in 1987. There were high hopes for this provincewide organization, which was formed through a process put in place by Action Child Care. Before long, however, it was clear that the SCCA's birth had actually tempered the provincial advocacy bite. A change in who was leading the advocacy charge was immediately apparent—the new leaders were primarily people who worked in centre-based care. This made sense, but it also meant a directional shift toward professionalizing child care workers and providing necessary services to this group. While this emphasis made the SCCA more attractive to child care professionals, it also changed advocacy politics in the province. Given the evolution of child care policy in this province, it can be argued that, in taking the direction they have, the SCCA forfeited the two ingredients—a broad base of supporters (many of whom are not directly linked to child care) and public displays of concern—that had proven effective in encouraging the community to have more say about child care spending. My sense is that during the 1990s, child care advocates as represented by the SCCA, have not been very influential in pushing government to take specific action on child care (as was the case in 1974, 1981 and 1984). Still it could be said that the improvements that government has made since 1991 have been influenced by advocates. The lack of a strong voice in the province advocating child care as an accessible service for the average working family and the SCAA's new, less populist agenda has meant that the government is increasingly comfortable in targeting new funds toward government (not advocates') priorities.

As of summer 2000, plans are underway to formalize the evolution of the SCCA from a child care advocacy group to an organization dedicated to the advancement of early childhood education. It is a change that is likely music to the ears of government and professionally oriented groups who do not want to hear the drumbeat for child care for working families. This is also an honest change, in that the SCAA is not currently advocating for child care. When I interviewed the executive director, I asked about the organization's main child care policy priority and was told that they did not have a list per se, but that their main priority was building support for a continuum of early childhood education services.[15] Apparently, the group has found little public support for child care and, due to budget constraints, has not emphasized awareness with the general public. Other advocates point out that the SCCA's failure to lobby for child care was the impetus for a new formation in spring 2000. This emergent group organized a Day of Action (May 16, 2000)[.16] which twelve out of twenty centres endorsed by closing. The action gathered directors, child care teachers, parents and board members to walk through Saskatoon calling on government for a more serious provincial child care agenda.

It would seem that citizen-based child care advocacy has played a less critical (and certainly a less dramatic) role in shaping child care policy from 1992–2000 than it did in the two earlier periods discussed. Recent political activity in Saskatoon at the grassroots level, however, points to new advocacy energy which may yet challenge the provincial government's passive approach to child care. Likewise, the upcoming metamorphosis of the SCCA may create more public support for childhood programming including child care.

Whether there will ever be a lasting, broadly based, unified public voice in Saskatchewan that demands public policy support for average-income, employed families with dependent children, remains to be seen.

The Lessons of History: What Seems to Have Worked; What Needs to Change

A review of the Saskatchewan experience yields one clear conclusion: child care advocacy has played a major role in shaping child care policy in Saskatchewan. This review also suggests that occasions of effective child care advocacy in this province share several key features.

One such feature is the engagement of a broad range public citizens: that is, advocates ought to be sceptical of moving to the stakeholder model usually favoured by government. Maintaining the active involvement of individuals whose careers or jobs are not directly connected to a particular issue has proven difficult, but it seems to be a key to effective advocacy. Another such feature involves public displays of concern accompanied by media attention. The presence of a diverse critical mass of supporters is crucial for a positive, inclusive representation of the issue. It seems better to have, for example, three church groups, two trade unions and the boards of several centres all meet with a variety of politicians than it is to have an association president deliver a brilliant brief to the minister in charge of child care. Unfortunately, when advocates become tied into dealing with government, they frequently spend more time preparing documents and/or presentations that will impress educated professionals than they do listening and talking to individuals in their local communities. Another feature of successful advocacy that stands out is its outreach to the "unconverted" through awareness work that is educational as opposed to promotional in nature. Those with advocacy goals must consider whether it is wise to combine both a service and an advocacy mandate within a single organization. Finally the most effective advocacy campaigns have consistently been those closely linked with and supported by a wide variety of national and international organizations and networks.

This brief review of some twenty-nine years of child care advocacy in Saskatchewan demonstrates that child care advocacy has been necessary in this province. Governments throughout this span of time (especially in the 1971–1991 period) have needed to be convinced to act in the better interests of child care.

Having said the above, the time for rethinking the direction (or vision) and style of child care advocacy is long overdue. However it would be foolish to suggest that the failure to achieve adequate child care, either in Saskatchewan or in the whole of Canada, can be attributed to those aspects of child care advocacy which I describe as problematic. It is important to acknowledge that a number of structural changes in Canadian society have mitigated against the implementation of adequate child care policy at both the provincial and federal levels. Neo-liberalism's attack on publicly funded services has made an expansion of the welfare state almost impossible. Changes in the structure of work and technology have raised issues about the appeal of child care. Further, it is often claimed that changing demographics have reduced public support for child care.

Although I publicly describe myself as an unrepentant supporter of child care, I have over many years been frustrated with what I call the "vision" and "style" of child care advocacy in Saskatchewan and in the country as a whole. A vision is an ideal that motivates one to achieve something even though the idealized state will never be reached. When advocating for new public policy, the particular "vision" that is conveyed is critical and should be chosen accordingly, because it needs to set up a picture of a desired state that the public believes in, is willing to speak out for and ultimately, is willing to pay for. The vision has to have emotional and cognitive appeal. Unless one is speaking primarily to those who are desperate, the speaker needs to appeal not only to the audience's immediate situation but to their dearly held beliefs and values.

The vision that child care advocates are pursuing is one of a service which provides affordable, accessible, publicly funded facilities staffed by professionals who provide high-quality care for children while the parents are at work. This vision appeals only to those who need and want this service. Such a vision lacks emotional appeal for the many people who are not sure of what they want for child care as well as for those who feel "boxed-in" by the very fact that they need child care in the first place. Further, this vision puts people in a passive position when many are looking to a participatory model. Given a choice, many people prefer that government and others do a variety of things to create more of an "enabling environment" in which parents can experiment with many options in a fluid and flexible fashion. The vision that informs the following scenario is very different than the one that informs most discussions about child care.

Imagine you are attending a discussion of family-tailored decision making around care for young children. Here you participate in a dramatization in which (after considerable discussion) the following is decided by a couple about to have their first child: for the first year both father and mother will work half-time, each claiming parental benefit. By year two, because of the career needs of mother, father will work half time, mother full time on a juggled-hours basis (having discussed their plan with the work/family committee at their workplace) so that nonparental care is needed for only two afternoons a week. This care will be provided by a stay-at-home mother who is not licensed, but who has become familiar with the parents through their mutual involvement in the neigh-bourhood Family Support Centre. When baby is about two-and-a-half years old, the parents will use the small, parent-controlled, licensed, primarily publicly funded child care centre attached to the Family Support Centre. Further, the employer of each parent will provide a paid half-day per month so that the parents can "work" in the centre—where, as it turns out, given the extensive work done with employers and unions, in general a parent is present every half day.

The above scenario is informed by a vision which grows out of an emancipatory analysis of gender issues and speaks of a collective desire and capacity to struggle for agency and impact on what society offers in terms of work. On the matter of gender, it seems that much of the current thinking about child care assumes that maternal employment necessitates nonparental care, even for very young children. Much liberal feminist thought in the last two decades perceived moving child care out of the family as a way of freeing women. The problem is, however, that this approach does little to alter gender roles within the family or to change children's highly gendered, early socialization. As feminist theorist Jean Cohen points out, it may be better to degender the familial tasks of raising children than to argue for commodifying the tasks that the family now does. She writes:

> Modernization has already involved the migration of work, (including education), from the home to the market. But surely a large part of a specifically feminist solution to the double burden of the working mother, to the subordination attached to the homemaker role and to labour market inequities must entail the degendering of the childrearing, nurturing, and homemaker roles along with a fight against the gendered division of labour in the workplace.[17]

Here, raising the gender issue, questions whether child care advo-cacy that presses almost singularly for spaces for nonparental care, is simply too adaptive to the dominant culture. The same issue comes up with respect to work. Why should child care advocates press for twenty-four-hour care when in many cases employees with young children would rather that someone support their desire for regular day work? Although there are inequities and, in many cases, a certain superficiality regarding the extent to which workplaces are becoming family-friendly, the broad and growing appeal of this issue reflects the interest employees have in adapting the workplace to their needs. Hence the vision of child care advocacy needs to be recast and broadened to speak to the larger issue of raising children in dual-income families instead of focusing solely on the legitimate struggle for more and better child care.

The narrow vision of much child care advocacy has created a focus on selling policy and programmatic solutions. It has the feel of "old politics." It pays scant attention to creating environments where people can come together to think about how to raise children, now that it is not simply a matter of relegating this task to mothers. These are not new concerns for me. In 1984, I failed to convince my colleagues in the Canadian Day Care Advocacy Association to press the federal Task Force on Child Care to engage Canadians in a discussion, which instead of focusing on child care per se looked at how we could facilitate equality for all women, including mothers, and raise happy, healthy children. Later, while chairing the 1992 Saskatchewan Task Force on Child Care, I was struck by the difference between talking with advocates versus parents; conversations with child care advocates were all about spaces and funding, while meetings with parents were about much more— wanting a husband to work less overtime, the desire for job sharing, the longing for a former supervisor who was herself a parent—alongside the need for more child care spaces. These observations are not intended to indict child care advocates or repudiate my own involvement in distributing standardized position papers to be "presented" by local activists. After all, the job of gaining a small bit of influence for constituencies which have little voice in this society is no small task. However, these examples illustrate the need to further democratize all politics, including community- and issue-based politics. Social theorists who have been thinking about how to support citizen democracy argue that what is needed are "social learning" venues where citizens, not stakeholders, can undertake a discourse that is aimed at influencing the political culture, which may in turn have an impact on parliamentary and electoral politics.[18] Such a participatory model is particularly necessary today as fewer people are willing to simply follow an established plan or "line" which is created by a leadership group. The point here is that an emphasis on direct lobbying often draws social movements too close to the status-quo thinking that ordinarily dominates government and the popular media.

Change in vision and style may make the quest for child care the popular and exciting social movement it ought to be (given that most parents are now employed and face many complications in combining earning and parenting). Obviously, child care will never have the support of those who yearn for a return of the traditional, male-breadwinner family. But it ought to have the active support (i.e., more than saying yes to a poll) of dual-earner families. An emancipatory child care agenda that speaks to the problems such families experience—lack of time/energy, stress, sexism, consumerism and such—in a style that emphasizes multiple family-tailored child care options may garner the needed energy to put up a good fight against the structural barriers to progressive public policy that currently characterize this society.

Notes

1. This chapter is dedicated to the memory of Janice Kell, who died in May 1999. Janice was involved in child care advocacy in Saskatchewan from 1979 to 1984–1985. Advocates from across the country may well recall her robust participation at the Winnipeg conference in 1982. Her generous spirit has been with me as I wrote this piece, since as a woman who was not involved in raising children and was not connected professionally in any way to child care, she in my mind, represents the very best of the "citizen-advocate," who tackles an issue simply because it needs to be dealt with if our communities are to be better places for more people.

2. Saskatoon Woman's Calendar Collective 1988: 52.

3. Saskatchewan NDP 1971: 14.

4. Information from files of Dayle Bowman of Saskatoon.

5. I obtained a copy of this memo from Dayle Bowman, Saskatoon.

6. Martin 1995: 38.

7. Hansard 1973–74: 624.

8. Hansard 1973–74: 1052.

9. "Universal daycare becomes an economically justified goal in different societies or periods of time when it is desirable [my emphasis] to have women as productive members in the work force outside the home ... at present there is no need to have more women in productive capacities outside the home ... we have an unemployment problem of major proportions" (Department of Saskatchewan Social Services 1974: 11.)

10. Ruggie 1984.

11. Gordon Dirks, letter to Dawn Shark, Chairperson Daycare Advisory Board, 1983.

12. Zazalenchuk 1984: 20.

13. Gordon Dirks, letter to R. Hnatyshyn, September 11, 1985.
14. Martin 1991: 249.
15. Interview with Susan Delanoy, May 9, 2000, Saskatoon.
16. Interview with Marta Jurio, May 18, 2000, Saskatoon.
17. Cohen 1992: 201–54.
18. Chambers 1995: 165–79.

Chapter 10

Federal Child Care Policy Development
From World War II to 2000

Rebecca Kelley Scherer

Introduction

In Canada, child care and other social policy issues have always been the responsibility of the provincial governments. The federal government has, however, influenced policy around social, health and education issues in a number of ways. Federal involvement has ranged from providing funding for programs considered important by the federal government, to facilitating cost-sharing programs, to utilizing the tax system to subsidize programs such as child care. Child care initiatives from the federal government have been accidental, as in the case of the Canada Assistance Plan, and deliberate, as in the introduction of Bill C-144, the national child care bill that died on the table. Historically, child care policy in Canada has emerged from multiple visions, few of them related to child care services per se:

> The origins of child care in Canada actually date back to late-nineteenth-century social reform, which has resulted in child care being placed in the historical context of the social welfare system.[1]

Subsequent funding programs have kept child care within a social welfare context by providing funding by way of cost-shared grants and subsidies for low-income families and the provision of tax deductions. These measures have been offered instead of a publicly funded system based on universal entitlement for all children.

This chapter provides a chronological review of federal initiatives that directly or indirectly influence child care policy. An appendix at the end compiles this evidence in a date line.

Dominion-Provincial Wartime Agreement

During World War II, the federal government under Prime Minister MacKenzie King offered funding for child care as part of the war effort:[2]

> World War II represented a departure from the custodial model of day care; the federal government became involved for the first time in day-care financing under the Dominion-Provincial War-time Agreement. This legislation emphasized that the nurseries were an emergency measure linked to mothers' participation in industries deemed essential to the war effort.[3]

The Dominion-Provincial Wartime Agreement provided start-up and operating costs for child care centers on a cost-shared basis. Initially, to receive funding, a province had to show that at least 75 percent of mothers using the service were working in war-related industries. While the federal government removed the 75 percent requirement, only Ontario and Quebec actually opened daycare centers under the program. Although Alberta signed the agreement, an advisory committee quickly refuted the need for child care in Alberta.[4] In 1945, the Dominion-Provincial Wartime Agreement was withdrawn and the federal government withdrew from funding child care. Since then, there has never been a national child care program.

Family Allowance

Following the Great Depression and World War II the federal government introduced a universal Family Allowance program in 1945.[5] Some authors have suggested that this payment to families with children under the age of eighteen reflected a federal recognition of the cost of raising children.[6] However, Durst and Ursel offer an alternate interpretation that family allowances were brought in as an attempt to keep wages low and maintain labour market competition.[7] The universal Family Allowance was introduced unilaterally by the federal government and designed by departments not usually involved in social policy, such as the Department of External Affairs, the Department of Finance and the Bank of Canada.[8]

Whether designed to support families and/or to suppress wages, the universal program was available to all families and therefore did not create an artificial hierarchy of deserving and undeserving recipients.

The program did not cost much more than a targeted program and had the added benefit of eliminating the need for eligibility criteria.[9] In 1989, Progressive Conservative Prime Minister Brian Mulroney introduced a clawback of the family allowance payments for middle- and upper-income families through the income tax system. Hence Family Allowance was no longer a universal program.[10] In 1993, under Prime Minister Jean Chretien's Liberal government, the Family Allowance program, the Child Tax Credit and the non-refundable tax credit were rolled together into a new income-tested program called the Child Tax Benefit. The Child Tax Benefit is an income support program targeted to low-income families.

Canada Assistance Plan

In 1966 the federal government, under Liberal Prime Minister Lester Pearson, introduced the Canadian Assistance Plan (CAP). CAP was a federal-provincial cost-sharing arrangement that allowed provinces to encourage the development of "non-profit services that have as their objective the lessening, removal or prevention of the causes and effects of poverty, child neglect, or dependence on public assistance."[11] Although CAP was never intended to fund child care, CAP allowed provinces to fund the costs of child care for low-income families within a welfare framework.[12] Cost-shared funding agreements allowed the federal government to support the development of child care programs in Canada, even though it was an area of provincial responsibility:

> Gradually, CAP's shared-cost agreements with the provinces and territories permitted expansion in the child care system. Yet, because CAP treated child care like other welfare services, subsidies for child-care spaces were made available only to lower-income families, barring the development of a child-care system designed to meet the needs of all children.[13]

In 1990, the federal government under Brian Mulroney placed a ceiling on CAP spending that resulted in a reduction of dollars for the richer "have" provinces of British Columbia, Alberta and Ontario. No longer did these provinces receive a matching federal dollar for every provincial dollar spent on welfare services. The cap on CAP had significant impact in reducing the expansion of regulated child care in those provinces affected.[14]

Local Initiatives Plan and Department
of Regional Economic Development

In 1970, the Liberal federal government under Prime Minister Pierre Elliott Trudeau introduced the Local Initiatives Projects (LIP), a federal job creation program. While in existence, this program allowed for the development and operation of community-based child care programs.[15] LIP was withdrawn in 1973. At the same time the federal government also introduced a plan under the Department of Regional Economic Expansion (DREE) that allowed the development of child care programs in rural areas for a target group of economically and socially disadvantaged families.[16] The development of child care programs through these projects was viewed particularly as an opportunity for job creation and service provision to an at-risk population rather than as a service for all children, families and communities.

Child Care Expense Deduction

In 1971, the federal government introduced the Child Care Expense Deduction (CCED) provision of the *Income Tax Act*. The CCED allows parents to deduct a percentage of their receipted child care expenses. This tax measure favours middle- and upper-income families in that the value of the deduction increases with income.[17] Lower-income families are more likely to use unregulated care with its generally lower cost. Unregulated care is frequently not receipted and consequently many lower-income families are unable to take advantage of the CCED. In 1978, the federal government introduced the Child Tax Credit through the *Income Tax Act*. The Child Tax Credit was means tested and targeted to low-income families. The Child Tax Credit was a supplement to low-income families, not a child care subsidy or expense deduction. In 1988, the Conservatives under Brian Mulroney tightened eligibility rules for the Child Tax Credit.

Katie Cooke Task Force

In 1984, the Liberal government appointed a task force to examine the issue of child care in Canada. The chair of the task force was Katie Cooke, the first president of the Canadian Advisory Council on the Status of Women. The other members of the task force were Renee Edwards, executive director of the Victoria Day Care Services in Toronto; Jack R. London, professor of law at the University of Manitoba; and Ruth Rose-Lizee, professor of economics at the University of Quebec. The assembly of these individuals was a direct response to prevailing social concerns of the time:

Providing quality child care for today's and tomorrow's children, and adequate leave policies for parents are major challenges of the 1980s. The federal government recognized the concern of parents and leading professionals in the field when, in May 1984, it appointed a Task Force on Child Care to study the issue and make recommendations to the government.[18]

The *Report of the Task Force on Child Care* was released in March 1986 and covered a wide range of issues. The task force evaluated child care in Canada by examining numerous facets of family life: changing family dynamics and needs; parental leave needs and their current provisions; current child care arrangements (both formal and informal); needs of parents; needs of caregivers; and issues pertaining to quality as well as the economic costs and benefits of public child care. The task force also looked at child care provisions in other countries as well as the delivery of other social programs in Canada to suggest means of delivering a national child care program. The task force made a number of recommendations that included immediate, short-term and long-term goals in the development of a national system of quality child care. These recommendations recognize both the need for a federal role and the jurisdictional issues and individual needs of each province and territory.[19]

Parliamentary Committee on Child Care
Following the appointment of the task force, the Progressive Conservatives were elected in 1984. During the election campaign the Progressive Conservatives included a national child care program in their campaign platform. In November 1985, before the task force reported, the Mulroney government appointed a Special Parliamentary Committee on Child Care, chaired by Conservative MP Shirley Martin.[20] The committee was to examine and report on the child care needs of the Canadian family, bearing in mind a focus on the child. In the end, the Martin committee made thirty-nine recommendations. However, members did not agree on the need for child care nor on the role of government in providing such services.

The committee was deeply split, and in the end the Liberal and NDP members issued dissenting minority reports. The Conservative majority thought that the focus should be on giving money to parents to pay for child care; the Liberals and NDP wanted governments to invest in the building and operation of more child-care spaces.[21]

Bill C-144

By 1988, the Progressive Conservatives had developed their National Strategy on Child Care:

> The strategy was not a new national government program. Instead, it was a package of existing tax measures with some additional funding to create and operate new child-care spaces. The funding was seriously inadequate: it was targeted to create 200,000 new spaces over seven years, when the actual present need is over a million spaces.[22]

This strategy required negotiating with the provinces and undertaking the parliamentary committee process. Such a long process involved producing reports on issues requested by the committee, holding public hearings and having the bill read in the House and Senate. Many advocates were concerned with the content of Bill C-144 and worked at increasing public awareness of its shortcomings:

> Conclusion: in its own terms, as we think we have demonstrated above, Bill C-144 fails. It does not meet its own criteria of availability, affordability, quality or accessibility, and it puts at risk certain populations served by the existing child care arrangements. Other criteria could have been presented. CDCAA (Canadian Day Care Advocacy Association) wishes that this committee would measure the bill against additional principles suggested by CDCAA and other major groups.[23]

When the Progressive Conservatives called an election in 1988, Bill C-144 died on the order table in Senate. Following their re-election, the Progressive Conservatives did not revive Bill C-144, and in 1992 Don Mazankowski, Minister of Finance, announced there would be no national child care program.

Canada Child Tax Benefit

In 1997, the federal government announced the creation of the Canada Child Tax Benefit as part of its strategy to eliminate child poverty. This is a supplement to be paid to low-income families combining the Child Tax Benefit with the Working Income Supplement (WIS). "Its primary goal is to encourage people to move from welfare to work by offering income supplements to working-poor families."[24] This is a federal program of cash supports to individuals, negotiated with the provinces and territories, that allows the provinces and territories to deduct the payment from funds that social assistance recipients collect. This clawback from welfare families effectively makes it a supplement benefitting only working-poor families, not families on social assistance—the poorest of the poor. Provinces and territories agreed to "reinvest" their Social Assistance savings in programs for poor children. The argument was made that the new Child Tax Benefit would provide a disincentive to welfare parents, because the supplement was not enough to cover the cost of quality child care should the welfare recipient move into the workforce.[25] As well, a requirement for the provinces to provide child care was not included in the discussions.

Community Action Program for Children and Aboriginal Headstart

In 1991 the federal government announced two programs, the Community Action Program for Children (CAPC) and Aboriginal Headstart, that were to be 100 percent federally funded. These federally funded service-delivery programs were designed to benefit children, but were not designed to deliver child care. Aboriginal Headstart, modeled on the American Headstart program, was to provide targeted early intervention programs for aboriginal children. CAPC was to encourage the development of programs for children by facilitating a partnership of community groups. "CAPC was designed to support integrated health and social services for families with young children."[26] However, before the program actually began in 1993, it had already had its budget reduced. CAPC lost more funding in 1996. In 1997, the federal government announced additional funds for CAPC, but the budget was still less than the amount originally announced in 1991. CAPC is a complicated community development program with several layers of administration. It has yet to reach the goals set out in its 1991 announcement.[27]

The Debt/Deficit Era

In 1993 the Liberals included the development and expansion of a national system of child care in their election platform (their so-called Red Book). After they were elected, the Liberals became committed to the elimination of the deficit and the reduction of the debt. Social programs became the scapegoat of the deficit/debt agenda, despite evidence that social programs were not major contributors to the accumulated debt and deficit situation.[28] Consequent budget-cutting measures had negative impacts on social programs, including child care.[29] Despite the commitment of Health and Social Services Minister Lloyd Axworthy and his attempt to introduce a national program late in 1995, the government did not fulfill the Red Book promise on child care. Following a cabinet shuffle in January 1996 that resulted in a new Minister of Health and Social Services, who was not supportive of child care, the Liberals retreated from child care negotiations.[30] This shift in emphasis resulted in the removal of child care from the federal agenda. Following the cabinet shuffle of 1996, elimination of the National Day Care Information Center meant that there remained not a single federal bureaucrat to contact regarding child care issues.

Canada Health and Social Transfer
Prior to 1995, funds for child care were cost-shared between the federal and provincial/territorial governments. In 1995, the federal government introduced the Canada Health and Social Transfer that significantly changed the funding mechanisms for social programs, including child care.[31] The funds from the federal government for health, social services and education were moved to a block funding arrangement, the delivery of which did not require the provinces to maintain current levels of funding. At the same time, the amount of funding in the block from the federal government was decreased. Not surprisingly this loss of funding negatively impacted child care services across Canada.[32]

Social Union Framework Agreement
In February 1999, the federal government and all provincial and territorial governments except Quebec signed a social union framework known as SUFA. According to its negotiators, "the February 1999 Social Union Framework Agreement signals an era of more effective cooperation among governments on social issues, including children."[33] The social union framework is a three-year agreement encompassing the areas of health and social programs.[34]

While the agreement mentions commitments, guidelines and principles that are agreed upon, it does not mandate actions to implement these commitments, guidelines and principles. In order to develop a new program there must be the agreement of a majority of the provinces and territories and an established accountability mechanism.[35] There is potential under this agreement to have discussions around a more comprehensive child care system, but such a discussion would be contingent upon the agreement of a majority of provinces and territories even to begin talks. Given such a stipulation, a national child care program seems highly unlikely. In fact, it is probable that we would not have a medicare system had SUFA been in place then! SUFA is slated for review in 2002.

National Children's Agenda

In June 1999, the federal and provincial/territorial governments released the results of their discussions around a National Children's Agenda (NCA). The National Children's Agenda is a product of the Federal-Provincial-Territorial Council of Ministers on Social Policy Renewal. The council was created in 1996 by the first ministers to discuss social policy issues in the wake of the CHST. Despite recognizing "children are our country's strength today, and in the future,"[36] the *National Children's Agenda* is a document without substance, and it does not actually commit to creating better policies for children. The document states, "As a nation we aspire to have children who are (1) Healthy, physically and emotionally. (2) Safe and secure. (3) Successful at learning. (4) Socially engaged and responsible." These are the four goals of the NCA. The document then goes on to identify the following as six key areas where "cooperative effort can have positive effects on children": (1) supporting parents and strengthening families; (2) enhancing early childhood development; (3) improving economic security for families; (4) providing early and continuous learning experiences; (5) fostering strong adolescent development; and (6) creating supportive, safe and violence-free communities. Although the document discusses the importance of cooperative efforts, there are no concrete actions that will lead to nationwide policies for children. There is some discussion suggesting that the government's role is to make information accessible to the public and some talk of the role of the voluntary sector in program delivery. However, there is no discussion of using the NCA as a means of prioritizing government policy to benefit Canada's children and families. At the end of the document the council recognizes that child care is an important environmental influence in a child's life:

> At some point in time, all families use some form of supplemental child care. Children who have experienced good care, whether at home, or through formal or informal child care arrangements, have greater social competence, higher levels of language development and play, and fewer behavioural problems in elementary school than those who have experienced lower quality care.[37]

Recent Events

July 1999 saw the release of an internal Health Canada document on a comprehensive system of programs for children. The draft document shows that Health Canada bureaucrats are actually looking at a comprehensive system of programs for children and families that includes programs from conception through infancy, such as parent support programs, accessible, affordable child care, and junior/ senior kindergarten for four- and five-year-olds. Language in the document demonstrates a shift in policy formulation reflecting a greater recognition of the need for and benefits of high-quality early childhood care and education. In Calgary, the subsequent press was mostly negative, viewing programs for children as government interference in the private lives of families.[38]

July 1999 also saw a federal cabinet shuffle, with Jane Stewart replacing Pierre Pettigrew as the minister of Human Resource Development. The new minister of Human Resource Development is a strong child care supporter and a strong believer in social programs. On the CBC Radio 1 broadcast of *The House* on October 16, 1999, Jane Stewart said that the Liberals had always felt that parents were the ones ultimately responsible for their children. However, she went on to say, given the overwhelming body of research emphasizing the importance of the early years to lifelong health, school completion and success, and crime prevention, the government had come to realize that on a policy level the federal government needs to provide and support parent choices. She immediately pointed out that the federal government had put child care on the table in 1996 but that the provinces had refused to negotiate. Her recounting of the 1996 child care offer leaves out the fact that following a cabinet shuffle, the new minister, Doug Young, withdrew the said proposal, in effect pre-empting negotiation with the provinces. According to the official federal government position at the time, the provinces were ostensibly not interested.

In September 2000, following ongoing negotiations and policy discussions, the first ministers signed an agreement on early childhood development. The Canadian Intergovernmental Conference Secretariat put out a press release on September 11, 2000, stating that the first ministers were confirming their commitment to the well-being of children and that "Canada's future social vitality and economic prosperity depend on the opportunities that are provided to children today." The agreement was signed by all provinces and territories except Quebec. The federal government agreed to put $2.2 billion into the initiative over five years, and the provinces and territories agreed to spend it in any or all of four key areas for action: promoting healthy pregnancy, birth and infancy; improving parenting and family supports; strengthening early childhood development, learning and care; and strengthening community supports. While this initiative allows federal money to support programs for the early years, it does not provide for any consistency of services across the country.

The mounting evidence in favour of and public support for programs that support early childhood development led to the first ministers' agreement in September 2000. This agreement provides a framework within which more comprehensive programs could be developed at the provincial and territorial level. However, the funding attached to the initiative is not sufficient to substantially address any of the above key areas for action.

Discussion

Federal involvement in child care has taken a variety of intentional and unintentional forms. The Dominion-Provincial Wartime Agreement was a federal policy to provide child care to working mothers in order to support the war effort. The Canada Assistance Plan was never intended to fund child care. It was a cost-shared program designed to assist with the cost of supporting welfare programs for those with low incomes. The provinces quickly realized that the language was vague enough that they could cost-share subsidies to low-income parents who needed child care. The Local Initiatives Plan and the Department of Regional Economic Expansion were never designed to develop child care but were used for child care in some provinces. Child care as an issue that may require federal support was first recognized by the Royal Commission on the Status of Women in 1970 and has since been variously echoed: in 1984 by Judge Rosalie Abella in the Royal Commission Report on Canadian Employment Equity; in the 1986 Liberal Task Force on Child Care; and in National Council on Welfare Reports of 1988 and 1999. Not to be left behind, the Conservatives also appointed a Parliamentary Committee on Child Care. The two bodies, the Liberal task force and the Conservative parliamentary committee, came to similar conclusions regarding the need for a comprehensive child care program with federal support, each with a different emphasis. The Liberal task force favoured the development of a system of child care, while the Conservative parliamentary committee stressed tax measures. Child care was an issue in the 1986, 1990 and 1994 campaigns, although election promises regarding child care were never fulfilled. More recent language has moved child care away from a welfare model and towards a more comprehensive definition recognizing the lifelong impacts of the early years and the attendant role quality child care plays.

Conclusion

Federal child care policy in Canada has been inconsistent. A number of initiatives between 1945 and 1999 have impacted child care in either a direct or an indirect way. However,

> There is no Canada-wide consensus about the goals for child care; instead different provinces espouse different goals. As a result there is no society-wide perspective on the characteristics of quality child care.[39]

A Health and Welfare Canada report suggests that the lack of a national policy is also the result of particular assumptions about balancing work and families needs:

> The implicit assumptions underlying existing child care policy seem consistent with a combination of patriarchal and individual responsibility models of the family. For example, existing tax policy requires that, in two-parent families, deductions for child care must be taken by the parent with the lowest income. The underlying assumption seems to be that child care is not the responsibility of the primary income earner (usually the father) nor a requirement for his ability to work, so he may not claim the child care expense. Rather, child care is the responsibility of the secondary earner (usually the mother) and often is a requirement for her to undertake paid work, so she may claim the expense. This is consistent with the assumptions of gender inequality and gendered division of labour common to the patriarchal model of the family and the separate spheres model of the work-family relationship.[40]

The suggestion that tax policy hinges upon a patriarchal and individualistic world view offers one explanation for the lack of consistent child care policy development in Canada. Individuals have been expected to care for their families without government assistance or interference. Child care when viewed as a private responsibility belongs in the private market; in this view government child care policy would be seen as an interference. Government policy involving child care has occurred when the government perceives that it is in the best interest of the government or society to breech such individualism:

> The values and norms of society, including gender roles, have varying influences on the health and well-being of children. Societal values help determine governments' social, health and economic policies. Public policies define the social expectations, rights and responsibilities that determine the resources available to children as they grow.[41]

Notes

1. Atkin 1998: 57.
2. Pence 1992a.
3. Atkin 1998: 59.
4. Read et al. 1992.
5. Bashevkin 1998; McQuaig 1993.
6. Bashevkin 1998; McQuaig 1993.
7. Durst 1999; Ursel 1992.
8. Durst 1999.
9. Ursel 1992.
10. Durst 1999; Bashevkin 1998; McQuaig 1993.
11. Pence 1992a: 27.
12. Friendly 1994.
13. Atkin 1998: 59.
14. Friendly 1994.
15. Friendly 1994; Atkin 1998.
16. Friendly 1994; Atkin 1998; Rochon and Rice 1992.
17. Bach and Phillips 1998.
18. Canada 1986: xxiii.
19. Canada 1986.
20. Canada 1987.
21. MacIvor 1996: 374.
22. MacIvor 1996: 375.
23. House of Commons 1988: 7-9.
24. Bach and Phillips 1998: 249.
25. August 1999; Battle 1999.
26. National Council of Welfare 1999.
27. National Council of Welfare 1999.
28. Pulkingham and Ternowetsky 1996.
20. Doherty, Oloman and Friendly 1998; Swimmer 1997; Pulkingham and Ternowetsky 1996.
30. Bach and Phillips 1998.
31. Pulkingham and Ternowetsky 1996.

32. Doherty, Friendly and Oloman 1998.
33. Canada 1999: i.
34. PMO office 1999.
35. PMO office 1999; Government of Saskatchewan 1999.
36. Canada 1999: 1.
37. Canada 1999: 36.
38. *Calgary Herald* July 30, 1999: A18, B1, B9.
39. Doherty 1999: 70.
40. Health and Welfare Canada 1989: 803–804.
41. Canada 1999: 37.

Appendix
Federal Chronology

1940	Liberals win election under Mackenzie King.
1942 (WWII)	Dominion-Provincial Wartime Agreement is created in response to the need to have mothers working. The program provided start-up funds and operating costs for child care centers on a federal–provincial 50/50 cost-shared basis. To receive funding, provinces initially had to show that at least 75 percent of mothers using the service were working in war-related industries.
1945	Liberals win election under Mackenzie King.
1945	Dominion-Provincial Wartime Agreement withdrawn.
1945	Introduction of the universal Family Allowance program.
1949	Liberals win election under Louis St Laurent.
1953	Liberals win election under Louis St Laurent.
1957	Progressive Conservatives win election under John Diefenbaker.
1958	Progressive Conservatives win election under John Diefenbaker.
1962	Progressive Conservatives win election under John Diefenbaker.
1963	Liberals win election under Lester Pearson.
1965	Liberals win election under Lester Pearson.
1966	Canadian Assistance Plan (CAP) introduced. This cost-shared program sought to develop "non-profit services that have as their objective the lessening, removal or prevention of the causes and effects of poverty, child neglect or dependence on public assistance."
1968	Liberals win election under Pierre Elliott Trudeau.
1970	Local Initiatives Program (LIP)—a job creation pro-

	gram that allowed for the creation of child care centers introduced.
1971	Child Care Expense Deduction (CCED) provision in *Income Tax Act* introduced.
1971	First national conference on daycare is held in Winnipeg and co-sponsored by the Federal Department of Health and Welfare and the Canadian Council on Social Development. Out of this conference came the recommendation for the establishment of a Federal Day Care Information Office.
1972	Royal Commission on the Status of Women established.
1972	National Day Care Information Center established within the Federal Department of Health and Welfare.
1972	CAP was amended to expand the definition of daycare services that could be cost-shared.
1973	LIP funding withdrawn.
1973	First annual *Status of Daycare in Canada* report issued.
1978	Child Tax Credit introduced. It is means tested.
1979	Progressive Conservatives win under Joe Clark.
1980	Liberals win under Pierre Elliott Trudeau.
1982	Second National Conference on Day Care is held in Winnipeg and leads to the formation of the Child Care Advocacy Association of Canada and the Canadian Childcare Federation.
1982	Canadian Advisory Council on the Status of Women release *Report on Day Care Centers.*
1984	John Turner takes over as Liberal leader and prime minister.
1984	Progressive Conservatives elected under Brian Mulroney.
1984	John Turner appoints a four-person task force on child care.
1986	Release of the report of Katie Cooke Task Force on Child Care.
1986	Brian Mulroney establishes a Special Parliamentary Committee on Child Care.
1987	Release of the report of the Special Parliamentary Committee on Child Care.
1988	Brian Mulroney introduces Bill C-144, the child care

	bill. C-144 dies in Senate following the election call.
1988	Introduction of Child Care Initiatives Program (CCIP). The program funded research, training projects and pilot projects.
1988	Progressive Conservatives re-elected under Brian Mulroney.
1989	Introduction of the clawback of Family Allowance.
1990	Cap on CAP.
1991	Community Action Program for Children (CAPC) introduced (100 percent federally funded).
1991	Aboriginal Head Start introduced (100 percent federally funded).
1993	Kim Campbell takes over as PC leader and prime minister.
1993	Liberals elected under Jean Chretien.
1993	Family Allowance, Child Tax Credit and the non-refundable tax credit are combined in a new income-tested Child Tax Benefit (CTB).
1993	Working Income Supplement (WIS) announced.
1994–5	Social Security Review led by the Parliamentary Committee on Human Resource Development.
1995	Canada Health and Social Transfer (CHST) introduced.
1995	CAP abolished.
1995	CCIP funding ended.
1995	Axworthy attempts to introduce a child care bill in December.
1996	Cabinet shuffle sees Doug Young become responsible for child care. Negotiations drop due to lack of provincial interest, although there had been no official negotiations.
1996	Elimination of the National Day Care Information Center results in no longer having a federal contact person for child care.
1998	Canada Child Tax Benefit (CTB) introduced.
1999	Social Union Framework Agreement signed.
1999	National Children's Agenda announced.
1999	Health Canada document suggests a comprehensive system for children should include community based planning, evaluation and monitoring of the following: • a perinatal system for prenatal, birth and infant care

- a parent resource system for families with children up to six years of age
- an accessible, affordable child care system
- a junior and senior kindergarten system for all four- and five-year-olds

1999   Cabinet shuffle replaces Human Resource Development Minister Pierre Pettigrew with Jane Stewart.

(Federal chronology reviewed by Christine Blaine)

Bibliography

"Alberta Association for Young Children Information Bulletin." 1974. AAYC Archives file.

Arnup, Katherine. 1994. *Education for Motherhood: Advice for Mothers in Twentieth Century Canada.* Toronto: University of Toronto Press.

Arnup, Katherine, Andree Levesque, and Ruth Roach Pierson with Margaret Brennan (eds.). 1990. *Delivering Motherhood.* London: Routledge.

Atkin, Wendy. 1998. "Babies of the World Unite: The Early Day-Care Movement and Family Formation in the 1970s." In Lori Chambers and Ed Montigny (eds.), *Family Matters: Papers in Post-Confederation Canadian Family History.* Toronto: Canadian Scholars' Press.

August, R. 1999. "Income Security and the Labour Market: Saskatchewan Perspectives on Child Benefit Reform." In D. Durst (ed.), *Canada's National Child Benefit: Phoenix or Fizzle?* Halifax: Fernwood.

Bach, Sandra, and Susan D. Phillips. 1998. "Constituting a New Social Union: Child Care Beyond Infancy?" In Gene Swimmer (ed.), *How Ottawa Spends 1997–98. Seeing Red: A Liberal Report Card.* Ottawa: Carleton University Press.

Baillargeon, Denise. 1996. "Les politiques familiales au Québec." *Lien social et Politiques—RIAC* 36.

Barber, Marilyn. 1991. *Immigrant Domestic Servants in Canada.* Ottawa: Canadian Historical Association.

Bashevkin, Sylvia. 1998. *Women on the Defensive,* Toronto: University of Toronto Press.

Battle, K. 1999. "The National Child Benefit: Best Thing Since Medicare or New Poor Law?" In D. Durst (ed.), *Canada's National Child Benefit: Phoenix or Fizzle?* Halifax: Fernwood.

BC Task Force on Child Care. 1991. *Showing We Care: A Child Care Strategy for the 90s, Complete and Summary Reports of the Task Force on Child Care.* Victoria: Government of British Columbia.

Beauvais, Caroline, and Jane Jenson. 2001. *Two Policy Paradigms: Family Responsibility and Investing in Children.* Ottawa: Canadian Policy Research Network F-12. Available at www.cprn.org/publications.

Beck, J.M. 1968. *Pendulum of Power: Canada's Federal Elections.* Scarborough: Prentice-Hall.

Bélanger, Paul R., and Benoît Lévesque. 1992. "Le mouvement populaire et communautaire: de la revendication au partenariat (1963–1992)." In Gérard Daigle (ed.), *Le Québec en jeu.* Montreal: Presses de l'Université de Montréal.

Bella, Leslie. 1978. *The Origins of Alberta's Preventive Social Service Program.* Edmonton: Department of Recreation Administration, University of Alberta.

Bergeron, Josée. 1997. Les frontières imaginaires and imaginées de I, État-providence. Unpublished PhD Thesis, Carleton University.

Blais, André, Donald Blake and Stéphane Dion. 1993. "Do Parties Make a Difference? Parties and the Size of Government in Liberal Democracies." *American Journal of Political Science* 37(1).

Boggs, C. 1986. *Social Movements and Political Power.* Philadelphia: Temple University Press.

Boisvert, Maurice. 2000. Speech to the World Summit on Social development. Geneva, June 26. Available at www.famille-enfance.gouv.qc.ca.

Boutilier, Beverly, and Alison Prentice (eds.). 1997. *Creating Historical Memory: English-Canadian Women and the Work of History.* Vancouver: UBC Press.

Bouwsma, W.J. 1990. *A Usable Past: Essays in European Cultural History.* Berkeley: University of California Press.

Boychuk, Gerard William. 1998. *Patchworks of Purpose: The Development of Provincial Social Assistance Regimes in Canada.* Montreal: McGill-Queen's.

Brennan, Deborah. 1998. *The Politics of Australian Child Care: Philanthropy to Feminism and Beyond.* Revised edition. Melbourne: Cambridge University Press.

Briskin, L. 1991. "Feminist Practice: A New Approach to Evaluating Feminist Strategy." In J. Wine and J. Ristock (eds.), *Women and Social Change.* Toronto: Lorimer.

British Columbia. 1992. *Special Needs Day Program: Report on Survey Results.* Victoria: Ministry of Social Services.

British Columbia, Ministry for Children and Families. 1996. *Practice Guidelines and Procedures for Supported Child Care.* Victoria: Ministry for Children and Families.

British Columbia. Special Needs Day Care Review Reference Committee. 1993. *Supported Child Care: The Report of the Special Needs Day Care Review in British Columbia.* Victoria: Ministry of Social Services.

Brush, L. 1996. "Love, Toil and Trouble: Motherhood and Feminist Politics." *Signs,* 21.

Burt, Sandra. 1997. "Gender and Public Policy: Making Some Difference in Ottawa." In V. Strong-Boag and A.C. Fellman (eds.), *Rethinking Canada: The Promise of Women's History.* Third edition. Toronto: Oxford University Press.

Calgary Herald. 1976. "Location of Commercial Day Care Centres (July, 1974)." July 23.

_____. 1978. "'Day care has turned full circle,' says city consultant." August 3.

Campbell, Sheila. 1997. "The Importance of The Early Years: The Beginning of AAYC." *Altachild* 10(3).

Canada. 1986. *Report of the Task Force on Child Care.* Ottawa: Supply and Services Canada.

_____. 1987. *Sharing the Responsibility: Report of the Special Committee on Child Care.* Canada: Queen's Printer.

_____. 1999. *Social Union Framework Agreement.* Ottawa: Ministry of Supply and Services.

Canada. Task Force on Program Review (Nielsen Task Force). 1986. *Introduction to the Process of Program Review.* Ottawa: Minister of Supply and Services.

Canadian Coalition on the Rights of Children, 1999. *The UN Convention on the Rights of the Child: How Does Canada Measure Up?* Ottawa: Canadian Institute for Child Health.

Canadian Council on Social Development (CCSD). 1971. "Day Care Legislation in Canada." *Report on the National Study of Day Care.* Ottawa: CCSD.

Carroll, W. (ed.). 1997. *Organizing Dessent: Contemporary Social Movements in Theory and Practice.* 2nd ed. Toronto: Garamond.

Castles, Francis (ed.). 1982. *The Impact of Parties, Politics and Policies in Democratic Capitalist States.* Beverly Hills: Sage.

Chambers, Simone. 1995. "Feminist Discourse/Practical Discourse." In Johanna Meehan (ed.), *Feminists Read Habermas.* New York: Routledge.

Charette, Donald. 1996. "Les jeunes claquent la porte." *Le Soleil*, November 1.

Child Care Advocacy Association of Canada (CCAAC). 1995. *Taking the First Steps. Child Care: An Investment in Canada's Future.* Ottawa: CCACC.

Child Care Resource and Research Unit. 1995. "Interprovincial Comparisons in Child Care." July. Child Care Resource and Research Unit, Centre for Urban and Community Studies, University of Toronto.

_____. 1997. *Child Care in Canada: Provinces and Territories, 1958.* Toronto: Child Care Resource and Research Unit, Centre for Urban and Community Studies, University of Toronto.

_____. 1998. *Child Care in Canada: Provinces and Territories, 1995.* Toronto: Child Care Resource and Research Unit, Centre for Urban and Community Studies, University of Toronto.

_____. 2000. *Child Care in Canada: Provinces and Territories, 1998.* Toronto: Child Care Resource and Research Unit, Centre for Urban and Community Studies, University of Toronto.

Child Welfare League of America (CWLA). 1965. *Standards for Day Care.* New York: CWLA.

Childhood and Youth Division. Health Canada. 1999. "The Early Child Development System and its Program Components." Draft Discussion Paper (July). Available at www.hc-sc.gc.ca/english/archives/releases/ecdreport.htm.

Clark, K. 1993. "The Unfinished Toll of Psychic Violence." *Newsweek*, January 11.

Clarke, Christopher. 1998. *Canada's Income Security Programs.* Ottawa: Canadian Council on Social Development.

Cleveland, Gordon, and Michael Krashinsky. 1998. *The Benefits and Costs of Good Child Care: The Economic Rationale for Public Investment in Young Children.* Toronto: Childcare Resource and Research Unit, Centre for Urban and Community Studies, University of Toronto.

Cloutier, Mario. 1996. "Le sommet sur l'économie et l'emploi." *Le Devoir,* November 1.

Coalition of Child Care Advocates of British Columbia (CCCABC). 1999a. *Child Care Advocacy Forum.* Available at www.cccabc.bc.ca/links.html.

_____. 1999b. *Publicly Funded Child Care Essential for Social and Economic Development.* Available at www.cccabc.bc.ca/links.html.

Cohen, Marcy, Nancy Duggan, Carol Sayre, Barbara Todd, and Niki Wright. 1973. *Cuz There Ain't no Daycare (Or Almost None, She Said): A Book About Daycare in BC.* Vancouver: Press Gang.

Cohen, Marjorie Griffin. 1993. "Social Policy and Social Services Documents." In Ruth Roach Pierson, Marjorie Griffin Cohen, Paula Bourne, and Philinda Masters (eds.), *Canadian Women's Issues. Volume I: Strong Voices.* Toronto: Lorimer.

Cohen, Jean. 1992. "The Historicist Critique." In Jean Cohen and Andrew Arato (eds.), *Civil Society and Political Theory.* Cambridge: MIT Press.

Collectif, Clio. 1992. *L'Histoire des femmes au Québec depuis quatre siècles.* Montreal: Le Jour.

Colley, Susan. 1981. "Day Care and the Trade Union Movement in Ontario." *Resources for Feminist Research* 10 (2).

_____. 1983. "Free Universal Day Care: The OFL Takes a Stand." In Linda Briskin and Linda Yanz (eds.), *Union Sisters: Women in the Labour Movement.* Toronto: Women's Press.

Commager, H.S. 1967. *The Search for a Usable Past and Other Essays in Historiography.* New York: Knopf.

Dandurand, Renée B. 1987. "Une politique familiale: Enjeux et débats." *Recherches sociographiques* XXVIII (2–3).

_____. 1992. "La famille n'est pas une île." In Gérard Daigle (ed.), *Le Québec en jeu.* Montreal: Presses de l'Université de Montréal.

Davin, Anna. 1978. "Imperialism and Motherhood." *History Workshop Journal* 5.

de Massy, P.R. 1997. "The Eaton Case Before the Supreme Court of Canada: A 'Constructive' Reading of the Decision." *entourage* 10 (3/4).

Department of Labour. 1964. *Day Care Services for Children of Working Mothers.* January. Ottawa: Women's Bureau.

Department of Saskatchewan Social Services. 1974. *Daycare Proposals.* Regina: Department of Social Services.

Desjardins, Ghislaine. 1991. *Faire garder ses enfants au Québec ... une histoires toujours en marche.* Quebec: Office des services de garde à l'enfance.

Division of Early Childhood (DEC) Council for Exceptional Children. 1993. DEC

Position on Inclusion. Reston, VA: Council for Exceptional Children.

Doherty, G. 1999. "Elements of Quality." In *Research Connections Canada. Volume 1*. Ottawa: Canadian Child Care Federation.

Doherty, G., D.S. Lero, H. Goelman, A. LaGrange, and J. Tougas. 2000. *You Bet I Care! A Canada-wide Study on Wages, Working Conditions and Practices in Child Care Centres*. Guelph: Centre for Families, Work and Well-Being, University of Guelph.

Doherty, Gillian, Martha Friendly, and Mab Oloman. 1998. *Women's Support, Women's Work: Child Care in an Era of Deficit Reduction, Devolution, Downsizing and Deregulation*. Ottawa: Status of Women Canada.

Doherty, Gillian, Ruth Rose, Martha Friendly, Donna Lero, and Sharon Hope Irwin. 1995. "Child Care: Canada Can't Work Without it." Toronto: Child Care Resource and Research Unit, Centre for Urban and Community Studies, University of Toronto.

Dolphin, R. 2001. "A Tale of Two Cities." *Edmonton Journal*, January 27.

Durst, D. (ed.). 1999. *Canada's National Child Benefit: Phoenix or Fizzle?* Halifax: Fernwood.

Dyhouse, Carol. 1978. "Working-Class Mothers and Infant Mortality in England, 1895–1914." *Journal of Social History* 12.

Edmonton Journal. 1964. "Creche Board Explains Closure." May 15.

_____. 1966a. "Meet to Discuss Day Nurseries." February 2.

_____. 1966b. "Day-Care Expansion Endorsed By Club." February 23.

_____. 1978. "City Rejects Role in Day-care Plan." May 24.

Edmonton Social Services Department. 1968. *Annual Report*. Edmonton: Social Services Department.

Esping-Anderson, G. 1989. "The Three Political Economies of the Welfare State," *Canadian Review of Sociology and Anthropology* 26, 1 (Feb).

Federal–Provincial–Territorial Council of Ministers on Social Policy Renewal. 1999. *A National Children's Agenda: Developing a Shared Vision*. Catalogue No. H39-4941-199E. Ottawa: Queen's Printer.

_____. 2000. *Public Report—Public Dialogue on the National Children's Agenda: Developing a Shared Vision*. Catalogue No.: SC-133-05-00. Ottawa: National Children's Agenda.

First Ministers, Prime Minister and Territorial Leaders. 1997. "Reaffirmed Their Commitment to New Cooperative Approaches to Address Children's Needs Through a *National Children's Agenda*. Responsibility for this Important Work Was Given to the Federal/Provincial/Territorial Council on Social Policy Renewal." In Federal–Provincial–Territorial Council of Ministers on Social Policy Renewal, *A National Children's Agenda: Developing a Shared Vision*, 1999. Ottawa: Queen's Printer.

First Ministers. 2000. "First Ministers Meeting Communique on Early Childhood Development." News release, September 11. Ref: 800-038/005. Available at www.scics.gc.ca/cinfo00/800038005 e. html.

Fraser, N. 1989. "Struggle over Needs." In N. Fraser (ed.), *Unruly Practices*.

Minneapolis: University of Minnesota Press.

_____. 1997. *Justice Interruptus: Critical Reflections on the "Post-Socialist" Condition.* New York: Routledge.

Friendly, Martha. 1994. *Child Care Policy in Canada: Putting the Pieces Together.* Toronto: Addison-Wesley.

_____. 2000. "The Social Union and Its Implications for a National Child Care Strategy," *Socialist Studies Bulletin* 59 (March).

Friesen, Bruce. 1995. "A Sociological Examination of the Child Care Auspice Debate." Toronto: The Childcare Resource and Research Unit, Centre for Urban and Community Studies, University of Toronto.

Gallagher Ross, Kathleen. 1986. "Parents' Choice." *Policy Options* 7 (7).

Globe and Mail. 1996. "Cuts Leave Disabled Children Without Day Care." June 13.

Goldstein, Judith, and Robert Keohane (eds.). 1993. *Ideas and Foreign Policy: Beliefs, Institutions and Political Change.* Ithaca: Cornell University Press.

Gordon, L. 1990. "The New Feminist Scholarship on the Welfare State." In L. Gordon (ed.), *Women, the State and Welfare.* Wisconsin: University of Wisconsin Press.

_____. 1994. *Pitied But Not Entitled: Single Mothers and the History of Welfare.* New York: Free Press.

Gorham, Deborah. 1997. "Making History: Women's History in Canadian Universities in the 1970s." In Beverly Boutilier and Alison Prentice (eds.), *Creating Historical Memory: English-Canadian Women and the Work of History.* Vancouver: University of British Columbia Press.

Government of British Columbia, Task Force on Child Care. 1993. *Showing We Care: A Child Care Strategy for the 90's: Complete Report.* Victoria: Government of British Columbia.

Government of Canada. 1961. *Report of the Royal Commission on the Status of Women.* Ottawa: Department of Supply and Services.

_____. 2000. "What Canadians are telling us about the National Children's Agenda." Press Release. June 21.

Government of Canada. Governor General. 1999. "Building a Higher Quality of Life for All Canadians." Speech from the Throne to open the Second Session of the Thirty-Sixth Parliament of Canada (October 12). Available at www.pco-bcp.gc.ca/sft-ddt/doc/fulltext_e.htm.

Government of Ontario. Ministry of Community and Social Services. 1995. *Interprovincial Comparisons in Child Care.* Unpublished government document.

Government of Ontario. Ministry of Community and Social Services, Child Care Branch. 1988. *Integrating Children Experiencing Special Needs in Day Nurseries: A Background Report.* Toronto: Queen's Printer.

Government of Saskatchewan. 1999. *Saskatchewan's Action Plan for Children: Building on Community Success: Creating a Long Term Plan for Saskatchewan's Youngest Children and their Families.* Working Paper: Policy Framework.

Regina: Government of Saskatchewan.

Griffin, Sandra et. al.1991. "British Columbia Report." In Alan R. Pence (ed.), *Canadian National Child Care Study: Canadian Child Care in Context: Perspectives from the Provinces and Territories.* Ottawa: Statistics Canada.

Haney, L. 1998. "Engendering the Welfare State: A Review Article." *Journal of Comparative Study of Society and History* 40, 4.

Hansard, Saskatchewan Legislature. 1973–74. *Volume 14.* Regina: Queens Printers.

Health and Welfare Canada. 1989. *Status of Day Care in Canada 1989: A Review of the Major Findings of the National Day Care Study.* Ottawa: Health and Welfare Canada.

Hernes, H. 1977. *Welfare State and Woman Power: Essays in State Feminism.* Oslo: Norwegian University Press.

Hewitt, Margaret. 1958. *Wives and Mothers in Victorian Industry.* London: Rockliff.

Hibbs, D.A. Jr. 1992. "Partisan Theory After Fifteen Years." *European Journal of Political Economy* 8.

Hicks, Alexander M., and Duane H. Swank. 1992. "Politics, Institutions, and Welfare Spending in Industrialized Democracies, 1960–82." *American Political Science Review* 86 (3).

House of Commons. 1988. *Minutes of proceedings and evidence of the Legislative Committee on Bill C-144, an Act to authorize payments by Canada toward the provision of child care services and to amend the Canada Assistance Plan in consequence thereof.* Ottawa: Queen's Printer.

_____. 1995. *Canada: Security, Opportunities and Fairness: Canadians Renewing Their Social Programs.* Report of the Standing Committee on Human Resources Development. Ottawa: Canada Communications Group—Publishing, Public Works and Government Services.

Howe, R. 1996. "Gender and the Welfare State: Comparative Perspectives." *Gender and History* 8, 4.

Irwin, S.H. 1992. *Integration of Children with Disabilities into Daycare and After-School Programs.* Ottawa: Disabled Persons Unit, Health and Welfare Canada.

_____. 1993a. "Directory of Mainstream Advocates." In *The SpeciaLink Book.* Wreck Cove, NS: Breton Books.

_____. 1993b. "'Trach'—It Rhymes with 'Snake.'" In *The SpeciaLink Book.* Wreck Cove, NS: Breton Books.

_____. 1997. "Where the Provinces Stand with Respect to Inclusion of Children with Disabilities in Child Care Programs." Updated bi-annually. Available from SpeciaLink, PO Box 775, Sydney, Nova Scotia, B1P 6G1

Irwin, S., D.S. Lero, K. Brophy. 2000. *A Matter of Urgency: Including Children with Special Needs in Child Care in Canada.* Wreck Cove, NS: Breton Books.

Institute for Research in Public Policy (IRRP). 2000. "Quebec Family Policy: Impact and Options." *Choices* 6, 1 (January).

Jenson, Jane. 1998. "Les réformes des services de garde pour jeunes enfants en

France et au Québec: Une analyse historico-institutionaliste." *Politique et Sociétés* 17 (1–2).

Jenson, Jane, and Sherry Thompson. 1999 *Comparative Family Policy: Six Provincial Stories.* Ottawa: Canadian Policy Research Networks.

Jenson, Jane, and Sharon M. Stroick. 1999a. *What is the Best Policy Mix for Canada's Young Children?* Ottawa: Canadian Policy Research Networks F-09.

——. 1999b. *A Policy Blueprint for Canada's Children.* CPRN Reflexion Paper No. 3. Ottawa: Canadian Policy Research Networks.

Jenson, Jane, and Susan Phillips. 2000. "Distinctive Trajectories: Homecare and the Voluntary Sector in Quebec and Ontario." In K. Banting (ed.), *The Nonprofit Sector in Canada: Roles and Relationships.* Kingston: School of Policy Studies, Queen's University.

Judd, C.S. 1997. "The *Eaton* and *Eldridge* Cases: Same but Different?" *entourage* 10 (3/4).

Katzenstein, M.F., and C. Mueller. 1987. *The Women's Movements of the United States and Western Europe.* Boston: South End Press.

Keck, Margaret, and Kathryn Sikkink. 1998. *Activists Beyond Borders: Advocacy Networks in International Politics.* Ithaca: Cornell University Press.

Klingemann, Hans-Dieter, Richard Hofferbert, and Ian Budge. 1996. *Parties, Policies and Democracy.* Boulder: Westview Press.

Koven, S., and S. Michel (eds.). 1993. *Mothers of a New World: Maternalistic Politics and Origins of Welfare States.* Routledgee: London.

Krasner, Stephen. 1984. "Approaches to the State: Alternative Conceptions and Historical Dynamics." *Comparative Politics* 16 (2).

Kyle, Irene et. al. 1991. "Ontario Report." In Alan R. Pence, (ed.), *Canadian National Child Care Study: Canadian Child Care in Context: Perspectives from the Provinces and Territories.* Ottawa: Statistics Canada.

La Gazette des femmes. 1996. "La cause des femmes selon Louise Harel." July–August.

Lacroix, Isabelle. 2001. "La mise en oeuvre de la r/forme des services de garde et le principe de l'égalité des chances." Unpublished MA thesis, Université de Montreal.

Lamoureux, Diane. 1992. "Nos luttes ont changé nos vies. L'impact du mouvement féministe." In Gérard Daigle (ed.), *Le Québec en jeu.* Montreal: Presses de l'Université de Montréal.

Lefebvre, Pierre. 1998. "Les nouvelles orientations de la politique familiale du Québec: une critique de l'allocation unifiée." In R.B. Dandurand, et al. (eds.), *Quelle politique familiale à l'aube de l'an 2000?* Paris: L'Harmattan.

Léger, Huguette, and Judy Rebick. 1993. *NAC Voters' Guide 1993.* Hull, Québec: Voyageur.

Legislative Assembly of Ontario, Standing Committee on Social Development. 1997. "Report on the Impact of the Conservative Government's Funding Cuts on Children and Children's Services in the Province of Ontario." First

Session, thirty-sixth Parliament. Toronto: Legislative Assembly of Ontario. December.

Lepage, Francine, and Marie Moisan. 1998. "L'assurance parentale: la nouvelle politique québécoise et les prestations réservées aux pères." In R.B. Dandurand, et al. (eds.), *Quelle politique familiale à l'aube de l'an 2000?* Paris: L'Harmattan.

Lero, Donna, and Karen L. Johnson. 1994. "Canadian Statistics on Work and Family. A Background Paper." Ottawa: Canadian Advisory Council on the Status of Women.

Lesemann, Frédéric. 1981. *Du pain et des services: la réforme de la santé et des services sociaux au Québec*. Laval, Quebec: Editions Saint-Martin.

Library of Parliament. 1997. *Canadian Prime Ministers Since 1867*. Available at www.parl.gc.ca/36/refmat/library/pm.

Lightman, Ernie, and Donna Baines. 1996. "White Men in Blue Suits: Women's Policy in Conservative Ontario." *Canadian Journal of Social Policy* 38.

Lind, Loren, and Susan Prentice. 1992. *Their Rightful Place: An Essay on Children, Families and Childcare in Canada*. Toronto: Our Schools/Our Selves Education Foundation.

MacIvor, Heather. 1996. *Women and Politics in Canada*. Peterborough, ON: Broadview.

Mahaffy, C. 2001. "Crisis in Alberta Daycare." *Alberta Views* 4 (1).

Mallan, Caroline. 1997. "Tax Credit to Help Low-Income Parents." *Toronto Star*, May 7.

Maloney, William A., Grant Jordan, and Andrew M. McLaughlin. 1994. "Interest Groups and Public Policy: The Insider/Outsider Model Revisited." *Journal of Public Policy* 14 (1).

Marsh, J. (ed.). 1985. *The Canadian Encyclopedia*. Edmonton: Hurtig.

Martin, J.A. 1991. "From Bad to Worse: Day Care in Saskatchewan, 1982–1989." In L. Biggs and M. Stobbe (eds.), *Devine Rule In Saskatchewan*. Saskatoon: Fifth House.

_____. 1995. "The Continuing Struggle for Universal Day Care." In Jim Harding (ed.), *Social Policy and Social Justice*. Waterloo, ON: Wilfred Laurier University Press.

Masson, J. 1985. *Alberta's Local Governments and Their Politics*. Edmonton: University of Alberta Press.

McAdam, Doug. 1996. "Conceptual Origins, Current Problems, Future Directions." In Doug McAdam, John D. McCarthy, and Mayer N. Zald (eds.), *Comparative Perspectives on Social Movements: Political Opportunities, Mobilizing Structures, and Cultural Framings*. Cambridge: Cambridge University Press.

McCain, Margaret, and Fraser Mustard. 1999. *Reversing the Real Brain Drain. Early Years Study Final Report*. Toronto: Children's Secretariat of Ontario.

McClintock, Ann. 1995. *Imperial Leather: Race, Gender and Sexuality in the Colonial Contest*. New York: Routledge.

McCord, M. 1988. "Child Care: A History." *First Reading* January/February.

McIlroy, Anne. 1999. "Canadians Want New System of Care for Children,

Report Says." *Globe and Mail,* July 30.

McNamara, Kathleen. 1998. *The Currency of Ideas: Monetary Politics in the European Union.* Ithaca: Cornell University Press.

McQuaig, Linda. 1993. *The Wealthy Banker's Wife: The Assault on Equality in Canada.* Toronto: Penguin.

McQuinty, Dalton. 1998. "First Steps. Report of the McQuinty Task Force on Children." Toronto: Ontario Liberal Party.

Meisels, S.J. 1988. "A Functional Analysis of the Evolution of Public Policy for Handicapped Young Children." *Educational Evaluation and Policy Analysis* 7 (2).

Metro Community Services (MCS). 1990. "Infosheet," Children's Services Division, Toronto, September 31.

_____. 1996. *Implications for Metro of Recommendations in Ontario's Child Care Review.* September 16.

Michalski, Joseph H. 1999. *Values and Preferences for the "Best Policy Mix" for Canadian Children.* CPRN Discussion Paper No. F/05. Ottawa: Canadian Policy Research Networks.

Michel, Sonya. 1999. *Children's Interests/Mothers' Rights: The Shaping of America's Child Care Policy.* New Haven: Yale University Press.

Mickleburgh, Rod. 2000. "B.C. Gives Parents $7-a-day Child Care." *Globe and Mail,* June 6.

Ministère de la Famille et de l'Enfance. 2000. June 6, 9, 22.

Ministère de la Santé et des Services sociaux (MSSS). 1991. *Un Québec fou de son enfants. Rapport du Groupe de travail pour les jeunes.* (The "Bouchard Report). Quebec: Ministère de la Santé et des Services sociaux.

Ministry of Community and Social Services. Ontario. 1992. "Ontario Child Care Management Framework." July 30. Toronto: Ministry of Community and Social Services.

_____. 1993. "MCSS Area Child Care Management Plan. Quarterly Report Ending December 1993." Toronto: Ministry of Community and Social Services.

_____. 1994a. "MCSS Area Child Care Management Plan. Quarterly Report Ending June 1994." Toronto: Ministry of Community and Social Services.

_____. 1994b. "MCSS Area Child Care Management Plan. Quarterly Report Ending March 1994." Toronto: Ministry of Community and Social Services.

_____. 1996a. "Report Recommends More Child Care Choices and Thousands of New Subsidized Spaces for Children." News Release. September 5. Toronto: Ministry of Community and Social Services.

_____. 1996b. "Improving Ontario's Child Care System. Ontario's Child Care Review." August. Toronto: Ministry of Community and Social Services.

Ministry of Women's Equality. 1995. *British Columbia Initiatives for Women's Equality,* Victoria: Government of British Columbia.

_____. 1998. *Annual Report, 1996–97 and 1997–98.* Victoria: Government of

British Columbia. Available at www.weq.gov.bc.ca/about/annualreport98/ mwe_annual.html

Moscovitch, A., and G. Drover (eds.). 1982. *Inequality: Essays on the Political Economy of Social Welfare.* Toronto: Garamond.

Moscovitch, A., and J. Albert (eds.). 1987. *The Benevolent State: The Growth of Welfare in Canada.* Toronto: Garamond.

Myles, John, and Paul Pierson. 1997. "Friedman's Revenge: The Reform of 'Liberal' Welfare States in Canada and the United States." *Politics & Society* 25 (4).

Naples, Nancy. 1998. *Community Activism and Feminist Politics: Organizing Across Race, Class and Gender.* New York: Routledge.

National Action Committee on the Status of Women (NAC). 1986. *A Brief to the Special Committee on Child Care.* Toronto: NAC.

_____. 1988. *Feminist Action News.* Toronto: NAC.

National Action Committee on the Status of Women (NAC). Child Care Subcommittee. 1988. *Child Care Bulletin/sur les Garderies.* Toronto: NAC (April).

National Center for Early Development and Learning. 1999. *The Children of the Cost, Quality, and Outcomes Study Go To School.* Cost, Quality, and Outcomes Study Report. Chapel Hill, NC: Frank Porter Graham Child Development Center, University of North Carolina at Chapel Hill. Available at http://www.fpg.unc.edu/~NCEDL/PAGES/cqes.htm.

National Children's Agenda (NCA). 1999. *Developing a Shared Vision.* Ottawa: NCA.

National Council of Welfare (NCW). 1988. *Child Care: A Better Alternative.* Ottawa: Minister of Supply and Services.

_____. 1999. *Preschool Children: Promises to Keep.* Ottawa: Minister of Public Works and Government Services Canada.

National Institute on Mental Retardation. 1977. *Children with Special Needs: A Guide to Integration.* Ottawa: Health and Welfare Canada.

National Post. 1999a. July 29.

_____. 1999b. July 30.

Noël, Alain, 1996. "La contrepartie dans l'aide sociale au Québec." *Revue française des Affaires sociales* 50 (4).

Norpark Computer Design, Inc. 1991. *A Comparative Analysis of Child Care Legislation.* Toronto: Ministry of Community and Social Services, Child Care Branch.

Nova Scotia, Department of Social Services. 1971. *Regulations under the Day Care Services Act.* Halifax: Department of Social Services.

O'Connor, J. 1996. "From Women in the Welfare State to Gendering Welfare State Regimes." *Current Sociology.* 44 (2).

O'Connor, J., and G. Olsen (eds.). 1997. *Power Resource Theory and the Welfare State: A Critical Approach.* Toronto: University of Toronto Press.

O'Handley, K., and C. Sutherland (eds.). 1997. *Canadian Parliamentary Guide.* Scarborough: Gale Canada, a Division of Thomson Canada Limited.

Office of the Provincial Auditor, Ontario. 1995. "1995 Annual Report." Toronto: Office of the Provincial Auditor.

Olsen, G. 1994. "Locating the Canadian Welfare State: Family Policy and Health Care in Canada, Sweden and the United States." *Journal of Canadian Sociology* 19, 1.

Ontario Coalition for Better Child Care (OCBCC). 1981. *Daycare Deadline 1990: Brief to the Government of Ontario on the Future of Daycare Services in Ontario*. Don Mills, ON: Ontario Federation of Labour.

_____. 1993. "Child Care in Metropolitan Toronto." April. Toronto: OCBCC.

_____. 1994. *Annual Report 1993–94*. Toronto: OCBCC.

_____. 1995a. "The Impact of Bill 26 on Early Education and Care Programs for Young Children." December 18. Toronto: OCBCC.

_____. 1995b. "Think About the Children: They are the Future. Report of the Public Inquiry Into Cuts to Regulated Child Care in Ontario." November. Toronto: OCBCC.

_____. 1996a. "Your Efforts Make Provincewide Day of Action Huge Success." *Network News* 5, 7. Toronto: OCBCC.

_____. 1996b. "Child Care Workers to Minister Ecker: We're Worth It—and So Are the Children!" September 26. Toronto: OCBCC.

_____. 1997a. "Brief to the Standing Committee on Bill 104—The Fewer School Boards Act." March. Toronto: OCBCC.

_____. 1997b. "A Brief to the Standing Committee on Finance, Government of Ontario." March 6. Toronto: OCBCC.

_____. 1997c. "Urgent: Municipal Guidelines/Update." January 29.

_____. 1997d. "Facts About Workfare." December. Toronto: OCBCC.

_____. 1998. "The Harris Government Record on Child Care. The OCBCC Response to the Crisis." January. Toronto: OCBCC.

_____. 1999a. "Child Care at the Centre. Brief to the Provincial Legislature." March 29. Toronto: OCBCC.

_____. 1999b. *Government Submission*. Available at www.web.net/~ocbcc.

Ontario New Democrats. 1996. "First Priority to Hold Public Hearings on Child Care." *Information* September 17. Toronto: Ontario New Democratic Party.

Orloff, A. 1993. "Gender and the Rights of Citizenship: The Comparative Analysis of Gender Relations and Welfare States." *American Sociological Review* 58.

_____. 1996. "Gender in the Welfare State." *Annual Review of Sociology* 22.

Osborne, David, and Ted Gaebler. 1992. *Reinventing Government*. Don Mills, Ont: Addison-Wesley.

Ottawa Citizen. 1996. "Child Care Gets Low Priority." Editorial. September 9.

_____. 2001. "The Cost of Child Care." April 11.

Peck, C.A., Carlson, P., and E. Helmstetter. 1992. "Parent and Teacher Perceptions of Outcomes for Typically Developing Children Enrolled in Integrated Early Childhood Programs: A Statewide Survey." *Journal of Early Intervention* 16 (1).

Pence, A. (ed.). 1992a. *Canadian National Child Care Study; Canadian Child Care in Context: Perspectives from the Provinces and Territories. Volume 1.* Ottawa: Health and Welfare Canada.

_____. 1992b. *Canadian National Child Care Study; Canadian Child Care in Context: Perspectives from the Provinces and Territories. Volume 2.* Ottawa: Health and Welfare Canada.

Pence, A., S. Griffin, L. McDonell, H. Goelman, D. Lero, and L. Brockman. 1997. *Shared Diversity: An Interprovincial Report on Child Care in Canada.* Ottawa: Statistics Canada.

Philip, M. 1998. "Public Daycare Pays Off for Whole Society, Study Says." *Globe and Mail,* March 5.

Phillips, Susan. 1989. "Rock-A-Bye, Brian: The National Strategy on Child Care." In K.A. Graham (ed.), *How Ottawa Spends 1989-90: The Buck Stops Where?* Ottawa: Carleton University Press.

Pierson, P. 1993. "When Effect Becomes Cause: Policy Feedback and Political Change." *World Politics* 45, 4 (July).

Pierson, Ruth Roach. 1986. *They're Still Women After All: The Second World War and Canadian Womanhood.* Toronto: McLelland and Stewart.

Prime Minister's Office. 1999. *The New Social Union Framework.* Available at pm.gc.ca/publications/factsheets=fact_sh19990204925_e.htm.

Prentice, Susan. 1988a. "Kids are not for Profit: The Politics of Childcare." In Frank Cunningham, Sue Findlay, Marlene Kadar, Allan Lennon, and Ed Silva (eds.), *Social Movements/Social Change.* Toronto: Between the Lines, Socialist Studies 4.

_____. 1988b. "The 'Mainstreaming' of Daycare." *Resources for Feminist Research* 17 (3).

_____. 1989. "Workers, Mothers, Reds: Toronto's Postwar Daycare Fight." *Studies in Political Economy* 30.

_____. 1999. "Less, Worse and More Expensive: Child Care In an Era of Deficit Reduction." *Journal of Canadian Studies* 34, 2 (Fall).

Pulkingham, J., and G. Ternowetsky (eds.). 1996. *Remaking Canadian Social Policy: Social Security in the Late 1990s.* Halifax: Fernwood.

Québec. 1999. *Un portrait statistique des familles et des enfants au Québec.* Québec: Gouvernment de Québec.

_____. 2000. *Budget de dépenses 2000–2001,* volume III: *Plans ministériels de gestion des dépenses.* Québec: Gouvernment de Québec.

Rankin, L. Pauline. 1997. "Experience, Opportunity and the Politics of Place: A Comparative Analysis of Provincial and Territorial Women's Movements in Canada." Unpublished Ph.D. thesis, Department of Political Science, Carleton University, Ottawa.

Read, M., M. Greenwood-Church, L. Hautman, E. Roche, and C. Bagley. 1992. "An Historical Overview of Child Care in Alberta." In A. Pence (ed.), *Canadian National Child Care Study; Canadian Child Care in Context: Perspectives from the Provinces and Territories. Volume 1.* Ottawa: Health and

Welfare Canada.

Rebick, J. 1998. "Five-dollar Day Care." *Elm Street* (Summer).

Rochon, K., and C. Rice. 1992. "An Historical Overview of Child Care on Prince Edward Island." In A. Pence (ed.), *Canadian National Child Care Study; Canadian Child Care in Context: Perspectives from the Provinces and Territories. Volume 2*. Ottawa: Health and Welfare Canada.

Roeher Insitute. 1993. *Right Off the Bat: A Study of Inclusive Child Care in Canada*. North York: Roeher Insititute.

Rose, Richard, and Phillip Davies. 1994. *Inheritance in Public Policy: Change Without Choice in Britain*. New Haven: Yale University Press.

Rose, Ruth. 1998. "Politiques pour les familles pauvres: supplément au revenu gagné et revenus minumums garantis." In R.B. Dandurand et al. (eds.), *Quelle politique familiale à l'aube de l'an 2000?* Paris: L'Harmattan.

Ross, Ellen. 1993. *Love and Toil: Motherhood in Outcast London, 1870–1918*. New York: Oxford University Press.

Roy, Maurice. 1987. *Les CLSC. Ce qu'il faut savoir*. Montreal: Editions Saint Martin.

Ruggie, Mary. 1984. *The State And Working Women—A Comparative Study of Britain and Sweden*. Princeton: Princeton University Press.

Rusk, James. 1996. "Day-care Wage Subsidies Should be Cut, Ontario Says." *Globe and Mail*, September 6.

Sainsbury, D. 1994. *Gendering Welfare States*. London: Sage.

Saskatchewan New Democratic Party. 1971. *A New Deal for People*. Regina: Saskatchewan NDP.

Saskatoon Woman's Calendar Collective. 1988. *Herstory 1988: The Canadian Women's Calendar*. Regina: Coteau.

Schmidt, Manfred. 1996. "When Parties Matter: A Review of the Possibilities and Limits of Partisan Influence on Public Policy." *European Journal of Political Research* 30.

Schulz, Patricia. 1978. "Day Care in Canada: 1850–1962." In Kathleen Gallagher Ross (ed.), *Good Day Care*. Toronto: Women's Press.

Scott, A. 1990. *Ideology and the New Social Movements*. London: Sage.

Scott, Joan, and Louise Tilly. 1978. *Women, Work and Family*. New York: Holt, Rinehart and Winston.

Smith, W. 1994. *Equal Educational Opportunity for Students with Disabilities: Legislative Action in Canada*. Vancouver Office of Research on Educational Policy, Centre for Education, Law and Society, Simon Fraser University.

Speirs, Rosemary. 1986. *Out of the Blue: The Fall of the Tory Dynasty in Ontario*. Toronto: Macmillan of Canada.

Strain, P.S. 1999. *Least Restrictive Environment (LRE) for Preschool Children with Disabilities: What We Know, and What We Should be Doing* Denver: University of Colorado.

Stroick, Sharon, and Jane Jenson. 1999. *What Is the Best Policy Mix for Canada's Young Children*. Canadian Policy Research Networks Study No. F/09.

Ottawa: Canadian Policy Research Networks.

Strong-Boag, Veronica, and Anita Clair Fellman. 1991. *Rethinking Canada: The Promise of Women's History.* Second edition. Toronto: Copp Clark Pittman.

Swimmer, G. (ed.). 1997. *How Ottawa Spends: 1997–8; Seeing Red: A Liberal Report Card.* Ottawa: Carleton University Press.

Tarrow, Sidney. 1998. *Power in Movement: Social Movements and Contentious Politics.* Second edition. Cambridge: Cambridge University Press.

Teghtsoonian, Katherine. 1996a. "Promises, Promises: 'Choices for Women' in Canadian and American Child Care Policy Debates." *Feminist Studies* 22 (1).

_____. 1996b. "Who Pays for Caring for Children? Public Policy and the Devaluation of Women's Work." Paper presented at the Annual Meeting of the Canadian Political Science Association, St. Catharines, Ontario, June 2–4.

Tilly, C. 1988. "Social Movements, Old and New." *Research in Social Movements, Conflicts and Change* 10.

Torjman, Sherri, and Ken Battle. 1995. "The Dangers of Block Funding." Ottawa: Caledon Institute of Social Policy.

Toronto Star. 1996. "Hitting the Vulnerable." Editorial. September 8.

_____. 1997. "Tories Dump Costs on Municipalities." Editorial. January 15.

Touraine, A. 1988. *Return of the Actor: Social Theory in Postindustrial Society.* Minneapolis: University of Minnesota Press.

Tyyskä, Vappu. 1995. *The Politics of Caring and the Welfare State. The Impact of the Women's Movement on Child Care Policy in Canada and Finland, 1960–1990.* Helsinki: Finnish Academy of Science, Series B.

_____. 1998. "Insiders and Outsiders: Women's Movements and Organizational Effectiveness." *Canadian Review of Sociology and Anthropology* 35 (3).

Ursel, J. 1992. *Private Lives, Public Policy: 100 Years of State Intervention in the Family.* Toronto: Women's Press.

Vaillancourt, Yves. 1988. "Quebec." In J.S. Ismael and Yves Vaillancourt (eds.), *Privatisation and Provincial Social Services in Canada.* Edmonton: University of Alberta Press.

Vander Ven, K. 1992. "Military Strategy and the Economic Base of Child Care: A Radical Proposal for Our Future." In S.H. Irwin, *The SpeciaLink Book.* Wreck Cove, NS: Breton Books.

Varga, Donna. 1997. *Constructing the Child: A History of Canadian Day Care.* Toronto: Lorimer.

Vérificateur Général du Québec. 1999. *Rapport à l'Assemblée nationale pour l'année 1998–1999.* Québec: Gouvernement de Québec. Available at www.vgq.gouv.qc.ca.

Vron, Ware. 1992. *Beyond the Pale: Racism, White Women and History.* London: Verso.

White, Linda A. 1997. "Partisanship or Politics of Austerity? Child Care Policy Development in Ontario and Alberta, 1980 to 1996." *Journal of Family Issues*

18 (1).

_____. 1998. "Welfare State Development and Child Care Policies: A Comparative Analysis of France, Canada, and the United States." Unpublished doctoral dissertation, University of Toronto.

_____. 2001. "The Child Care Agenda and the Social Union." In Herman Bakvis and Grace Skogstad (eds.), *Federalism in the New Millenium: Performance, Effectiveness and Legitimacy*. Toronto: Oxford University Press.

Wilson, E. 1977. *Women and the Welfare State*. London: Tavistock.

Wolfensberger, W. 1991. "Reflections on a Lifetime in Human Services and Mental Retardation." *Mental Retardation* 29 (1).

World Health Organization. 1962. *Deprivation of Maternal Care; A Reassessment of Its Effects*. Geneva: World Health Organization.

_____. 1964. *Care of Children in Day Centres*. Geneva: World Health Organization.

Zazalenchuk, J. 1984. *Directions for Child Care in Saskatchewan: A Report*. Regina: Saskatchewan Department of Social Services.